W9-ARW-861

ANDREW JACKSON

Symbol for an Age

ANDREW JACKSON

Symbol for an Age

JOHN WILLIAM WARD

OXFORD UNIVERSITY PRESS

LONDON   OXFORD   NEW YORK

OXFORD UNIVERSITY PRESS

London   Oxford   New York
Glasgow   Toronto   Melbourne   Wellington
Cape Town   Ibadan   Nairobi   Dar es Salaam   Lusaka   Addis Ababa
Delhi   Bombay   Calcutta   Madras   Karachi   Lahore   Dacca
Kuala Lumpur   Singapore   Hong Kong   Tokyo

Copyright 1953, 1955 by John William Ward
© John William Ward, 1955
Library of Congress Catalogue Card Number: 55-8125
First published by Oxford University Press, New York, 1955
First issued as an Oxford University Press paperback, 1962

This reprint, 1973

Printed in the United States of America

FOR BARBARA

PREFACE

A FELLOWSHIP awarded by the American Council of Learned Societies made it possible for me to devote one whole year to this work without the distraction of other duties. It also financed research in various libraries which otherwise would have been beyond my reach and without access to which this study would have been fruitless. A grant from the Princeton University Research Fund aided in the final preparation of the manuscript.

The intellectual resources I have mined are less easy to name. I can only indicate the richest. Leo Marx and Bernard Bowron read my manuscript and gave me valuable criticism on it. I owe them much more, however. The intellectual stimulus which has accompanied their friendship did, in a real sense, make it possible for me to undertake this study. The influence of Henry Nash Smith on me and my work is so pervasive that it is difficult to describe. My method is derived from his work, *Virgin Land, The American West as Symbol and Myth* (Cambridge, Mass., 1950), but far more important than his practical aid to me has been the example of his own teaching and scholarship. I would like to think that his mark is discernible on every page of mine. Where it isn't, my work is that much the less.

One happy feature of the intellectual world is that debts are never called; here, at least, resources are appropriated in behalf of the whole community. I cannot name them but I hope I have not wasted the help of so many.

Lastly, my wife. I can only put her name at the beginning, confident she will know what it means.

J. W. W.

Princeton, New Jersey
March 1955

CONTENTS

SYMBOL FOR AN AGE
        I   In the Beginning Was New Orleans, 3

NATURE
       II   'The Hunters of Kentucky,' 13
     III   Nature's Nobleman, 30
     IV   The Plowman and the Professor, 46
      V   The Whigs Take to the Woods, 79

PROVIDENCE
     VI   God's Right-Hand Man, 101
    VII   Extending the Area of Freedom, 133

WILL
   VIII   The Man of Iron, 153
     IX   The Self-made Man, 166
      X   The Man of (Malleable) Iron, 181

SYMBOL
     XI   Coda, 207

NOTES, 215
INDEX, 267

ILLUSTRATIONS

PLATE I

Lithograph drawn on stone by Lafosse, 1856, after the daguerreotype by Mathew Brady. COURTESY OF THE LIBRARY OF CONGRESS.

PLATE II

Lithograph, artist unknown, c.1835. A political cartoon on the controversy with France during Jackson's second administration. COURTESY OF THE TENNESSEE STATE LIBRARY.

PLATE III

Lithograph, artist unknown, 1836. A political cartoon published by P. Desobry, New York, on the controversy with France. COURTESY OF THE TENNESSEE STATE LIBRARY.

PLATE IV

Lithograph, artist unknown, c.1834, probably in New York. A political cartoon on the decapitation of the figurehead of Andrew Jackson on the frigate *Constitution*. COURTESY OF THE LIBRARY OF CONGRESS.

PLATE V

Woodcut, artist unknown, sometime after 1835. A magazine illustration of the second figurehead of Andrew Jackson on the frigate *Constitution*. COURTESY OF THE LIBRARY OF CONGRESS.

PLATE VI

Stipple Engraving by Charles Phillips, 1842, after John Wesley Jarvis's portrait of Andrew Jackson (c.1819) which, despite the inscription on the engraving, was not taken from life or done in 1815 but probably copied from an earlier and lesser known portrait of Andrew Jackson. COURTESY OF THE LIBRARY OF CONGRESS.

PLATE VII

Lithograph by James Baillie, 1845, on the death of General Andrew Jackson. COURTESY OF THE LIBRARY OF CONGRESS.

PLATE VIII

Broadside, J. Pritts, Printer; Chambersburg, Pennsylvania, not dated. COURTESY OF THE LIBRARY OF CONGRESS.

PLATE I

PLATE II

SPIRIT OF THE TIMES.

PLATE III

The Decapitation of a great Block head by the Mysterious agency of the Claret coloured Coat.

PLATE IV

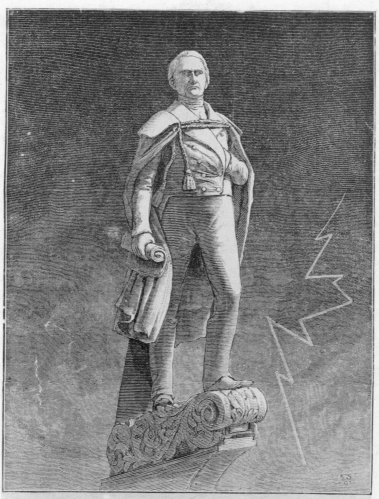

GENERAL JACKSON—FIGURE-HEAD OF THE "CONSTITUTION."

PLATE V

Engraved by Chas. Phillips from a Drawing in Marty's Levee. Hall's 6th 1815.
now in the Possession at Jonathan Reed Esq.

Andrew Jackson

PLATE VI

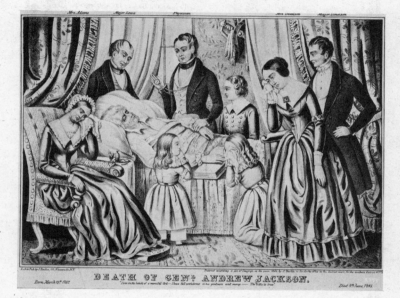

PLATE VII

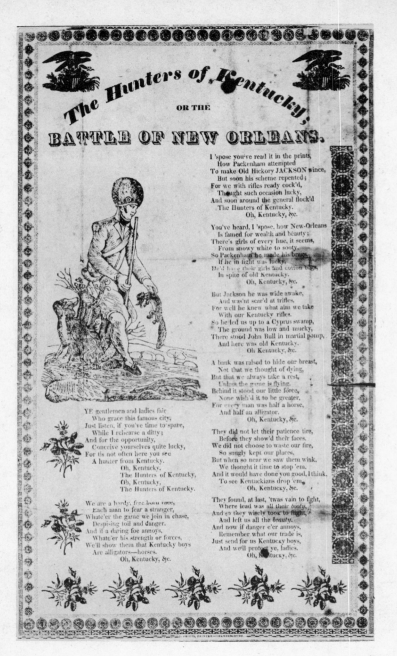

The Hunters of Kentucky,

OR THE

BATTLE OF NEW ORLEANS.

I 'spose you've read it in the prints,
How Packenham attempted
To make Old Hickory JACKSON since,
But soon his scheme repented;
For we with rifles ready cock'd,
Thought such occasion lucky,
And soon around the general flock'd
The Hunters of Kentucky.
Oh, Kentucky, &c.

You've heard, I 'spose, how New-Orleans
Is famed for wealth and beauty;
There's girls of every hue, it seems,
From snowy white to sooty.
So Packenham he made his brags,
If he in fight was lucky,
He'd have their girls and cotton bags,
In spite of old Kentucky.
Oh, Kentucky, &c.

But Jackson he was wide awake,
And was'nt scar'd at trifles,
For well he knew what aim we take
With our Kentucky rifles.
So he led us up to a Cyprus swamp,
The ground was low and mucky,
There stood John Bull in martial pomp,
And here was old Kentucky.
Oh, Kentucky, &c.

A bank was raised to hide our breast,
Not that we thought of dying,
But that we always take a rest,
Unless the game is flying.
Behind it stood our little force,
None wish'd it to be greater,
For every man was half a horse,
And half an alligator.
Oh, Kentucky, &c.

YE gentlemen and ladies fair
Who grace this famous city,
Just listen, if you've time to spare,
While I rehearse a ditty;
And for the opportunity,
Conceive yourselves quite lucky,
For tis not often here you see
A hunter from Kentucky.
Oh, Kentucky,
The Hunters of Kentucky,
Oh, Kentucky,
The Hunters of Kentucky.

We are a hardy, free born race,
Each man to fear a stranger,
Whate'er the game we join in chase,
Despising toil and danger.
And if a daring foe annoys,
Whate'er his strength or forces,
We'll show them that Kentucky boys
Are alligators—horses.
Oh, Kentucky, &c.

They did not let their patience tire,
Before they show'd their faces,
We did not choose to waste our fire,
So snugly kept our places,
But when so near we saw them wink,
We thought it time to stop 'em,
And it would have done you good, I think,
To see Kentuckians drop 'em.
Oh, Kentucky, &c.

They found, at last, 'twas vain to fight,
Where lead was all their booty,
And so they wisely took to flight,
And left us all the beauty.
And now if danger e'er annoys,
Remember what our trade is,
Just send for us Kentucky boys,
And we'll protect ye, ladies.
Oh, Kentucky, &c.

PLATE VIII

ANDREW JACKSON

Symbol for an Age

SYMBOL FOR AN AGE

What *was* Andrew Jackson, and what did he *do,* that he should receive such honors while living, and, when dead, should gather a nation round his tomb? What *was* he? He was the imbodiment [sic] of the true spirit of the nation in which he lived. What did he do? He put himself at the head of the great movement of the age in which he lived. . . Run the eye across the history of the world. You observe that there are certain cycles, or ages, or periods of time, which have their peculiar spirit, their ruling passion, their great, characterizing, distinctive movements. He, who imbodies in its greatest fulness, the spirit of such an age, and enters with most earnestness into its movements, received the admiration of his contemporaries. . . And why? because they see in him their own image. Because, in him is concentrated the spirit that has burned in their own bosom. Because in him exists, in bodily form, in living flesh and blood, the spirit that gives them life and motion. The spirit of God descended upon the Saviour of the world in the form of a dove. The spirit of an age sometimes descends to future generations in the form of a man. . . in proportion as an individual concentrates within himself, the spirit which works through masses of men, and which moves, and should move them through the greatest cycles of time, in that proportion, he becomes entitled to their admiration and praise. . . Because his countrymen saw their image and spirit in Andrew Jackson, they bestowed their honor and admiration upon him.

Washington McCartney, 'Eulogy
[on the death of Andrew Jackson]'

I

In the Beginning Was New Orleans

REMEMBERING the War of 1812 some years after the event, Samuel G. Goodrich wrote:

> All that could be maintained was, that we had made war, charging the enemy with very gross enormities, and we had made peace, saying not one word about them! . . . 'Let us, however,' [said Mr. Madison and his party], 'put a good face upon it: we can hide our shame for the moment in the smoke of Jackson's victory; as to the rest, why we can brag the country into a belief that it has been a glorious war!' Madison set the example in a boasting message, and his party organs took up the tune, and have played it bravely till the present day.[1]

Even discounting New England's bias against 'Mr. Madison's War,' Samuel Goodrich's estimate is historically valid. The War of 1812 was a war of anomalies: the United States went to war in part over Great Britain's Orders-in-Council which were repealed two days before war was declared; the main issues of the war were completely ignored in the treaty that brought the war to an end; and the greatest battle of the war was fought when the war was over.[2]

In a war replete with military reverses for the United States, the harshest blow dealt America was not military, however, it was moral. The war threatened to destroy the young nation's pride. The buoyant optimism which had marked the opening of the war had given way by the end to gloom and despair. At the beginning of 1815, Washington was in ashes, the Hartford Convention was in session, holding out the threat of disunion, and rumors of a British armada had the cities along the east coast in a panic.[3]

When the news began to filter through from the South that the British were before New Orleans, the only assurance the administration press could give the nation was negative: 'if the British succeed, they will know they have been in a fight'; there is an expectation of the British 'not being ineffectually resisted.'[4] The opposition press was more emphatic but hardly in a way to bolster the nation's sagging morale. The *New-York Evening Post* editorialized that 'if an attack has been made on Orleans, the city has fallen' since the British have 'perfect command' of the strategical situation. A few days later it surmised that the enemy had spent Christmas in New Orleans.[5] It was believed by some that the administration was in possession of the official account of the capture of New Orleans and feared to release the news.[6]

Into this atmosphere of gloom and doubt burst the news of Andrew Jackson's crushing victory over the British before New Orleans. As a contemporary later remembered, the news of victory 'came upon the country like a clap of thunder in the clear azure vault of the firmament, and travelled with electromagnetic velocity, throughout the confines of the land.'[7] The newspaper headlines give some measure of the nation's reaction:[8]

ALMOST INCREDIBLE VICTORY!!
GLORIOUS NEWS.

GLORIOUS!!!
UNPARALLELED VICTORY

SPLENDID VICTORY

RISING GLORY OF THE AMERICAN REPUBLIC!

Hard on the heels of Jackson's victory came the news of the peace.[9] The terms of the Treaty of Ghent were hardly satisfactory, but comment on that score was invariably answered by reference to the glory of Jackson's victory. When the Federalists asked, 'What Have We Gained by the War?' 'A Good Name' was the answering chorus.[10] The *National Intelligencer,* favorable to the administration, carried a series of editorials in vindication of the peace treaty and the final remark of the final number was that 'considering Gen. Jackson's splendid victory at New Orleans just at the close of the war, we have also *won the odd trick.*'[11]

Modern treatments of the War of 1812 traditionally regret that the Atlantic Cable had not yet been laid in 1815 so that the needless carnage of the Battle of New Orleans could have been averted; not so contemporary accounts of the battle. 'How fortunate it is for the U. S. [observed the editor of *The Enquirer*] that the peace did not arrive *before* the attack was made on N[ew] Orleans. How elegantly does it round off the war! It is the last touch to the picture!' [12] Mr. Ingersoll, in the House of Representatives, agreed: 'The terms of the treaty [of Ghent] are yet unknown to us. But the victory at Orleans has rendered them glorious and honorable *be what they may* . . . The nation now . . . is above disgrace.' [13] And in Paris, Henry Clay, hearing of the outcome of the battle of New Orleans, is supposed to have said, '*Now,* I can go to England without mortification.' [14] It was true, as one editor observed, that 'the brilliant and unparalleled victory at *New-Orleans,* has closed the war in a blaze of Glory' and the nation agreed with him that Jackson's victory 'placed America on the very pinnacle of fame.' [15]

Through Andrew Jackson, the American people were vicariously purged of shame and frustration. At a moment of disillusionment, Andrew Jackson reaffirmed the young nation's self-belief; he restored its sense of national prowess and destiny. It means nothing, however, to say that Andrew Jackson reinvigorated American nationalism without exploring further the terms in which the United States celebrated its self-love. What needs stressing at this point is that the various concepts which give substance to the abstraction, nationalism, were articulated in terms of Andrew Jackson, so that Andrew Jackson easily became a counter for the ideas themselves.

— 1 —

On February 16, 1815, twelve days after the *National Intelligencer, Extra* had announced the 'ALMOST INCREDIBLE VICTORY' of Andrew Jackson at New Orleans, Mr. Troup, of Georgia, rose to address the House of Representatives. The occasion was the proposal of a resolution offering the thanks of the House to General Jackson and his brave associates for their glorious defense of New Orleans. 'Mr. *Troup of Geo.* said that he congratulated the House on the return of peace — if the peace be honorable, he might be permitted to congratulate the House on the glorious termination of the war. He might be permitted to congratulate them on the glorious termination of the most glorious war ever waged by any people. To the glory of it Gen. Jackson and his army have contributed not a little.'

I cannot, sir [continued Mr. Troup] — perhaps language cannot, do justice to the merits of General Jackson and the troops under his command . . . it is a fit subject for the genius of Homer. But there was a spectacle connected with this subject upon which the human mind would delight to dwell — upon which the human mind could not fail to dwell with peculiar pride and exultation. It was the yeomanry of the country marching to the defence of the City of Orleans leaving their wives and children and firesides at a moment's warning. On the one side, committing themselves to the bosom of the mother of rivers, on the other side taking the rout [sic] of the trackless and savage wilderness. . . The farmers of the country triumphantly victorious over the conquerors of the conquerors of Europe. I came, I saw, I conquered, says the *American Husbandman,* fresh from his plough. The proud veteran who triumphed in Spain and carried terror into the warlike population of France was humbled beneath the power of my arm. The God of Battles and of Righteousness took part with the defenders of their country and the foe was scattered as chaff before the wind. It is, indeed, a fit subject for the genius of Homer[,] of Ossian or Milton. . . that regular troops, the best disciplined and most veteran of Europe, should be beaten by undisciplined militia with the disproportionate loss of an hundred to one is . . . almost incredible. . . Europe have seen [sic] that to be formidable . . . we need *but will it.* Europe will see that to be invincible . . . it is only necessary that we judiciously employ the means which God and Nature have bountifully placed at our disposal.[16]

Beneath the turgid idiom endemic among nineteenth-century politicians one can detect certain key concepts in Representative Troup's speech. I wish to do no more here than to suggest that contemporary estimates of the Battle of New Orleans, at the very outset of Andrew Jackson's career, present in embryo the dominant conceptual strains which later characterize the fully developed symbol of Jackson. I do not wish to develop the implications of these ideas now, but simply use them to delineate the major themes of the subsequent discussion.

After an opening which well exemplifies the agency of Andrew Jackson in swelling national self-esteem, the ideas which underlie Troup's words are, in the order of their appearance:

1. The victory at New Orleans was a victory of the American farmer. This is the major point of the speech, the one that calls forth Troup's utmost rhetorical embellishment. The grandeur of the fact is suggested by the echo of Caesar and the invocation of the age's favorite epic poets. The phrase, 'fresh from his plough,' implies a causative relation between the life of the farmer and the victory of the American husbandman over Europe's finest. In some fashion, the militia because of its normal life *vis a vis* nature has been able to overcome the conquerors of the conquerors of Europe. The yeoman of the western world seems to have a storehouse of energy at his command which enables him to surpass the best strength that Europe has to offer.

Involved in this victory of the farmer is the careful attention paid to the fact that he is 'undisciplined' in comparison to the veteran troops of Britain who have had the benefits of long training and military discipline. There is a spontaneous element connected with the strength of the American farmer which allows him to forego the regimen required by European troops and still surpass them.

2. God is on our side; not only the God of Battles but God and Nature (a synonym for God?) have shown their special concern for the United States by the bountiful means placed at America's disposal.

3. Will, the process of self-determination, brought victory to our side. Despite the seeming odds, an exertion of the self conquered and did the impossible. It might be

pointed out that such a concept is antithetical to the idea
that the God of Battles had decreed the American victory;
the cosmic determinism of the latter precludes self-determination. However in the larger suggestion that God and
Nature have placed the means of national greatness at our
disposal, Troup, with dialectical brilliance, yokes these in-
compatible concepts by suggesting that we are favored by
God, but with one stipulation — we must prove ourselves
worthy of God's favor by improving the opportunity he so
bountifully provides. To the assurance that God is on our
side, that we *cannot* fail, is added a psychological injunction
to act.

Thus, we have national pride apparently resting upon
three main concepts, which for brevity may be designated
as 'Nature,' 'Providence,' and 'Will.' My purpose is to show
that these general concepts are the structural underpinnings
of the ideology of the society of early nineteenth-century
America, for which Andrew Jackson is *one* symbol.

NATURE

In history the great moment is when the savage is just ceasing to be a savage. . . Everything good in nature and the world is in that moment of transition, when the swarthy juices still flow plentifully from nature, but their astringency or acidity is got out by ethics and humanity.

Ralph Waldo Emerson, 'Power'

Ralph Waldo Emerson

'The Hunters of Kentucky'

In the spring of 1822, Noah M. Ludlow, prominent in the
beginnings of the theater in the western United States, was
in New Orleans. One day early in May he received, as was
the custom in the early theater, a 'benefit' night. Remembering the occasion some years later, Ludlow could not
recollect what pieces had been acted on that evening but he
did recall doing something that was as a rule 'entirely out
of [his] line of business.' As an added attraction he had sung
a song he thought might please the people. The song was
'The Hunters of Kentucky.'

The lyrics of 'The Hunters of Kentucky' had been written by Samuel Woodworth, better known today for having
written 'The Old Oaken Bucket.' Noah claimed his brother
had seen the poem and since it 'tickled his fancy' had sent it
along to New Orleans. Noah adapted the words to the tune

'Miss Baily,' which was taken from the comic opera *Love Laughs at Locksmiths,* and decided to sing it for his New Orleans audience.

> When the night came [remembered Noah] I found the pit, or parquette, of the theatre *crowded full* of 'river men,' — that is, keel-boat and flat-boat men. There were very few steamboat men. These men were easily known by their linsey-woolsey clothing and blanket coats. As soon as the comedy of the night was over, I dressed myself in a buckskin hunting-shirt and leggins, which I had borrowed of a river man, and with *moccasins* on my feet, and an old slouched hat on my head, and a rifle on my shoulder, I presented myself before the audience. I was saluted with loud applause of hands and feet, and a prolonged whoop, or howl, such as Indians give when they are especially pleased. I sang the first verse, and these extraordinary manifestations of delight were louder and longer than before; but when I came to the following lines: —

> > 'But Jackson he was wide awake, and
> > > wasn't scared with trifles,
> > For well he knew what aim we take
> > > with our Kentucky rifles;
> > So he marched us down to "Cyprus Swamp";
> > > The ground was low and mucky;
> > There stood "John Bull," in martial pomp,
> > > *But here was old Kentucky.'*

> As I delivered the last five words, I took my old hat off my head, threw it upon the ground, and brought my rifle to the position of taking aim. At that instant came a shout and an Indian yell from the inmates of

the pit, and a tremendous applause from other portions
of the house, the whole lasting for nearly a minute,
and, as Edmund Kean told his wife, after his first
great success in London, 'the house rose to me!' The
whole pit was standing up and shouting. I had to
sing the song three times that night before they would
let me off.[1]

Thus was launched one of America's most popular songs.
Its popularity quickly became a source of annoyance to Ludlow since he was forced to sing it two or three times wherever
he appeared. It plagued him so that he gave it to the local
papers thinking to kill it but he achieved the opposite result; he simply created a wider audience for the song. 'The
Hunters of Kentucky' became so popular 'that you could
hear it sung or whistled almost any day as you passed along
the principal thoroughfares of the city.'[2] The widespread
circulation of the song was helped along by friends of Andrew Jackson who recognized its use and printed and circulated large editions of it;[3] Thomas Low Nichols remembered that in 1828 'the land rang with "The Hunters of
Kentucky."'[4] At Jackson Day Dinners on the anniversary
of the Battle of New Orleans the song was rendered as part
of the entertainment and sometimes sung by the whole company seated at dinner.[5] As one anonymous student of campaign songs says, ' "The Hunters of Kentucky" had much
to do with arousing sentiment [for Jackson in 1828].'[6]

A contemporary of the period in which 'The Hunters
of Kentucky' had its greatest vogue remarked about campaign songs in general that 'it is not necessary that [a song]
should possess much literary merit; if it condenses into some

rhythmic form, a popular thought, emotion or purpose.' [7] The question then is: what popular thought or emotion is expressed in 'The Hunters of Kentucky'?

Taken over almost immediately for political purposes, [8] the song is the final expression given to a widely held assumption why Andrew Jackson was able to defeat the British at New Orleans. In 'The Hunters of Kentucky' version of the battle, the terrible slaughter inflicted upon the British was the result of the skill of the frontier rifleman. As might be anticipated from the fact that it worked its way into a popular song, this version of the Battle of New Orleans was widely current from 1815 until it received its classic enunciation in Ludlow's presentation in 1822.

Before we examine 'The Hunters of Kentucky' version of the victory at New Orleans and its popular acceptance, it can be flatly asserted that Jackson's overwhelming victory can in no way be attributed to the sharpshooting skill of the American frontiersman; further, that fact was recognized by those who took part in the battle and also in the immediate newspaper accounts of the battle. So what we have in 'The Hunters of Kentucky' is the imputation to a historical event of a cause which has no basis except in the widespread desire of Americans to believe their own imaginative construction of the battle.

– 1 –

The Battle of New Orleans was the sort that stirs the imagination. Hastily summoned to New Orleans, Andrew Jackson took command of an ill-organized and ill-equipped body of men recruited from the city of New Orleans and the states of Louisiana, Mississippi, Tennessee, and Kentucky. The force under Jackson was vastly outnumbered and, except for his own Tennessee troops, had little or no battle experience.[9] Facing them was the finest body of troops at England's command, veterans under Wellington of the peninsular campaign in Spain, led by one of Britain's foremost generals, Sir Edward Packenham. The result still seems incredible. At the main attack on the morning of January 8, 1815, the British lost more than 2000 in killed, wounded, and missing.[10] The American loss was approximately eight killed and thirteen wounded.[11] Little wonder that few popular accounts of the battle rested on what might be called rational grounds.[12]

The Battle of New Orleans has been well described in many places.[13] I want here to touch only upon the main features of the battle, particularly upon those that account for the disparity of loss suffered on each side.

Despite all precautions taken by Andrew Jackson, the British were able to land a force from their transports and to penetrate within approximately six miles of New Orleans by December 23, 1814. Jackson attacked the enemy immediately and, as many writers on the battle have pointed out, the Battle of New Orleans was probably won on that night. The British command, unused to American offensive action, assumed that Jackson had a large force in New Orleans or he would not have dared to risk an attack. As a member of the British expedition wrote, 'We held them too much in contempt to fear their attack.' [14] At that moment, however, Jackson was at his weakest. He had less than 5000 troops at his disposal but, what was more important, no fortifications had yet been built to impede the march of the British toward New Orleans.[15] The British, because of Jackson's unexpected offensive thrust, elected to await reinforcements and when the wait was over Jackson was well entrenched before New Orleans and had received needed additions to his fighting force.

The battle ground on the plains of Chalmette was topographically a simple one. The armies were encamped within view of each other on a broad, flat plain. Jackson sheltered his troops behind a wall made of Mississippi mud about breast high which varied in depth along the line.[16] The wall itself was behind an abandoned mill-race, whose sides had fallen in to give it the appearance of a shallow drainage ditch. This ditch extended across the American front from the river levee on the right to a cypress swamp on the left.[17] The British thus could not turn either flank and had to advance directly against the American wall. To make possible an enfilading fire along the ditch a redoubt was constructed on the American right flank which, although tactically sound, proved to be the weakest spot in the American defensive line. Jackson also had troops on the right bank of the Mississippi with cannon that could enfilade the plain with cannister during an enemy attack.

The British attempted various skirmishes against the American line, first hoping that a show of power would frighten away the American militia, then hoping to breach the American wall by cannon fire. Neither hope was warranted, and the British command decided to take the American position by direct assault and planned to attack at dawn, Sunday, January 8. Their plan was to send a body of troops across to the right bank and seize the battery there, which would save them from a galling fire and enable them to turn these guns on the American position. A small attack body was to advance up a road by the river and seize the redoubt on the American right flank so as to clear the ditch of fire during the assault. The main attack was to be made along the line of cypress trees against what was approximately the center of the American line. The British had been told by a deserter that militia manned that sector and therefore chose it as the weakest spot in the line. After the battle they hanged their informant, believing that he must have given them false information.

The British plan of attack required one heroic task. That muddy ditch before the American lines had to be crossed under direct fire and the British could not afford to founder there. Packenham decided to fill the ditch with fascines made of bound sugar cane and in accord with approved contemporary tactics to put ladders against the wall behind the ditch. The nature of such a mission describes itself. The task was assigned to the 44th Regiment of Foot under the command of Lieutenant-Colonel Thomas Mullins.[18]

Things went badly for the British in every sector on the morning of the eighth. The attack on the right bank was delayed and did not reach the line of departure at the appointed time. Packenham decided to move out anyway and gave the attack signal, a rocket launched into the air. The small attack group advancing along the river road gained the redoubt on the American right flank despite the fact that it had to advance under the fire of the battery on the opposite bank of the river; a heavy morning fog on the Mississippi prevented accurate fire from the other side of the stream. However, the group was ahead of the main attack body (for reasons to be discussed in a moment) and, thus isolated and suffering heavily, was forced to retreat and surrender its local victory. With the rocket signal the main attack body moved along the line of woods on the American left. It advanced to within about two hundred yards of the American line when it was discovered that Colonel Mullins and the 44th were not in the van with the fascines and ladders. Confusion was inevitable and the British, massed in orthodox (1815) close formation, halted momentarily.[19] What follows seems incredible. General Gibbs, who was in command of the assault, literally parked his force under the guns of the American line and attempted to locate the 44th and to bring up the fascines and ladders. Even when the material was gathered it meant that the main body had to incline to the left in order to create a passage for the troops coming up. The attempt was fruitless and Packenham came to the front to urge on the attack without the equipment to bridge the ditch. All this time the American line was pouring cannon and rifle shot into the massed British soldiery. Their nerve was broken and when Packenham tried to lead them to the attack they wavered, and when he fell they broke completely, fleeing the field.[20] An observer present at the battle described for the *New-York Evening Post* the halting of the British in mass formation before the American guns, but mistakenly ascribed the act to cowardice.[21]

Although it is true that the British were sitting-ducks for the American army, the fact does not *necessarily* detract from the skill of the American riflemen, although skill would seem to be irrelevant in the circumstances. Two other considerations, however, clinch the case against the marksmanship brief. One is that the Americans simply could not see well enough to bring to bear any skill they may have possessed. A participant's letter, although marked by a certain lack of critical balance, suggests this: 'The atmosphere was filled with sheets of fire and volumes of smoke. . . Our men . . . took steady and deliberate aim, and almost every shot told.' [22] Not only was the field obscured by the smoke of battle, but the attack was made in the half-light of dawn and fine shooting was impossible. One of the actual riflemen recalled that it was so dark that little could be seen, until just about the time that the battle ceased. . . the smoke was so thick that everything seemed to be covered up in it.' [23]

Contemporary accounts contained some ambiguous statements, such as the one in the letter to the *National Intelligencer* just quoted, but in general the first news of the battle correctly attributed the havoc done among the British to the American cannon, rather than to rifle fire. The *National Intelligencer, Extra,* the first eastern announcement of the battle, carried a letter from an American officer who referred to the terrible toll of British dead and wounded as 'being generally from our cannon.' [24] Another on the scene account said, 'Our artillery was fired upon their whole columns, about an hour and a half, within good striking distance, whilst advancing and retreating, with grape & cannister; and the slaughter must have been great.' [25] Andrew Jackson's victory address to his troops on January 21, 1815, also recognized the prime importance of the American cannon fire.[26] The condition of the British casualties testified further to the source of their wounds: 'their wounds are horrible — they are indeed mutilated — there is none of them who have less than three or four wounds, and some have even eight and ten; *they have been thus crippled by our grape shot.'* [27] Even when those on the scene attributed the American victory to 'sheer superiority in firing' there was no mention of what kind of firing.[28]

– 2 –

Despite available records as to what did happen at New Orleans, there gradually arose the legend that the British were slaughtered because of the sharpshooting skill of the American frontiersman. The first anecdotes which circulated through the nation were plausible, even if, as one suspects, apocryphal. One particularly went the rounds. It was copied from paper to paper, always under the same heading, 'Sharp Shooting.' It told of the death of the British officer who led the attack on the American right flank and who was killed after taking possession of the isolated redoubt there. After the battle there was some argument among the American militia about who had been responsible for killing the officer, a Colonel Rennie. 'One said if Rannie [sic] had been shot just below the left eye he would claim the merit, otherwise not — for that is where he had aimed the ball. On inspection, it was found that Rannie had been shot as predicted by the marksman!' [29] Since Rennie had penetrated right to the American iine there is a possibility that this anecdote might have been founded in truth and that such a feat of marksmanship had been executed. However, the British officer who conveyed the news of Rennie's death to his relatives in England, and who had examined his body after the battle, reported that Rennie had died of two bullet wounds in the head which suggests that he fell under a hail of bullets and not by the act of a single marksman.[30] Similar to this story was the one about the 'Humane Rifleman.' This concerned a Tennesseean who beckoned to an English officer reconnoitering the American line prior to the battle to come in and surrender, which the officer did. When asked why, the Englishman replied, 'I had no alternative; for I have been told these *d—d Yankee riflemen can pick a squirrel's eye out as far as they can see it.*' [31] Neither of these anecdotes, be it observed, relates to the main battle area, although both obviously attest to the belief in the frontiersman as an excellent rifleman.

In 1820, two years before Noah Ludlow enshrined the legend of 'The Hunters of Kentucky' in song, Marshal Count Bertrand Clausel, who at Salamanca had commanded the French division that had been defeated by Packenham, and Count Desnoettes, who had been with Napoleon at Moscow, visited the battlefield of New Orleans.

These gallant and distinguished Frenchmen [relates Walker, the contemporary historian of the Battle of New Orleans] . . . were greatly puzzled to know how such good soldiers as the English could be repulsed by so weak a force from such trifling fortifications. 'Ah!' exclaimed Marshall Clausel, after some moments of reflection, 'I see how it all happened. When these

Americans go into battle they forget they are not
hunting deer or shooting turkeys and try never to
throw away a shot.' And there [remarks Walker] was
the whole secret of the defeat, which the British have
ascribed to so many different causes.[32]

Thus the story grew until the author of *An Epick Poem*
on the Battle of New Orleans could characterize Jackson's
fighting force in this fashion:

. . . Rude their sun-burnt men,
In simple garb of foresters are seen —
But mark — they know with death the bead to sight,
And draw the centre of the heart in fight.[33]

And the account of the Battle of New Orleans in *The
Jackson Wreath* could sum up the conflict with the statement that 'the fatal aim of the western marksmen was
never so terribly exemplified.' [34]

It would not be worth establishing the fact that contemporaries were mistaken in ascribing the cause of the victory at New Orleans to the skill of the western frontiersman, if there were nothing more to the matter than a mis-
take. But in singling out 'the western farmer,' or 'the
frontiersman,' as the cause of the victory, the imagination
of the American people was trying to make the account
of the Battle of New Orleans buttress one of its favorite
concepts; that, as I suggested in commenting on Representative Troup's speech,[35] 'The Hunters of Kentucky'
version of the Battle of New Orleans is an attempt to establish the empowering force of nature as the cause of the

American victory over the disciplined soldiery of Europe. The point is not that frontier life did not create good marksmen, which it may have, but that a prevailing attitude toward nature caused Americans to ascribe the victory at New Orleans to the frontier farmer although the facts did not support such a version.

Jackson himself implicitly accepted the view that nature was somehow in the background of the American victory. In his address, 'To the Embodied Militia,' on December 28, 1814, before the main engagement, Jackson complimented his 'fellow citizens and soldiers' on their noble ardor. 'Inhabitants of an opulent and commercial town [he went on to say], you have by a spontaneous effort shaken off the habits, which are created by wealth, and shewn that you are resolved to deserve the blessings of fortune by bravely defending them.' [36] Jackson's thought is here stated in terms of historical primitivism.[37] It is assumed that the advance of wealth and material well-being saps moral and physical strength. Negatively there is the implication that the condition of man in a state of nature is somehow superior.

One will notice, however, that Jackson is addressing the inhabitants of an opulent and commercial town; there would be no sense in making a statement such as this to farmers from the frontier regions of Kentucky. We thus come to realize that 'The Hunters of Kentucky' account of the Battle of New Orleans has drastically altered the facts to fit its particular version. Concentration on the marksmanship of the frontiersman has required the neglect of a large number of others who were also engaged in the defense of New Orleans. Thus, what is the most popular account of Jackson's victory has no place for the part played by the French Creoles,[38] the Free Men of Color, the regular troops, the Barratarian Pirates, or the citizens of the city of New Orleans. Of the 3,569 troops *on the line* on the morning of the eighth, only 2100, Coffee's and Adair's men, fit the frontiersman category. This means that 'The Hunters of Kentucky' version has, by its focus, been forced to dismiss more than 41 per cent of the total from consideration, a considerable alteration of the facts.[39] Of the Kentucky troops on hand, most were held in reserve, back of the main line of defense, for the very good reason that only 550 arrived with any arms.[40] Jackson complained that 'hardly one-third of the Kentucky troops, so long expected, are armed, and the arms they have are not fit for use.'[41] The fact that no more than one-third of the Hunters of Kentucky had rifles in their hands during the battle further depreciates the legend of their sharpshooting at New Orleans.

It is almost too happy for present purposes that after the Battle of New Orleans had ended a controversy arose over the relative shooting ability of General Coffee's famed mounted brigade of Tennessee Volunteers and Beale's Rifle Company which was composed of 'leading merchants and professional characters of the city, who had formed themselves into a volunteer corps.'[42] To decide the issue a shooting match was held; against the frontiersmen, fresh from their plows, the inhabitants of an opulent city won the trial of skill.[43]

The view that it was the special worth of the American frontiersman that accounts for Jackson's victory was not only unhistorical, it was astigmatic. The assertion of the frontiersman not only dictated a cause of victory which simply did not pertain, it demanded the rejection of all who did not fit its particular version, who did not spring from frontier life.

— 3 —

Contemporaries of Jackson shared his attitude that movement away from nature was a measure of moral and physical decline. Samuel Putnam Waldo, tracing the growth of the republic by way of introduction to Jackson's life, noted that after the Revolution 'sudden wealth was the result of the exertions of the different classes of Americans. The voluptuousness and effeminacy, usually attendants upon the possession of it, were rapidly diminishing that exalted sense of national glory.' [44] Waldo, preaching a doctrine of the strenuous life, welcomed the War of 1812, which arrested the moral and physical decline of the American people. Nathaniel H. Claiborne, reviewing the war in the South, asserted that the Battle of New Orleans 'shows that the United States can boast of a population possessing the faculty of fighting to a degree beyond the lot of most nations.' [45] Claiborne finished this sentence with the observation, 'whether this arises from the nature of our climate . . . is not material to determine,' but a few pages later he expanded the thought, as a good Virginian, in Jeffersonian terms.

The most obscure soldier in the American lines [wrote Claiborne] saw that the hour of peril was at hand, and instead of shrinking from the horrors of the approaching tempest, seemed by the cheerfulness of his countenance and the alacrity with which he obeyed the orders of his officers, to wait its coming with the composure and firmness that belongs to cultivated minds. This is not to be wondered at; they were almost to a man freeholders, or the sons of freeholders; they were not taken from the streets of dissipated and corrupt cities, or enlisted into the army to prevent their becoming victims to the shivering pangs of want.[46]

In Claiborne's account, written in 1819, we have a precise recognition of the element that was to be somewhat disguised in the song, 'The Hunters of Kentucky.' The same sentiment was expressed in a volunteer toast at a Fourth of July dinner in Cincinnati in 1815: 'The Backwoods militia — from the lakes to the gulph [sic] they have repulsed the enemy — and shown that, the forest, which they inhabit is not more fertile of the bounties of nature than of valour and patriotism.' [47] Representative Troup's stress on the fact that the American militia were 'fresh from the plough' was widely echoed: 'Fresh from the plough, our gallant people rushed to the seaboard to meet the invader, and beat and discomfit the best proved veterans of the old world, provided with all the needed requisites for the fight, and led on by one of the ablest and most experienced generals'; [48] 'unpractised militia, whose hands were yet callous from the labours of husbandry'; [49] 'The pride of Albion in the dust is low, / To be thus handled by their western foe — / Men, late from managing the simple plough'; [50] 'they were the sons of the forest and the plain, hastily summoned from their daily and necessary toil.' [51]

The quotations here plainly exhibit the force that was at work in accounting for the Battle of New Orleans as a victory of the American frontiersman. From Crèvecoeur and Jefferson to modern American historians, there has been a persistent tendency in American thought to account for the development of the United States by appeals to nature and the frontier.[52] 'The Hunters of Kentucky' is another and remarkably clear example of this process. The spontaneous popular acceptance of the selective character of 'The Hunters of Kentucky' points to the fact that we are in the area of imaginative play, which is less concerned with history than with objectifying concepts which are the chief supports of culture.

'The Hunters of Kentucky' had then a significance for the contemporary American mind greater than *simply* the victory at New Orleans. Its nationalistic appeal derived from and supported an idea already present in American society and destined to be of increasing importance as America turned away from Europe and westward to its own development.

I I I

Nature's Nobleman

IF 'The Hunters of Kentucky' reflects a prevailing assumption about the positive force of nature in the universe, it only indirectly connects Andrew Jackson with that force.

Foreign commentators, speaking within the context of a type of European romanticism, called Jackson 'one of nature's noblemen.' [1] Usually in this sense, nature was used abstractly. As a normative idea, it was negative, meant to deny certain vices of European civilization rather than to affirm nature in the concrete. In the United States, however, nature was not simply an abstraction. The categories for a philosophy of nature were to a large extent imported from Europe; the substance was indigenous.[2]

A rudely fashioned notebook still exists in which the historian, George Bancroft, in his crabbed and nearly unreadable hand, made random notes on the life of Andrew

Jackson. There is a rough chronology to these notes, which
are generally the staccato fragments of half-formulated
thoughts. On one page, however, the hesitant character
of the writing disappears for one brief phrase. In bold,
large letters, across half a page Bancroft wrote, 'from
17[?]8 to 1812 He grew as the forest trees grow.' [3]

Both the image and the dates of Bancroft's phrase are
significant. The year 1812 marks the emergence of Andrew
Jackson on the national scene. Bancroft is suggesting that
Jackson's early preparation for the successful role he was
to fill on the national stage was analogous to the natural
growth of the forest. Another Jacksonian had suggested
the same thought when he said of Jackson, 'he grew up in
the wilds of the West, but he was the noblest tree in the
forest.' [4] Senator Hugh Lawson White, while still an ardent Jacksonian, drew the lesson more clearly. In accounting for the comprehensiveness of Jackson's mind, White
derived it from the fact that Jackson had been 'educated
in Nature's school.' [5]

These appraisals of Jackson suggest more than the
eighteenth-century belief that all men are endowed with
certain natural powers. They imply a dynamic relation
between physical nature and human character. Such an
attitude possesses enormous implications. Because of the
geographical situation of the United States it lends itself
to national pride and the rejection of Europe, not simply
because Europe is not-America (although this gives the
idea its emotional appeal), but because Europe is not-
nature. It also lends itself to a preference for the natural
over the artificial, the intuitive over the logical, with all

the ramifications inherent in such a point of view. But before developing and demonstrating the presence of concepts that derive from a certain attitude toward nature, it will be useful to define with greater precision what was generally meant by 'nature.'

Two political cartoons survive the controversy during Jackson's second administration between the United States and France over the payment of spoliation claims to this country.[6] The intent of both cartoons was the same: to present graphically the contrast between a virile republican government and a debilitated monarchical government. One cartoonist made the basis for the contrast explicit. He attached as a motto to his cartoon (Pl. II) lines from Byron's *Childe Harold's Pilgrimage:*[7]

> Can Freedom find no champion and no child
> Such as Columbia saw arise when she
> Sprung forth a Pallas, arm'd and undefiled.
> Or must such minds be nourish'd in the wild,
> Deep in the unpruned forest, 'midst the roar
> Of cataracts, where nursing nature smiled
> On infant Washington. Has earth no more
> Such seeds within her breast, or Europe no such shore?

In the second cartoon (Pl. III), the basis for contrast is implicit, it is rendered pictorially rather than overtly stated. The background of the European side of the Atlantic is a large building, symbolizing France's advance in civilization and movement away from the 'unpruned forest' and suggesting that such material advancement is organically connected with political debility. But the crucial element in the second cartoon is the background of the American scene. Rather than the 'unpruned forest' of Byron's primitivistic statement, America is represented by a cornfield surrounded by a split rail fence. Americans were willing to accept the idea that nature, symbolized by the forest, was the source of vitality, but their attitude was ambivalent. They celebrated nature, but not wild nature. The tension in American thought concerning nature is suggested by comparing the two cartoons we have been discussing. In overt statement, the wild nature of Byron's words is accepted. In the covert form of pictorial statement, although nature is still accepted as a source of strength, the image which it calls up for the artist is the rudimentary beginning of civilization which, however, the artist rejects when it has advanced to the stage of urban development represented by the large masonry building of France.[8] The problem implicit in the contrast of the two cartoons is how to avoid the disadvantages of both extreme civilization and savage nature; phrased positively, how to combine the best advantages of nature and civilization.

My interpretation of the cartoons can be demonstrated better by reference to a theme in 'The Hunters of Kentucky' that was purposely neglected in the preceding chapter. Most practical-minded accounts of the Battle of New Orleans stressed that Jackson's victory saved the 'emporium of the West,' but the mission of the defenders of New Orleans in 'The Hunters of Kentucky' is to save the ladies of the city from being ravished by a victorious British army. This chivalric interpretation of the role of the vic-

torious West had its beginning immediately after the battle
in a letter written by George Poindexter to the editors of
the *Mississippi Republican.*

> The watch-word and countersign of the enemy on the
> morning of the 8th [wrote Poindexter], was BEAUTY
> and BOOTY. — Commentary is unnecessary on these sig-
> nificant allusions held out to a licentious soldiery. Had
> victory declared on their side, the scenes of Havre de
> Grace, of Hampton, of Alexandria, & of St. Sebastian,
> would without doubt have been reenacted at New
> Orleans with all the unfeeling and brutal inhumanity
> of the savage foe with whom we are contending.[9]

For present purposes the importance of this letter lies
in the characterization that Poindexter finds fitting for the
British. They are a 'savage foe'; they are, in other words,
uncivilized. This stigma was widely imputed to the British.
The editor of the *Spirit of the West,* in taking notice of
the Ohio legislature's vote of thanks to Jackson, referred
to the victory at New Orleans as the 'splendid defeat of
that host of modern Vendals [sic].' [10] In likening the British to the barbarian forces of the North that swept down
over Roman Civilization, the intent of the writer is not
only to affirm the new Rome of the western world but also
to derogate Britain by a scale of values based on the concept, civilization. The ladies of New Orleans, in a card accompanying an offer of blankets to Jackson's army, expressed the hope that their husbands, brothers, and sons,
directed by Jackson, 'will be instrumental in defeating the
purposes of those Modern Vandals, who have invaded their
land.' [11] Before the battle, Jackson made the same criti-

cism of the British in positive terms: 'You are to contend [he told his men] . . . against an enemy . . . who avows a war of vengeance and desolation, proclaimed and marked by a cruelty, lust and horrours unknown to civilized nations.' [12]

At first glance, it seems inconsistent to affirm American troops in terms of nature, as in 'The Hunters of Kentucky,' and at the same time to derogate the foe in terms of civilization. The conflict between two value systems, organized around antithetical concepts, can even be detected in accounts of the American mode of fighting. Prior to the main battle of the eighth of January, the Americans harassed the British lines constantly, all through the night, either singly or in small parties. This Indian style of fighting was approved by the contemporary historian of the battle, Alexander Walker, who was quite proud of the 'natural restlessness and nomadic tendency' of the American militia.[13] However, this mode of operations struck the British as 'uncivilized,' and they censured the American raiding habits as 'an ingenious return to barbarity,' finding the same epithet appropriate for the Americans that the editor of the *Spirit of the West* had for the British.[14] Now, while Walker was proud of the frontiersman's 'natural' skill, he was bothered by the British accusation and felt the need to apologize. The only excuse he could find, however, was a pragmatic evasion of the issue: 'Whatever may be the opinion of ethical and historical writers, on the abstract question of duty and chivalry in this matter, there can be no doubt as to the fact, that the British soldiers had but little rest or quiet.' [15]

The problem here is one that was introduced by Na-thaniel Claiborne's use of the word 'cultivated' in describ-ing the special worth of the yeomen who conquered the British at New Orleans.[16] Claiborne's choice of language is singularly useful in getting at the problem. 'Cultivated,' as a figure of speech applied to the mind or character, is derived from the language of agriculture; in either its literal or its figurative sense, the significance is that some-thing artificial has been introduced into the natural order, that man has interposed in some way to improve the processes of nature.[17] Followed to its logical conclusion, cultivation should be greater to the degree that it departs from nature. This is not, of course, what Claiborne is say-ing. The British, unlike the Americans, have been recruited from the streets of cities, whereas the Americans are 'free-holders,' with the implication of being close to the land and nature.[18] It is an *extreme* departure from nature that makes the British 'dissipated and corrupt' as opposed to 'culti-vated.'

Implicit in Claiborne's remarks is an attitude toward the development of society. It is that history is the record of progression from 'nature' to 'civilization,' either ex-treme of which is undesirable; one might chart this pro-gression in Claiborne's own terms, as the movement from the soil to the city. In Claiborne's view of the War of 1812, Europe, represented by the British troops, has already passed into the extreme phase of civilization which is cor-ruption and degeneracy; whereas America is still on the upward slope of the curve and is in the area which is nourished by *both* nature and civilization. This attitude was so widespread that it informed Charles A. Goodrich's *History of the United States*. Goodrich's *History* was the most widely used textbook in America's secondary schools before the Civil War.[19] In it he wrote: 'A marked distinction undoubtedly exists between the inhabitants of the commercial and maritime towns and the villages of the country. The former, in a more considerable degree, as to luxury and vice, resemble the great towns of Europe. Those of the country, who lead an agricultural life, preserve much of the simplicity, with something of the roughness of former days; but they enjoy all that happiness which proceeds from the exercise of the social virtues in their primitive purity.'[20]

The attitude of Claiborne and others can be demonstrated further by reference to two addresses by Andrew Jackson to his troops. In the first Jackson is addressing his Tennessee troops after their victory over the Creek Indians at Horseshoe Bend. After recounting the particulars of the victory, Jackson remarks that the Indians too had anticipated victory. But, he goes on to say, 'They knew not what brave men could effect. . . Barbarians they were ignorant of the influence of civilization and government over the human powers. . . The fiends of Tallapoosa will no longer murder our Women and Children. . . They have disappeared from the face of the earth. In their places a new generation will arise who will know their duties better. The weapons of warfare will be exchanged for the utensils of husbandry; and the wilderness which now withers in sterility and seems to mourn the disolation [sic] which overspreads it, will blossom as the rose, and be-

come the nursery of the arts.'[21] In his affirmation of civilization in this quotation, Jackson, as Claiborne does in his
use of the word, 'cultivated,' seeks an image of man's intervention in the natural order. The second address is the
one to the embodied militia before the Battle of New Orleans which I have quoted before.[22] In that address, Jackson congratulates the 'inhabitants of an opulent and commercial town [who] have by a spontaneous effort, shaken
off the habits which are created by wealth.'

In these two addresses, Jackson is praising his troops.
In one, he lauds them as civilized men; in the other, as
men able to resist the debilitating effects of civilization.
It would seem that Jackson is violating the canons of logic
in saying that civilization is both good and bad. If, however, one reads Jackson's addresses in the light of a rejection of two extremes the logic is impeccable. A letter Jackson wrote to Governor Blount, of Tennessee, after the first
taking of Pensacola leads to the suggestion that the latter
is the case. 'The good order and conduct of my troops
whilst in Pensacola [wrote Jackson], has convinced the
Spaniards of our friendship, and our prowess, and has
drawn from the citizens an expression, that our Chactaws
are more civilized than the British.'[23] Compare this sentiment with that of a writer in 1815 giving an imaginative
account of the Creek campaign. The British tell the Red-
sticks, the warring Creek Indians, that after victory they
can rape the American women, to which an Indian chief
replies, 'We red people whom you Christians call savages,
that know nothing about your Christian God, do not force
the women of any nation or people, but when we take

prisoners in battle, the laws of female virtue and chastity are sacred to us; and even the beasts in the field and the cattle on a thousand hills teach us better human modesty than this.' [24] In these two statements the Indians are affirmed and the British derogated by their opposites; in other words, the Indians are good because they are more civilized than the British, the British are bad because they are more savage than the Indians. The optimum condition then becomes an admixture of the best of each state. Who better symbolizes this midway point than a man who defeated both the Indians and the British? George M. Dallas, Vice-President of the United States, in his eulogy on the death of Jackson, pointed to Jackson's midway position in the cultural spectrum, the extremes of which are the savagery of unqualified nature and the degeneracy of overdeveloped civilization: 'The *sagacity* of General Jackson was the admiration of the sophist, and the wonder of the savage; it unravelled the meshes of both, without the slightest seeming effort.' [25]

The ideas that are only implicit in the comments of Jackson, Claiborne, and others are explicit in a Fourth of July address by William Foster Otis in Boston in 1831. 'If we seek examples for our country and for ourselves [said Otis], let us resort to the new-created West. There the fountains are uncorrupted. There civilization meets nature unimpaired. There we can behold how the young American grapples with the wilderness, and thence we can return and imagine how our fathers lived.' [26] Although nature is obviously the source of strength to which civilization must resort for reinvigoration, one cannot fail to notice that it

is the *meeting* of the two that is important. Thus we have
the 'new-created West.' Prior to the meeting of civilization
and nature there is only the primordial chaos which pre-
cedes creation; there is, in a very literal sense, nothing, before civilization impinges upon nature.

The conflict between the two sets of ideas with which
Claiborne and Jackson and Otis were grappling became
crucial when Americans had to establish some tolerable
conformity between their ideas and their actions toward
the Indians. As they advanced into the interior of the continent, pushing the Indians before them, Americans tended
to see themselves as the advancing frontier of civilization,
the carriers of government, religion, and social order. But
always at their backs was Europe, the culmination of the
process of civilization, which was inextricably involved in
the American mind with tyranny and decadence. The problem Americans faced was to reject savage nature, as embodied by the Indians, and decadent civilization, as embodied by Europe. One attempt to resolve the dilemma
in satisfactory terms fell to the lot of Andrew Jackson under
whose administration the project of removal of all Indians
to the western country was fulfilled.[27] The idea, attributed
to Jefferson, to transplant all the Indians beyond the settled
areas of the United States was a practical, if temporary,
answer to the needs of the frontier. The plan for removal of
the Indians, however, ran counter to the idea that the role
of the United States was to redeem the Indian from benighted savagery. Some rationalization had to be formu-
lated before the problem could be effectively disposed of.
In his last formal message to the American people, Andrew

Jackson offered a resolution. The answer was incredibly simple. America would save the Indians *for* civilization by rescuing them *from* civilization.

> The States [said Andrew Jackson in his 'Farewell Address'] which had so long been retarded in their improvement by the Indian tribes residing in the midst of them are at length relieved from the evil, and this unhappy race — the original dwellers in our land — are now placed in a situation where we may well hope that they will share in the blessings of civilization and be saved from the degradation and destruction to which they were rapidly hastening while they remained in the States . . . the philanthropist will rejoice that the remnant of that ill-fated race has at length been placed beyond the reach of injury or oppression.[28]

Through the paternalistic care of the Federal government, the Indians would be rescued from the corruption of civilization but would still enjoy its benign influences. This line of reasoning, if generalized, however, posed a real problem for America itself. How was it to continue in the advance of civilization if at the same time it faced the weakness incurred by an alienation from nature? For a society facing this problem, the Hero is the one who brings order out of chaos by conquering nature; he is the boon-giver of civilization who ventures forth to bring back the power that reinvigorates the world. In Jackson's America he was the frontier farmer; the plow was his symbol and his weapon, the farm his realm, and the property deed his title to legitimacy.

In 1828, the opponents of Andrew Jackson bitterly bewailed the fact that 'some very honest folks' thought Andrew Jackson was a farmer.

> The advocates of General Jackson for the Presidency [wrote an anonymous pamphleteer] have pressed into his support every circumstance and every epithet which they have supposed might influence the popular feeling in his favor. 'The modern Cincinnatus,' 'The Second Washington' (what an abuse of language!) 'The Hero of two wars,' (In 1780 he was only thirteen years of age) are given to him with a degree of impartiality almost ludicrous. Of all these epithets, one of the most ill-fitted is that of the 'farmer of Tennessee,' which was intended, no doubt, to operate upon the feelings of our own northern farmers, by holding up the General to their view as one of themselves, engaged in the same employment, and actuated by the same feelings. The comparison of the occupation of our hardy yeomanry to that of a man whose plantation is worked by slaves and superintended by an overseer . . . is almost too ridiculous to be seriously noticed.[29]

This statement is as important for what it assumes as for what it says. The assumption is that if Andrew Jackson did work the soil himself, rather than at one remove through slave labor, he *would* be actuated by the same feelings as the hardy yeomen of the nation. It grants the thesis that underlies the attempt to present Andrew Jackson to the nation as a farmer; it only denies its application. A later and more widely attended critic of Andrew Jackson was still faced with the need to combat the assumption that Andrew Jackson was a farmer. 'It aint tu be understood here [wrote some anonymous person in the character of Jack Downing] that the Farmer warn't still the gineral. . . This wou'dnt be jist rite for as tu the matter of farmin, I guess he didn't know much about it. He cou'dnt tell the chronology of a cow by the rinkles on her horns; but as tu hosses, chickens and niggurs, he was up tu trap.[30]

Looking back over the career of Andrew Jackson, one can sympathize with his opponents in their fury at the widespread image of Jackson as a farmer. He was, as a modern student of Jackson has observed, what we should now call a member of the *rentier* class.[31] His personal tastes might favor French hand-printed wallpaper for the hallway of 'The Hermitage' and express themselves in orders for $1500 worth of cut glass for his personal use,[32] but when Jackson arrived in Washington his opponents expected to see a savage armed with a tomahawk and with a scalping knife in his teeth. 'Many here [in Washington, Jackson wrote to a friend] . . . had expected, I understand, to see a most uncivilized, unchristian man.'[33] Unsympathetic observers sneeringly referred to Jackson's pre-inauguration headquarters at Gadsby's hotel as 'the Wigwam.'[34]

Andrew Jackson's opponents saw his relation to nature as that of the savage; Jackson's name was synonymous with barbarism.[35] Jackson's friends and political managers preferred to stress his relation to nature in more honorific terms. Thus, Jackson referred to himself in his correspondence as 'a plain cultivator of the soil' and expressed the desire to remain on 'my own farm.'[36] A Democratic meeting in Philadelphia in 1823 referred to Jackson as the 'American Cincinnatus' retired on his farm, 'cultivating with his own hand the soil that he defended from the grasp of a foreign foe.' [37] The Cincinnatus theme was echoed throughout the land and the Pittsburgh Committee of Correspondence, friendly to Jackson's election, invoking Washington as well as Cincinnatus, beseeched the nation to 'call him from the plough to direct the destinies of his country.' [38] Amos Kendall, when he had occasion to refer to Jackson's military exploits, liked to call him the 'farmer soldier.' [39] Supporters toasted Jackson as the 'Farmer of Tennessee.' [40] John Henry Eaton, writing under the pseudonym of 'Wyoming,' concluded his series of letters in behalf of Jackson's candidacy in 1824 by saying if he had consulted Jackson's personal happiness he would have preferred 'that he should remain upon his farm and at his plough.' [41] It was made clear by reference to his neat and prosperous acres that Jackson was a good farmer.[42] When he died a eulogist summed it up: 'He wielded the axe, guided the plough, and made, with his own hands, the most of his farming utensils — as nature had made him a farmer and a mechanic, besides making him a statesman and soldier.' [43]

Despite the fact that Andrew Jackson was no 'farmer,' that he did not work his land 'with his own hand,' and that as the owner of 'The Hermitage' he hardly qualified as a 'plain cultivator of the soil,' he was so presented to the American people. Friendly portrayals pictured Jackson at his plow and stressed the fact that he worked his farm himself. Adverse comments attempted to push Jackson out beyond the pale of civilization into the chaotic regions of unorganized nature. Both versions embodied a rejection by the American mind of the extreme of nature which was savagery, but the image of Jackson apparently accepted by the majority of the people just as carefully rejected a complete acceptance of the advanced stages of civilization. This ambivalent attitude was possible as long as the United States fronted free land so that its progress in civilization was constantly regenerated by contact with nature. The solution of a periodic return to nature was an uneasy one, however, since it had an obvious temporal limit. What was more important, the ideal of the admixture of nature and civilization was a static one. It could be achieved only in the pioneer stage when the wildness of nature had been subdued but the enervating influence of civilization had not yet been felt. As America moved toward a denser civilization, the conflict in logic implicit in the two ideas made ideological adjustment to a new social stage difficult. Jacksonian democratic thought, built upon a philosophy of nature in the concrete, was oriented toward a period in American social development that was slipping away at the very moment of its formulation.

I V

The Plowman and the Professor

WHEN the Battle of New Orleans was over, Andrew Jackson drew a moral from it for his troops:

> Reasoning always from false principles, [the British, said Jackson] expected little opposition from men whose officers even were not in uniform, who were ignorant of the rules of dress, and who had never been caned into discipline. Fatal mistake! a fire incessantly kept up, directed with calmness and unerring aim, strewed the field with the brave officers and men of the column, which slowly advanced, according to the most approved rules of European tactics, and was cut down by the untutored courage of the American militia.[1]

We know now why the British reasoned from false principles; I cite Jackson's speech here to draw attention

to the effortless character which was ascribed to the superiority of Jackson's troops, the theme which I suggested
was implied in Troup's speech in the use of the word 'untrained.' The Americans are not in uniform, that is, they
do not wear the badge of training; their obedience is freely
given, it is not the artificial product of coercion; ignorant
of the most approved rules of European tactics they are
victorious by virtue of their untutored courage. As Jackson's chief engineer, Major Latour, described 'those modest and simple sons of nature': 'Instinctively valiant, disciplined without having passed through the formal training
of reviews and garrison manoeuvres, they evinced [attri-
butes] which were of far more avail than scientific tactics.' [2]
The rejection of formalism and training here is based on
the assumption that there is a superior strength that is
spontaneous.

Descriptions of the militia constantly stressed their lack
of training. 'With their long unkempt hair and unshorn
faces [wrote a contemporary historian], Coffee's [Tennessee
troops] were not calculated to please the eyes of the mar-
tinet, of one accustomed to regard neatness and primness
as essential virtues of the good soldier. . . But the sagacious judge of human nature could not fail to perceive beneath their rude exterior those qualities, which . . . are
far more formidable than the practised skill and discipline
of regulars.' [3] 'Their system [the same author observed], it
is true, is not to be found in Vauban's, Steuben's or Scott's
military tactics, but it nevertheless proved to be quite effective.' [4] The same point was made before the House of
Representatives:

> Hasty levies of half-armed undisciplined militia [said
> Mr. Robertson, of Louisiana] from the interior of our
> vast continent, from the banks of the Tennessee, the
> Cumberland and Ohio [descended to New Orleans]
> . . . There the hardy sons of the West, with the yeo-
> manry of the adjacent territory . . . constituted the
> force from which the tremendous armament of our
> enemy was to experience the most signal overthrow the
> world has ever witnessed. But Jackson was their leader,
> and though inexpert in scientific warfare, they were
> animated by something more valuable than discipline,
> more irresistible than all the energy mere machinery
> can display; they were animated by patriotism.[5]

The theme prevailed to the extent that a contemporary account of the militia was hardly complete without the word
'untrained,' or 'unpractised,' or 'undisciplined.' [6]

The rejection of training and experience, which the
victory of the militia at New Orleans seemed to support,
was an important aspect of nineteenth-century American
thought. It may have been a rationalization of American
experience but it rested upon the belief, observed in a
different context, that 'there is only one thing better than
tradition, and that is the original and eternal life out of
which all tradition takes its rise.' [7]

The United States was founded in a period when reason was believed to be universally characteristic of man.
On this basis, the revolutionaries of the Age of Enlightenment believed that each generation was equally capable of
creating its own society and its own polity. On the basis of
the absolute character of reason, history was not so much

dispensed with as made secondary; history served as an illustration not as a precedent.[8] However, in the eighteenth century, as Ernst Cassirer has stressed, the emphasis was still upon the quality of reason; reason was to be developed by man, it did not simply exist in unalterable given form.[9] Jefferson in arguing for the natural aristocrat was arguing for the precedence of intellect over birth, not that intelligence was inevitably characteristic of man.[10] 'State a moral case [wrote Jefferson] to a ploughman & a professor. The former will decide it as well, & often better than the latter, because he has not been led astray by artificial rules.' [11] But the case under consideration was a *moral* one, and many have neglected the qualification. The whole cast of Jefferson's mind would have rejected the proposition that the plowman was intellectually superior to the professor in some absolute sense. Jeffersonian democracy may have rejected tradition as a value in itself, but it did not reject intellectual discipline along with it. Rather, it stressed the training of the mind, in pragmatic terms since America's first needs were pragmatic, but not with the implication that the intellect was somehow an inferior organ. A Jeffersonian could never characteristically speak, as a Jacksonian did, of 'a judgement unclouded by the visionary speculations of the academician.' [12]

One of the many indices to the difference between Jeffersonian and Jacksonian democracy is to observe the shift in mental attitude that supported each. The shift may be one of emphasis, as all shifts in intellectual history are, but it is fair to say that where the Jeffersonians rested their case on the power of man's mind, the Jacksonians rested theirs on the prompting of man's heart. However, the Jacksonian rejection of the mind was not as simple as this statement might make it seem. The reason of the university was rejected in behalf of the higher reason of nature. The attitude that underlies Jacksonian democracy can best be expressed in terms made current in America by New England Transcendentalism. The conjunction of Jackson and anything connected with New England may at first seem inappropriate, but the Jacksonians not only grappled with the same problem as the Transcendentalists (in different terms, perhaps) but arrived at a similar answer.

From Coleridge the Transcendentalists derived the categories 'Reason' and 'Understanding.' Understanding is a lower order of the intellect, arrived at through sensory perception and therefore improved by training in the use of the senses; Reason is intuitive, beyond empirical demonstration, and inherent in man's nature.[13] In rejecting tradition, the Jacksonians took the same ground as the Transcendentalists: against 'Understanding,' or methodical thought, they appealed to 'Reason,' that is, intuition.

When in the election of 1824 the selection of the President devolved upon the House of Representatives, an article in a western newspaper offered two reasons why Jackson should be the choice. The first reason was the simple one that he had received the most votes. The second was that he was the best qualified.

> In regard to the second point [wrote the editor] we conceive General Jackson to be the only man among the candidates, to whom it will apply, and for one sim-

ple, but all-powerful reason — he alone of the three is gifted with genius — with those great powers of mind that can generalize with as much ease as a common intellect can go through detail. Endowed with the faculties to see the whole, and grasp the most remote relations of vast and comprehensive designs, he is the most qualified to govern. We should blush, if we could say with truth, that he would make a good secretary of the Treasury, of the Navy, of State, or of the Post Office. We hope and we believe that he would not; we hope that he is above such works, incompetent he cannot be. But for great designs he is fashioned by nature, and therefore would he advance the general interest and glory of this republic, beyond any other man.[14]

One attribute of 'genius,' according to this account, is its superiority to detail, the area to which the understanding is restricted. Here again the Jacksonians anticipate the Transcendental scheme which opposed Genius to Talent, just as Reason is opposed to Understanding. In the next Presidential election of 1828, another publicist of the Jackson cause made the same point: 'As to the qualifications of Gen. Jackson . . . we shall say but little. His services . . . prove him. . . He has unfortunately, perhaps for himself, (but fortunately for his country,) been called to act on some most trying occasions, when safety was to be found only in that bold and decided course which is ever pursued by Nature's great men, but which is far above the reach of the man of official detail.'[15] In New Hampshire, it was suggested that the bold and decided course would necessarily be impeded by acquaintance with the forms of official detail. 'Nor have I much respect [said Nathan B. Felton] for the long unprofitable experience of a plodding politician, and diplomatist. . . Jackson is one of the most distinguished statesmen in our country; for acuteness and penetration of mind. He is one of the few great men, who, untrammeled by forms, are qualified, by nature, to innovate, successfully upon the maxims of those who have gone before them.' [16] The Jacksonians of New York City concurred: 'Jackson is recommended . . . by his *capacity*. He possesses in an extraordinary degree, that native strength of mind, that practical common sense, that power and discrimination of judgement which, for all useful purposes, are more valuable than all the acquired learning of a sage.' [17] The Jacksonians upstate agreed with the stress on Jackson's 'native' strength of mind: 'We do not claim for General Jackson the distinction of the academy . . . but we do claim for him those higher attributes which an active public life alone can teach, and which can never be acquired in the halls of the university — a knowledge of mankind. . . We claim for him, above all other qualities, an integrity never known to yield to interest or ambition, and a judgement unclouded by the visionary speculations of the academician.' [18] A Boston editor, also stressing Jackson's 'natural sense,' concluded that 'it can never be acquired by reading books — it can only be acquired, in perfection, by reading men.' [19] In the widely reprinted biographical sketch that Robert Walsh included in the *Jackson Wreath,* Jackson's 'native' cast of mind was again opposed to the learning acquired from books. 'He is artificial in nothing,' concluded Walsh.[20]

And a Fourth of July orator, in the year of Jackson's death, praised his power to 'grasp by his untutored genius, conclusions which other men reach by philosophical detail.' [21] To express his 'genius,' nearly every characterization of Andrew Jackson eventually came to such words as 'natural' or 'native,' 'instinctive' or 'intuitive.' [22] In 1834, the Washington Correspondent of *The New York Times,* in reviewing the course of Jackson's executive career, brought to its climax the strain of thought that attributed Jackson's success to the intuitive quality of his mind.

> There is [asserted *The New York Times* correspondent] a mysterious light which directs his intellect, which baffles all speculation upon philosophy of mind and the channels through which conclusions are reached without the aid of that mental operation which can alone shed light, upon the pathway of research. He arrives at conclusions with a rapidity which proves that his process is not through the tardy avenues of syllogism, nor over the beaten track of analysis, or the hackneyed walk of logical induction. For, whilst, other minds, vigorous and cultivated, are pursuing these routes, he leaves them in the distance, and reaches his object in much less time, and with not less accuracy. His mind seems to be clogged by no forms, but goes with the lightning's flash and illuminates its own pathway.[23]

The philosophy implicit in these characterizations of Andrew Jackson is one whose chief purpose is to restrain philosophizing. It is a philosophy of action in which thought is subordinate. Andrew Jackson not only profited by such a philosophy, he justified it.

— 1 —

Andrew Jackson received his famous nickname, 'Old Hickory,' in 1813. Mr. Madison and the War Department had conceived the grand idea of an offensive action against the Floridas in order to deprive the British of an obvious base of operations. In pursuance of this plan, Jackson and the Tennessee militia were ordered to New Orleans to augment the force of General Wilkinson. Jackson had long been awaiting the chance to take the field and moved swiftly.[24] He was soon at Natchez and there he stayed on the advice of Wilkinson until further developments.[25] At Natchez, Jackson received the laconic order that his services were no longer needed. He was directed to disband his troops and to turn over to the agent of the district commander, General Wilkinson, all the public property in his possession.[26] General Armstrong of the War Department, who issued this order, later said that he thought Jackson and his men would still be in Nashville when the order was received.[27] However, the order found Jackson and his men over 800 miles from home; obedience to it would have left them with neither stores nor the means of transportation by which to return to Tennessee. Jackson disobeyed the order.[28]

Jackson retained wagons to transport his sick and other necessary matériel and wrote General Wilkinson that he was so doing. Because he had little use for Wilkinson and suspected this might all be a plot to gain recruits for the regular army from among his stranded troops, Jackson ordered that no agent of the U. S. Army be allowed within the limits of his camp. He wrote to the governor of Tennessee to have provisions awaiting him at the border of Tennessee and suggested that if these were not awaiting him there was another alternative, 'which altho' it might alarm those who are enjoying plenty and comfort at home, yet it will be resorted to by soldiers who think that their country is not gratefull, and who are pinching under lean gripe of hunger. Provissions I must have and hope you will save me from the unpleasant necessity of procuring them *vie et armis.'* [29] Jackson then borrowed needed funds on his own note from the merchants of Natchez and started home.[30]

There were more than 150 men stricken with fever on Jackson's sick list and insufficient wagons and horses to transport them. Because of the shortage Jackson surrendered his own horse and walked most of the retrograde march through the wilderness to Tennessee. On the trip his men gave Jackson the affectionate name, 'Hickory,' in testimony to his toughness.

Jackson's act endeared him to the Tennessee militia, who thereafter were always willing to take the field under him, and it established his closeness to his men. The democratic leader faces a delicate task. He must lead men and still be one of them. According to a naïve democratic philosophy of equality, the vertical distance that separates the leader from the led must be denied. One of the easiest ways to lessen that distance is through the nickname, which lessens the august character of the leader while at the same time it increases the emotional allegiance given him. After the march from Natchez to Nashville, Jackson was as well known by the name 'Old Hickory' as by his given name.[31] It is not unimportant that he was our first President to be accorded a nickname.

But over and above the affection and sense of oneness that Jackson achieved from his act, there was an added significance that his biographers and eulogists did not allow to pass unnoticed. Jackson's violation of the letter of his orders was interpreted as obedience to the higher law of justice. One biographer compared his action to that of Lord Nelson, who disregarded the signal that recalled him from the fight and thereby fulfilled the intention of the British government.[32] 'The course pursued by General Jackson [wrote another] in regard to Mr. Armstrong's order, and the Volunteers, may meet with the animadversion of the *mere* officer, who acquired his knowledge of tactics from *books,* and his ideas of subordination from reading the articles of war.' [33] 'An ordinary man [said a eulogist, recalling the affair], the mere slave of routine and detail, would have complied, followed strictly the letter of his order.' [34] But Jackson was no *mere* officer, no slave to the articles of war. 'He refused [said still another] to obey the order, because he could not obey it without violating a higher authority, than any that mortal man can give — his moral obligations.' [35] 'His love of justice was so great . . . he disobeyed the positive orders of his government.' [36] In language that precisely accords with the Transcendental distinction between the Reason and the Understanding, it was observed that 'nothing can be more obvious than the distinction between nominal and real obedience.' [37]

There always lingered about the famous name, 'Old

Hickory,' not only the sense of fraternity but the suggestion that here was a man who would act for justice untrammeled by forms. Jackson's nickname served as a constant reminder that he was less concerned with methods than with results, that, as a man of action, he was willing to let the law accommodate itself to his course even if it had to be after the act. Andrew Jackson represented the individual of native force who was able to transcend forms because he was in touch with the reality that gave the forms meaning.

— 2 —

The son-in-law of Jackson's intimate friend and close political advisor, John Overton, felt that it was the attack made by Congress upon Andrew Jackson during the Seminole controversy that assured him his fame.[38] Certainly Jackson's actions in occupying Spanish forts in Florida and executing two British subjects while pursuing the Seminole Indians kept him before the public. The debate over the Seminole affair was the first lengthy Congressional investigation — the first in a long series to which later generations have become somewhat more inured. As Jackson testily observed to President Monroe, the debate in the House caused him to 'be laboriously engaged for a longer time than I was employed in giving peace and security to our borders.' [39] The affair itself occupied the public prints from the early summer of 1818 until Jackson's final vindication and triumphant tour of the eastern cities in February 1819. The *National Intelligencer,* in its attempt to provide full coverage of the House debates, was not able to print the last speech on the subject until May 19, 1819, almost three months after a House vote had disposed of the affair in Jackson's favor.

The Seminole affair had many facets. It involved domestic politics as well as foreign relations, the philosophy of American expansionism as well as international law. But an aspect not generally noted was the way in which the Seminole affair disclosed the sharply activistic temper of the American people. The people approved Jackson's actions in Florida and resisted any efforts to translate his deeds into abstractions that had a relevance beyond the immediate situation. The opposition to Jackson in Congress attempted to censure Jackson on the high grounds of international law and to impugn his character by suggesting that his disregard for authority outside himself presented a grave threat to the democratic process. But, as in the affair which gave Andrew Jackson his famous nickname, the people cared little for the letter of the law; they admired the man of action, the man of self-reliance.

Andrew Jackson was connected with nearly every stage of the Seminole controversy.[40] The Seminoles were Creek Indians and Jackson's harsh treaty at Fort Jackson in 1814 had made them ripe for violence. The defeat of the British in the War of 1812, however, had deprived the Seminoles of their only strong ally and the British were hardly in a mood to intercede in their behalf. Jackson's victory at New Orleans was not unconnected with the British attitude. When settlers attempted to occupy the lands obtained under the treaty of Fort Jackson trouble threatened, and a large armed force was necessary even to survey the land. Once settlement took place depredations were common on both sides, but in addition to the ordinary complaints the white American settlers believed that British agents were inciting the Indians. At the moment when the border conflicts passed into formal warfare the command of the American troops on the southeastern frontier passed from General Gaines to General Andrew Jackson.[41]

Jackson responded to the demands of his new command in characteristic fashion. He was authorized to call on the governors of neighboring states for additional troops if they were needed. The governor of Tennessee was away, however, so Jackson rounded up his old officers and called out troops on his own initiative, and left the governor to approve the action when he returned to the state. Jackson was correct in assuming that the governor would approve, but the deed illustrates his whole course in the Florida campaign. Jackson acted and let the legal rationalization catch up with the deed. He swept through Florida, crushed the Indians, executed the Englishmen, Arbuthnot and Ambrister, and occupied the main Spanish towns in Florida. When his whirlwind course was over, Jackson seemed to have violated nearly every standard of justice. He had disobeyed orders, originally sent to Gaines, not to molest Spanish forts, and he had caused the death of two British subjects on what were flimsy legalistic grounds. Like many another general, Jackson had correctly estimated the military situation but had ignored the larger situation in which it was inextricably involved.

The *Richmond Enquirer* led the attack against the proceedings of the United States in Florida. On June 30, 1818, it suggested that Jackson had exceeded his authority; the July 3 issue quoted demands from southern papers that the government accept the situation as a *fait accompli* and retain the Floridas. The first long editorial attack came on July 14, signed 'Civis,' and was directed not against Jackson but against Monroe for executive usurpation. At the very outset, the *Enquirer* editorial gives us one key to the intensity of the argument over the whole affair in Florida. The attack was as much political as it was legal or ethical. The press that opposed the action was the Crawford press, led by the *Enquirer*. A fierce struggle for the succession underlay a dispute that was ostensibly international in character. This quickly became apparent and caused a general revulsion against the Crawford and Clay factions. *Niles' Weekly Register* ran a long editorial pointing out that the opposition has 'struck at another man over [Jackson's] shoulder. This is our serious *opinion.*' [42] The western papers admonished Clay for opening a breach with the President [43] and the *Boston Patriot* observed that the whole inquiry was an effort by 'the hostile combination against the executive.' [44]

Its obvious political bias weakened an argument which took as its basis the high ground of the law of nations. The argument was further weakened by a widespread contempt for the legal hair-splitting that accompanied the entire debate. This feeling was naturally strongest in the South, which stood most to gain by taking Florida, but it was shared nationally. The Nashville papers expressed the southern point of view.

> Some of the Eastern editors [commented a Nashville editor] are greatly incensed. . . With them, all is wrong that Puffendorf and Vattel [authorities on the law of nations] has [sic] not declared right. . . Let our Eastern friends look to the situation of the frontier in the western country [here follows a lurid description of the horrors of Indian warfare]. In such a situation what would be his feelings; would he go to some learned treatise on national law and enquire what was right to propose to be done; or would he complain of a general who would afterwards inflict the heaviest vengeance upon such lawless offenders.[45]

Colonel Robert Butler expressed the sentiment of the Southwest more nakedly in a toast given to Andrew Jackson on his return to Nashville from Pensacola: '*The Floridas* — Ours without 16 years of negotiation.' [46]

Probably no argument would have persuaded the Southwest that Jackson had acted wrongly, but the position taken by his opponents was ill-received in every section of the country. The opposition's argument was a legalistic one. The first long editorial of the *Richmond Enquirer* against Jackson's course was replete with quotations from Bynkershoek and Vattel.[47] It is a good example of the sophisticated position that characterized Jackson's adversaries throughout the debate. When Representative Cobb of Georgia made his attack on Jackson in the House, he held a copy of Vattel's *Law of Nations* in his hand and quoted from it freely.⁴⁸ The famous letters of 'Algernon Sidney' in the *Enquirer* were marked throughout with citations from authorities on international law.⁴⁹

The almost inevitable result was that the main themes of the opposition's argument were lost in the mass of references. The editor of *The Eastern Argus* simply confessed his inability to comprehend the force of the argument from law and approved the result of Jackson's action.⁵⁰ A Mr. Wright of Cincinnati expressed the same thought at a Fourth of July dinner when he offered the volunteer toast: 'Gentlemen — I am confident I express the sentiments of you all, when I say, we shall ever admire bravery. Let lawyers have their demurrers and exceptions, give the soldiers their declaration and execution. As citizens of the West and men capable of gratitude, you can never forget the hero who protected from capture and pillage the great reservoir of your trade. I give you *General Andrew Jackson* — The soldier whose hobby it is always to conquer, and his single fault to be too quick in planting his own standard at the headquarters of his enemy.' ⁵¹ After the Secretary of State, John Quincy Adams, gave both Spain and the administration's critics a lesson in the reading of Vattel, it did seem that Jackson's only fault was that he was too quick. The people approved and their approbation suggests that they subscribed to the view that the criticisms of Jackson were 'jesuitical distinctions between different parts of a noble action.' ⁵²

The significance of the popular reaction to Jackson's course in the Seminole affair is summed up by an anecdote in the reminiscences of Henry A. Wise. Long after the event, Wise had a conversation about Jackson and Florida with John Quincy Adams in the House of Representatives. Adams maintained that Jackson was a man of absolutely no principles because when Adams had defended him on the high ground of international law, as expounded by Grotius, Puffendorf, and Vattel, General Jackson's response was, 'D—n Grotius! d—n Puffendorf! d—n Vattel! — this is a mere matter between Jim Monroe and myself!'

> Jackson was the very man to d—n Grotius, Puffendorf and Vattel [commented Wise]; and Adams was the very man to condemn him for that above all other things as a great malefactor. Jackson cared only for his justification; but Adams was horrified at its mode. Jackson made law, Adams quoted it.[53]

'Jackson made law, Adams quoted it.' That single sentence puts it succinctly. Having once approved the end, the people were not inclined to make distinctions among means. In the Seminole affair, Jackson and Adams were on the same side of the question but less than a decade later the American people were presented with a choice between the doer and the thinker.

— 3 —

The origin of the name, 'Old Hickory,' and the Seminole affair foreshadow one of the reasons why the American electorate in 1828 preferred Andrew Jackson to John

Quincy Adams. One of the factors in Jackson's success seems to have been that the people believed that their will had been thwarted in the election of 1824.[54] Another was that, running against an ex-Harvard professor, Jackson embodied a rejection of the intellectual.

The followers of Adams never could bring themselves to believe that the American people in selecting a President could spurn a trained diplomatist and statesman like John Quincy Adams and embrace a man so eminently unqualified by background as Andrew Jackson. Their only solace finally had to be that of another Adams that the people, being coarse, preferred a coarse instrument.[55] But before a coarse people had laid rude hands on John Quincy Adams, he and his supporters made their appeal on the grounds of the intricacy of government and the need of training for its proper administration. 'General Jackson is not qualified [went the address of the friends of Adams in New Hampshire] . . . he has had little experience . . . If elected, could he possibly, even with the best intentions, discharge the complicated and arduous duties of President.' [56] To prove Jackson's lack of qualifications the friends of Adams were not above circulating forgeries which demonstrated Jackson's illiteracy.[57] An Adams campaign pamphlet purporting to be an impartial and true history of Jackson asked with horror, 'What will the English malignants . . . the Edinburgh and Quarterly reviewers, — who have hitherto defamed even the best writings of our countrymen, say of a people who want a man to govern them who cannot spell *more than about one word in four?*' [58] The answer should have been fairly obvious.

The people didn't give much of a damn what the English malignants thought and, as has been the case until recently in American politics, were disposed to support the candidate who stood at the farthest pole from English opinion. Adams's campaign on the basis of learning and experience was, as a student of Ohio has said, 'not of the sort to arouse popular enthusiasm.' [59]

In the election of 1828, the American people were presented with a choice between the plowman and the professor that was not limited to the area of morals, although morals figured prominently in the campaign. But the Jacksonians did not repudiate academic training, personified in the Harvard professor, simply to embrace ignorance in its stead. Pursuing the distinction between reason and understanding, they took the higher ground that the type of intelligence represented by Adams was the corruption of real intelligence.

That Mr. Adams is possessed of *learning* [wrote the Republican General Committee of New York City] we are willing to admit. We are not ignorant that he has received a college education — that he has been a professor of rhetoric . . . He may be a philosopher, a lawyer, an elegant scholar, and a poet, too, forsooth (we know he wrote doggerel verses upon Mr. Jefferson,) and yet the nation may be little better off for all these endowments and accomplishments. That he is *learned* we are willing to admit; but his *wisdom* we take leave to question . . . We confess our attachment to the homely doctrine; thus happily expressed by the great Englis[h] poet: —

> That not to know of things remote
> 'From use, obscure and subtle, but to know
> 'That which before us lies in daily life,
> 'Is the prime wisdom.'

That wisdom we believe Gen. Jackson possesses in an eminent degree.[60]

The contrast between learning and wisdom was also implicit in the sarcasm of a Boston editor, probably Theodore Lyman:

> Plain simple common sense [marks Jackson's style. One] will encounter few brilliant metaphors, no Greek quotations, no toilsome and painful struggles after eloquence — . . . But Mr. Adams is a learned man; he reads Byron and Puffendorf, and Jean Jacques Rousseau; has studied chemistry and meteorology, and metaphysics, and will dispute with any man 'de omnibus rebus et quibusdam aliis' . . . were I am [sic] a member of the Corporation at Harvard, I should certainly defer a selection of a president of that Institution till after the Ides of March.[61]

An Ohio paper stressed that Jackson did not secure his knowledge 'from Voltaire, and Oriental legends,' but it introduced another element by expressing confidence in the old hero because he was 'not raised in the lap of luxury and wealth.' [62] The corruption of wisdom by learning, of Reason by Understanding, is here linked to the material advance of society, the movement away from nature. In national terms the problem could then be phrased as the simple West *versus* the effete East; in a wider frame of reference, as the United States *versus* Europe. For the American mind Europe stood for tradition, training, and luxury. The repudiation of formal training was thus inextricably involved with the repudiation of Europe, and the two attitudes lent each other mutual support. This is part of the significance of the boast that Andrew Jackson had not spent his life in foreign courts.[63] To account for the fall from grace of another westerner, the western press said of Henry Clay that 'once he was the open and frank servant of the people. . . Since his return from Europe, he has been a changed man.'[64] The reason education and culture, represented by Europe, could be dismissed is that they were conceived to be at best no more than adornments to the natural intellect. Thus Levi Woodbury, while asserting that Jackson was a great statesman, did not wish to claim for him 'what he himself was the last man to tolerate as deserved — any deep researches into the writings of political economists, or that wide range of historical reading which *sometimes* instructs, no less than it adorns. . . He had been endowed, by nature, with a strong intellect.'[65] Even the suggestion of qualification was repugnant to another eulogist: 'Regular and classical education has been thought by some distinguished men, to be unfavorable to great vigour and originality of the understanding; and that, like civilization, whilst it made society more interesting and agreeable, yet, at the same time, it levelled the distinctions of nature. That whilst it strengthened and assisted the feeble, it was calculated to deprive the strong of their triumph, and beat down the hopes of the aspiring. . . Andrew Jackson escaped the training and dialectics of the schools.' [66]

Jackson's political friend, John Henry Eaton, played on these ideas in his famous *Letters of Wyoming.*

It is certainly necessary, remarked a gentleman the other day, [wrote Eaton] that the President of the United States should be acquainted with the particular etiquette and ceremonies which appertain to the intercourse of different courts. Of Jackson I entertain the most exalted opinion, but then he has been reared in the interior and having never been to any of the European courts it is impossible he should be informed on those rules of polite intercourse, which the head of a nation should be acquainted with. . . To wiser heads [commented Eaton], and to those who may be conversant in the sublime science of dancing, is it left for discussion, if in the choice of a Chief Magistrate, if it be a material inquiry, whether he may bow with the right or left foot foremast [sic]. Upon this subject the constitution is silent.

I am indeed sorry to see my country manifest such fondness and partiality for exotics. In manners, dress, and language we are imitators, and borrowers from abroad; native genius sinks. . . All that we have national, is our government, and even that, ere long, without much caution, will have introduced into it, many notions and idioms, other than the growth of this country; already have some appeared: witness for example those things called etiquette and courtly parade (and nonsense) so much in vogue at our metropolis. . .

But 'tis folly I know to rail against fashion; she is
a tyrant that has long ruled us and will bear sway. In
Europe she has decreed that kings shall rule, and the
people submit. In this wilderness, as if by magic, a new
and different order of things has appeared; but vigilance apart and that order will soon be encroached
upon. Well! be it so.[67]

In Eaton's conversation with his imaginary gentleman,
Jackson, simplicity, and native genius are counterpoised
against the metropolis, exoticism, and the influence of Europe. The diplomat, here reduced to the level of the dancing master, has nothing to bring to the United States except the corruption of Europe. The founding fathers have
embodied all necessary governmental wisdom in the Constitution, which needs no additions. More important is
the stress upon the wilderness as the magical source of
Republicanism, with the implication of a radical break
with Europe and civilization and the further suggestion
that the interior, the West, still in touch with the wilderness, maintains the promise of American life.[68]

Francis Boylies of Massachusetts had made the same point
when he said that '[Jackson] had not the privilege of visiting *the courts of Europe at public expense* and mingling
with the kings and great men of the earth and glittering
in the beams of royal splendor. He grew up in the wilds
of the West, but he was the noblest tree in the forest. He
was not dandled into consequence by lying in the cradle
of state, but inured from infancy to the storms and tem-
pests of life, his mind was strengthened to fortitude and
fashioned to wisdom.' [69] The West might not have the arti-

ficial brilliance of Europe, but it possessed substance which
Europe lacked. Employing an image that has remained a
favorite in American expression, a New York Jacksonian
drew an analogy between the first Adams and George
Washington and the second Adams and Andrew Jackson.
'The discernment of our fathers [he wrote], unseduced by
artificial splendour, knew well how little the value of the
diamond depends upon its polish. Undeceived by the sound
of learning and diplomacy, they saw and prized . . . those
intrinsic and substantial qualities, which their sons ap-
preciate in the Hero of New Orleans.' [70]

Perhaps the greatest irony of the campaign of 1828 was
the success of the Jacksonians in casting upon John Quincy
Adams the stigma of sensuality and profligacy. The imputation was achieved by connecting Adams, through his foreign service, to Europe. As one student of the period has
observed, 'To accuse that forbidding Puritan in the executive mansion of carousing all night with wastrels and sharp-
ers was a feat even for the Nineteenth Congress; but the
accusation was, after all, no more than the *reductio ad ab-
surdum* of the people's case against him.' [71]

In an attempt to dispose of Jackson's claim to simplicity,
the administration press made the facetious suggestion that
should he be elected President he could effect a great saving in the executive department by living upon acorns.[72]
The allusion was to a widespread story about Jackson concerning an incident supposed to have occurred after the
battle of Talledega in the Creek campaign. When the
troops were without provisions, a soldier spied Jackson

seated beneath a tree eating. Deciding that what was good enough for the officers was good enough for the men, he approached Jackson and reproached him for eating while his men were without bread. Jackson replied, 'I will most cheerfully divide with you such food as I have,' and offered the private a handful of acorns upon which he was dining.[73] The story varied in the telling. Some versions had Jackson offer the meal to his junior officers to drive home to them their duty to the troops, but the moral remained the same.[74] At first the story was used to stress Jackson's sacrifice in the field; later it was used to contrast the hard simplicity of Jackson's life with the soft degeneracy of Adams. As an Ohioan expressed it, 'Although General Jackson has not been educated at foreign courts and reared on sweetmeats from the tables of kings and princes, we think him nevertheless much better qualified to fill the dignified station of president of the United States than Mr. Adams.'[75]

Underlying the rejection of education and training, which were personified in John Quincy Adams, was the assumption that, at best, training was unnecessary and, at worst, it corrupted reason, which is intrinsic and not acquired.[76] The sentiment should have sounded familiar to an Adams whose Puritan forbears had argued in rejecting the embellishment of man-made ritual that 'God's Altar needs not our pollishings.'[77] In similar fashion, as in the 'diamond in the rough' analogy, Adams's contemporary opponents argued that God's handiwork, Man, needed not the ornamental polish of human institutions.[78]

– 4 –

George Bancroft succinctly expressed the philosophy that favored the untutored intellect over the trained mind when he wrote, 'There is nothing in books, which had not first, and has not still its life within us.' [79] James Hall, who would have liked to interest the West in books, subscribed to the same philosophy of mind in an article whose purpose was to demonstrate that trans-Allegheny people were as intelligent as easterners. Hall pointed out that travelers who maintained otherwise confused intelligence and education. 'Schools are not so abundant in the western as in the eastern states [Hall wrote], and of course the great mass of the people are not so well educated; but it does not follow that they are less intelligent.' Denied access to eastern colleges, Hall went on, 'the backwoodsman is generally his own schoolmaster, and his book is the volume of nature.' [80]

Any distinction that might have arisen between the wisdom of the inner self and the teaching of the outward book of nature was obliterated by the presence of God in the scheme of things. Although few went as far as Emerson in reducing man and nature to twin manifestations of a single spirit communing with itself, most of Emerson's contemporaries agreed with him that there was an intimate correspondence between the inner nature of man and the outward nature of the universe. This assumption, the logic of which ironically drove Emerson beyond the grasp of most of his contemporaries, was so widely accepted that it was a cliché of political rhetoric. In ascribing Jackson's political wisdom to his western origin, a eulogist at his

death could say that western statesmen 'imbibed together
the healthy air of the forest and the pure principles of
liberty, as they trod the pathless wood. In their own free
hearts, they found the latent feelings which carried them
straight forward in the path of building up their social institutions.' [81] The speaker saw no need to make a connection between the pathless wood and the straightforward
path of man's heart; it was taken for granted. With somewhat more flourish Bancroft made the same assumption.

> Behold, then, the unlettered man of the West, the
> nursling of the wilds, the farmer of the Hermitage,
> little versed in books, unconnected by science with the
> tradition of the past, raised by the will of the people
> to the highest pinnacle of honour, to the central post
> in the civilization of republican freedom, to the station
> where all the nations of the earth would watch his ac-
> tions — where his words would vibrate through the
> civilized world, and his spirit be the moving-star to
> guide the nations. What policy will he pursue? What
> wisdom will he bring with him from the forest? What
> rules of duty will he evolve from the oracles of his own
> mind? [82]

Bancroft's choice of language here, the use of the word
'oracles,' suggests the support for what otherwise might
seem a gratuitous assumption. The religious connotation
of oracles points the way to Bancroft's belief that the
prompting of man's heart was the voice of God speaking
through man. Likewise, external nature was God's word
writ large. The two were accepted as equivalent since God
was assumed to be beneficent and not capricious. The for-

est was not only a surer guide to wisdom because it was pure nature, the word of God without the interlineations of man, but also because it preserved man in the condition of self-reliance since it protected him by geographical distance from the false corruptions of learning. Bancroft's belief had led him to put great stress on the Quaker doctrine of the Inner Light in his *History* and to assert, elsewhere, that in addition to the senses opening outward on the external universe man has 'an internal moral sense, which places us in connexion with the world of intelligence and the decrees of God.'

> It is the possession of this higher faculty [Bancroft continued] which renders advancement possible. There is *a spirit in man:* not in the privileged few; not in those of us only who by the favor of Providence have been nursed in public schools: IT IS IN MAN: it is the attribute of the race. The spirit, which is the guide to truth, is the gracious gift to each member of the human family; not one is disfranchised; not one is cut off from the heavenly inheritance.
>
> Reason exists within every breast. I mean not that faculty which deduces from the experience of the senses, but that higher faculty, which from the infinite treasures of its own consciousness, originates truth, and assents to it by the force of intuitive evidence.[88]

After a long section on the importance of this belief for the arts in the United States, Bancroft applied it to the political realm.

> The absence of the prejudices of the old world leaves us here the opportunity of consulting independent

truth; and man is left to apply the instinct of freedom to every social relation and public interest. *We have approached so near to nature that we can hear her gentlest whispers;* we have made Humanity our lawgiver and oracle; and, therefore, principles, which in Europe the wisest receive with distrust, are here the common property of the public mind.[84]

The 'therefore' of this quotation conceals the quasi-logic that allowed the United States to cast off Europe, the humanist past, and all formalism. A eulogist at Jackson's death, using the same comparison as Bancroft, drew the same moral.

It is eminently true of all Americans [said General Benjamin Chew Howard], that they deal practically and familiarly with abstract principles which European philosophers can do little more than meditate upon in the recesses of their closets. But it is, perhaps, more eminently true of western statesmen, who have seen society grow up from the germ, and traced it through all its gradations, until the healthy plant has shot forth both luxuriant flowers and fruits. The hut in the primitive forest was the seed; a republican government the fruit.[85]

General Howard was as willing as Bancroft to accept the conjunction between the forest and the heart, between the inner light and the gentlest whispers of nature. Jacksonian democratic thought was able to build on these twin pillars because the common man of the early nineteenth century was generally thought to be in touch with nature. As the nineteenth century progressed, however, a split between the two ideas was inevitable. As industrialism advanced, man's intuitive wisdom could less and less rely upon the voice of nature. But until the heart and the forest were sundered by the emergence of a new society that was not organized around nature, they worked together to support an ideology that was ostensibly democratic. Yet by repudiating the relevance of the past, the heart and the forest also supported an ideology that was violently activistic. The material development of nineteenth-century America needed a philosophy less than it needed action, but Americans satisfied both needs by developing a philosophy of action. Jackson sanctified this philosophy in his own person.

> The deep earnest enthusiasm he possessed, springing up from his fiery heart [declared one eulogist at his death], was the source of all his greatness. The cold, the timid, and the plodding spirit, may follow on in well-known paths, but a fiery soul, like Jackson's, fearless, intuitive, bold, and trustful, must lead the way through untried and perilous scenes. It is the heart that inspires the intellect. Its warm and instinctive impulses are more to be trusted than the cold inductions of the understanding. Man lives and is governed by love. The heart sees farther than the head. In its deep and silent revelations — flashes, as it were, from another world — Jackson was made conscious that he was an instrument in the hands of Providence — a being consecrated for a great purpose.[86]

Just as in Henry Wise's epigram that Jackson made law while Adams quoted it, another orator, taking the ground of the heart against the head, drew from Jackson's first seizure of Pensacola in 1814 the lesson that 'statesmen see that the instincts of a heart and will devoted to the public weal, can anticipate the rule of public law.' [87]

These sentiments express the desire that the law conform to deeds rather than that deeds conform to the law. It was left for a later age to question whether America could safely disregard the law, whether action that was not subordinated to a philosophy that defined its ends might not call down ruin beyond repair after the event. In the more open society of the early nineteenth century the question simply never urged itself upon the people. The age of Jackson framed a philosophy that allowed it freedom of action and elected a President who provided content for the abstractions of its creed. Andrew Jackson captured the American imagination at the Battle of New Orleans, which rightfully stands for the point in history when America's consciousness turned westward, away from Europe toward the interior. Jackson not only symbolized the negative side of this phenomenon, the rejection of the old world, but also its positive side, the formation of a philosophy of nature (of which the new world had a virtual monopoly) with the further implication of the intuitive character of wisdom. Andrew Jackson embodied the latter two concepts for the contemporary imagination. He was presented as a child of the forest and the major incidents of his career were explained in terms of his untutored genius.

Implicit in the statements of Bancroft and Howard is the weakness of Jacksonian democratic thought. Although Bancroft and Howard rely upon a primitivistic philosophy of nature to support their belief in democracy, both are addressing themselves to the concept of progress. The end toward which the western statesmen of Howard's address are working is 'building up their social institutions.' The very title of Bancroft's article is 'On the Progress of Civilization,' and in his funeral oration the destiny of Andrew Jackson, 'the nursling of the wild,' is to have his words 'vibrate through the civilized world.' As long as the society could rely on nature to provide economic openness and philosophical justification, a democratic ideology based on nature could survive without jarring grossly with the facts of society. But the failure of Jacksonian democratic ideology lay in its rigidity. Just as the farmer was an unstable compromise between the poles of civilization and savagery, nature could not indefinitely provide support for a democratic faith.

V

The Whigs Take to the Woods

In February 1835, Major Jack Downing invited Colonel David Crockett to write for the *Downing Gazette*. 'You being away off there in the western country [the Major wrote] and I here away down east, who knows, if we should put our heads together, how much we could do towards keeping the government straight and making things go well.' [1] Crockett accepted and in the correspondence that ensued in the *Downing Gazette* from February to June 1835, the careers of two of America's most important comic figures converge for a brief moment. The circumstances that joined Downing and Crockett are not without interest for the student of political tactics.

The character of Jack Downing was the creation of Seba Smith, a newspaperman of Portland, Maine. David Crockett was, on the other hand, a real live Congressman from the

back country of Tennessee, although he soon passed into
the folklore of the American people. When Crockett responded to Major Jack Down·ng's invitation he referred
to Jackson's 'glorification spectacles' and Van Buren's teaching the deacon's 'darter' how to 'shuffle.' Seba Smith's success had attracted imitators and Crockett's references here
are to incidents in the letters of the spurious Jack Downing of Charles Augustus Davis, a New York merchant. The
Downing Gazette was, however, the project of Seba Smith.
Like most of his countrymen, Crockett did not know there
was more than one Jack Downing. The confusion is com-
pounded, however, by the fact that it was probably not
the real David Crockett, of Tennessee, who answered Major
Jack Downing's letter.[2]

The confusion concerning the identity of Jack Downing and Davy Crockett, if not caused, was at least furthered
by the Whig discovery of the usefulness of both Downing
and Crockett as weapons in the campaign against Andrew
Jackson. Jackson's opponents were slow to realize that they
profited little from insisting upon his lack of training for
the responsibilities of government. Jackson's case *was* his
lack of training and the people supported it. It took the
Whigs, who 'claimed all the decency, refinement, wealth,
and cultivation of practically all the States,' [3] until the election of 1840 to discover the source of their opponent's success but, once discovered, they exploited it with a vengeance.

– 1 –

In January 1830, when Jack Downing rode from Downingville to Portland, way down east in the state of Maine,

with a load of axe-handles, a cheese, and a bundle of foot-
ings, Seba Smith introduced a comic device into the field
of American humor which was to be followed and exploited by many successors. There were antecedents for
the type of comic figure which Jack Downing represents,
but the immense popular response which greeted Seba
Smith's shrewd and self-reliant hero suggests that the type
had at last come into its own.⁴ Jack Downing marks the
emergence and full acceptance in America of what one
scholar has named the 'unlettered philosopher.' ⁵ Jack
Downing succeeded in literature for approximately the
same reason that Andrew Jackson succeeded in politics:
both reflect the American emphasis on the sagacity of the
common man. Before the Jacksonian period the backwoods philosopher had found his medium in the oral tradition of the folk; in the 1830's the rustic critic achieved a
more public place in the subliterary media of the newspaper and almanac. Jennette Tandy suggests that his various guises, all representing the viewpoint of the common
man, are successive incarnations of Uncle Sam, the unlettered philosopher.⁶

Seba Smith, the creator of the original Jack Downing,
was, according to his biographer, a conservative, clinging
to the established order.⁷ But his object in creating the
homely character, Jack Downing, was not to serve his social
bias. It was to exploit his interest in the speech patterns
and mores of the down-easterners among whom he had
grown up. When Smith hit upon the idea of making his
folk-hero an imaginary associate of Andrew Jackson, his
treatment of the President, although humorously satirical,

was tempered with a certain warmth and kindness. But the role of Presidential advisor awakened another writer whose intention was not to explore the medium of folk speech and habits but to use the medium as a weapon against Andrew Jackson.

It was during the President's 'Grand Tower' of the northeastern states in 1833 that spurious Downing letters began to appear in the newspapers of the country. Although more than one letter-writer tried to cash in on the popularity of Downing, Seba Smith had only one serious competitor, the New York merchant, Charles Augustus Davis. It is still easy to differentiate the letters of Davis and Smith. The former dwells almost solely upon political matters, particularly the bank problem, and is bitter in his caricature of Jackson. Smith, although making humorous use of the incidents of Jackson's Presidency, tends to keep both Downing and Jackson on the same level of homely wisdom. Beneath his foibles, the Andrew Jackson of Seba Smith's creation is still a character of some appeal.

Charles Augustus Davis was a wealthy Whig, close friend of the aristocratic Philip Hone, and an enemy to everything democratic. He was among the select group of Whigs who gave a dinner to Daniel Webster in November 1842. No one could have been further removed in social status from Jack Downing. Davis began his series of letters (which with a curious scrupulosity he signed 'J. Downing, major,' to distinguish them from Smith's signature, 'Major Jack Downing') in June 1833, describing for the *New York Daily Advertiser* the accident which befell the Presidential party at Castle Garden when the bridge to the mainland gave way, plunging many of the Presidential group into the bay. Davis' letter of June 25 was published in the *Advertiser* before Seba Smith's letter of June 14 in the *Portland Courier* could reach New York City.[8] From that time on, two series of letters circulated through the country and most Americans failed to distinguish between them although they differed strikingly in tone and subject matter.

The difference between Seba Smith's and Charles Augustus Davis' letters can best be demonstrated by taking a look at the letter describing Jackson's reception of an honorary Doctor of Laws degree at Harvard at the June commencement, 1833. Of all of Seba Smith's letters this was the one most widely circulated and imitated.[9] It is, perhaps, the one that most interests modern students of Jack Downing. It marks the point at which the two sets of letters by Smith and Davis go their separate ways and it is also the letter which has caused the greatest confusion for historians of both Jack Downing and Andrew Jackson.

When it was apparent that the President was to visit Boston on his tour, the overseers of Harvard decided to confer upon him the honorary degree of Doctor of Laws as had been the custom of the college with previous Presidents.[10] There was opposition, of course. John Quincy Adams asked the president of the college if there were not some way to avoid conferring the degree. 'Why no,' replied President Quincy, 'as the people have twice decided that this man knows law enough to be their ruler, it is not for Harvard College to maintain that they are mistaken.' [11] So the ex-President went home and confided in his diary that he 'would not be present to witness [the college's] disgrace in conferring her highest literary honors upon a barbarian who could not write a sentence of grammar and hardly could spell his own name.' [12] There was other opposition in New England, not all so bitter as that of Adams, but it was at its weakest in the spring of 1833. Jackson's Nullification Proclamation was one act that New England could heartily endorse, and Jackson had not yet outraged State Street by removing the deposits from the Second Bank of the United States. The aide assigned to Jackson by the Commonwealth of Massachusetts attributed the hearty ovation he received in Boston solely to the enthusiasm over the Nullification Proclamation.[13] Uncle Joshua Downing amusingly described 'what a tussle they had in Downingville to keep the Federalists from praising the President's Proclamation against the Nullifiers.' [14]

According to custom, the address to President Jackson preceding the presentation of the degree was in Latin. The situation was a happy one for the wags and a considerable amount of folklore, still perpetuated in the halls of Harvard, has grown up around what happened at the time. Seba Smith's letter concerning the reception of the degree has it that Jackson 'never said a word, only once in a while bowed a little.' The President acted on the advice of Jack Downing 'jest to say nothing, but look as knowing as any of them.' It seems that he may have bowed in the wrong places once in a while since some of the 'sassy' students snickered, but Smith's Jack Downing concluded that the 'Gineral stood it out like a hero, and got through very well.' [15] Charles Augustus Davis did not write a letter on the Harvard Commencement but he introduced the matter of the honorary degree in a letter which purported to be a description of Jackson's reception at Downingville, Maine. In Seba Smith's letters, the President's actual itinerary was followed and the reception at Downingville had to be called off when Jackson turned about at Concord, New Hampshire, and headed back for Washington.[16] Davis, however, had the President continue his tour and carried through the reception at Downingville which Seba Smith had prepared for in his letters. In Davis' account, Jackson finished his speech of thanks to the residents of Downingville; 'Here [says Jack Downing] the Gineral was goin to stop, but, says I, in his ear, "You must give 'em a little Latin, Doctor." Here he off hat again — "E pluribus unum," says he, "my friends, sine qua non." ' [17] The intent here was to ridicule Jackson's pretensions since a little before in the same letter Jack Downing had told Zekiel Bigelow that 'the Gineral can't stomack any thing now without its got Latin in it, ever since they made a Doctor on him down there to Cambridge t'other day.' The story had other variants until finally the Latin speech by Jackson followed immediately upon the reception of the degree.[18] Josiah Quincy quoted a passage of an outrageous satire upon a Latin speech and remembered that 'mimics were accustomed to throw social assemblies into paroxysms of delight by imitating Jackson in the delivery of his Latin speech.' [19]

Before developing the final significance of the LL.D. episode, it is worth inquiring whether or not Jackson actually said anything when he received the degree at Harvard. One of those present recalled that 'the General submitted graciously to the Latin, bowed generally in the proper places, and *received his parchment in eloquent silence,* which was broken by general applause.' [20] This account, with its allowance of some misplaced bows, follows Seba Smith's letter. Josiah Quincy, who was present as Jackson's aide, however, remembered that there 'were a few modest words, presumably in the vernacular, though scarcely audible, from the recipient of the doctorate.' [21] It seems that, if he did speak, Jackson did not speak in Latin.

The intent of Charles Augustus Davis was to ridicule Jackson's lack of learning, but the two phrases he hit upon to do it, chosen probably because they would be known even by the least educated, had a meaning which could be turned about with some ease. Jacksonians pointed out their President may not have read all the books in the Harvard library but he knew enough Latin to strike to the heart of a fundamental truth which his much acclaimed Nullification Proclamation had already demonstrated in action. 'E pluribus unum, sine qua non.' What have we here but 'Our Federal Union, it must be preserved.' [22] Josiah Quincy said that 'the story was, on the whole, so good, as showing how the man of the people could triumph over the crafts and subtleties of classical pundits, that all Philistia wanted to believe it.' [23] Precisely. The people cared so little for formal learning that it was of no purpose to create stories to demonstrate their hero's lack of it; they simply turned them around to reaffirm their belief in the unacquired wisdom of the natural man.[24]

— 2 —

The letters LL.D. made possible several puns at the expense of Andrew Jackson. One writer, attempting to impute an anti-democratic bias to Jackson, took the letters to mean 'Long Live Dionysius,' and a note reminded the reader that Dionysius was first the general and afterward the tyrant of Syracuse.[25] The crudest play upon Jackson's receipt of the degree, however, was reserved for a public banquet in well-bred New England. At a Fourth of July dinner in Salem the toast was offered, 'Andrew Jackson — In War a Hero — In Politics a Statesman; in literature an LL.D. and an A.S.S.'[26] Although eventually Seba Smith took the sting out of this toast by having Jack Downing appropriate the 'A.S.S.' to himself as a degree for an 'Amazin' Smart Skoller,'[27] the pun proved so popular in New England that in commemoration of Jackson's degree a copper token was struck bearing on one side the figure of an ass labelled LL.D.[28]

The image of the jackass was often used to ridicule Andrew Jackson. In New York, after the removal of the deposits from the bank, another token was struck which combined the LL.D. with the action taken by Jackson. He was represented as a jackass, branded with an LL.D., and the coin bore the motto, 'The Constitution as I Understand It.'[29] Shinplaster notes were circulated picturing Jackson as a jackass loaded with saddlebags marked 'deposits' and headed down the road 'to ruin.'[30] Contemporary cartoons made use of the motif, and Thurlow Weed, the New York politician, was sufficiently convinced that the jackass was identified in the popular mind with the Democratic party to parade the animal at election time while henchmen gibed at Democratic voters calling out 'Long Ears, Long Ears.'[31]

The Whigs, in their use of the jackass, intended to make an invidious comparison between its stupidity and the head of the Democratic party. However, as a beast of burden, the jackass also carried connotations of humble origins and lowliness and thus became translated, as many symbolic devices do, from an epithet of opprobrium into a mark of distinction. The creation of the jackass symbol for the Democratic party has been credited to Thomas Nast in the post-Civil War days, but it seems to belong more appropriately to the days of Andrew Jackson.[32] Rather than being the creation of a single artist, it evolved gradually, the product of the community, finally making itself available to the cartoonist who must take his devices from the minds of his contemporaries in order to reach them most effectively.

– 3 –

The opponents of Andrew Jackson had at first argued that he was incompetent by training and background to lead the nation as President. In the mouth of John Quincy Adams this argument was unavailing. Consequently when Whig leaders at last became aware of the appeal of the crackerbox philosopher, they arranged to have criticism of Jackson expressed in his own terms, that is through such folk figures as Major Jack Downing and Colonel Davy Crockett. The important thing is that to attack Jackson the opposition had to assume the pose in which Jackson had been standing for some time. This is more obviously the case with Davy Crockett than with Jack Downing. And as with the down-easterner, the confusion about who was the real Davy Crockett was caused by the unmerciful exploitation of Crockett for political purposes. Crockett provided excellent propaganda, at first for Jackson, later against Jackson, because, as Walter Blair has pointed out, 'he happened to offer very good material for a type of political argument which was being discovered in his heyday — the argument based on the great respect in America for mother wit.' [33] Crockett's lack of education was rationalized in precisely the same terms as Jackson's. Crockett justified his rough, rule-of-thumb dispensation of justice by asserting that he 'relied on natural born sense, and not on law learning.' [34] An old timer remembered that Crockett's best appeal to the crowd was 'a dry witty allusion to his educated opponents, which would bring thunders of applause.' [35] Even the mythical Davy Crockett, who chiefly survives today embodied in the fantasies of frontier folk tales, was given practical chores to perform in the stubborn world of physical reality, thus maintaining, even in the wild extravaganzas that cluster about him, the American emphasis on the practical and common-sense matters of the world and the rejection of the speculative and the intellectual.

The opposition had at last discovered the sentiment that had made Andrew Jackson President. [36] The introduction to Charles Augustus Davis's *Letters of J. Downing, Major* played heavily on the simple wisdom of Jack Downing. An anonymous reviewer of Davy Crockett's *Life* found it valuable not for the humor but for the homely experience common to all frontiersmen. 'The work, therefore, is valuable, as it presents accurate descriptions of border life, and shows how such men as the Colonel are *raised,* and what they are made of.' [37] The reviewer emphasized his play on the word 'raised' so that his readers would not miss his wit. The colloquial verb is appropriate here since in its obvious sense 'raised' refers to the social mobility dramatized by Crockett's career; it also, however, has agricultural overtones which suggest the 'natural' quality which made Crockett's rise possible. In this one word, 'raised,' the reviewer of Crockett's *Narrative* has indicated the purpose which the cult of natural man served in American society: to abolish distinctions (say of learning and descent) and to foster social mobility. Thus, the pose of Charles Augustus Davis, the wealthy New York merchant, as Jack Downing, the barefoot boy who works his way up in the world, adumbrates the myth that culminates in the Horatio Alger legend later in the century.[38] The concept of the natural man was democratic in that it denied class distinctions, but there was always the danger that the argument could be reversed, that one could say if men rise by their natural endowments then there is no logical case to be made against the man on top. As we have seen, in the way the people regarded Jackson, it was widely believed that man did owe his position to his native capacity and that success was proof of that capacity.

By the end of Jackson's career as President the Whigs

had at last seized upon one aspect of his secret of success, but their use of it was still negative. They simply turned it against Jackson. The pose of the untutored philosopher was designed to overturn its counterpart in Jackson. By the election of 1840, however, the Whigs found that the best manipulation to be made of the attraction mother wit had for the American mind was to go out and find a man of nature for *their* candidate. So they discovered, in William Henry Harrison, the 'Farmer of the North Bend.'

– 4 –

As one scholar has observed, 1840 was the 'year of the great straddle.' [39] The Whigs were united on little but their opposition to the Jacksonians. Their greatest difficulty was in setting aside their avowed leader, Henry Clay, who was too involved with Whig economics to serve as a good Presidential candidate. Harry of the West was finally shunted aside through a complicated procedure of nomination and the Harrisburg convention came up with General William Henry Harrison, our first 'dark-horse' Presidential candidate.[40] As Seward observed, 'General Harrison's strength lay in the fact that he was the most unobjectionable and therefore the most suitable candidate.' [41] The Whigs made Harrison even less objectionable by framing no platform and Harrison intoned that 'the people of this country do not rely on professions, promises and pledges [because] they know that if a candidate is unprincipled he will not scruple to give any pledge that may be required of him.' [42] Since Harrison was nothing if not principled, he pledged nothing. A joke went the rounds that Harrison, once asked how he was feeling, had to check with his confidential committee.

In addition to the character of the Whig candidate there were minor indications as to how the campaign of 1840 was to be conducted. When a then unknown young newspaperman, Horace Greeley, was sounded out to be editor of a Whig campaign sheet, he suggested *The Jeffersonian* as a name for the paper.[43] It was adopted and the Whigs wrapped themselves in the mantle of the leader of the Democratic party in order to oust that party from power. The lesser icons were not neglected; they too were enrolled in the Whig cause. Governor Metcalf of Kentucky seconded Harrison's nomination by assuring the convention that ' "The Hunters of Kentucky" will be found true to the great Whig party of the Union.' Mr. Bates, of Michigan, in another seconding speech, said, 'he liked the eccentric Crockett's motto, "Be sure you're right, then go ahead." With General Harrison, said Mr. Bates, we are right, and I assure the convention we will "go ahead." ' And Sargent Joel Downing, cousin to the major, wrote to Jackson that the canny Uncle Joshua, who had fought to replace Adams with Jefferson and the second Adams with Jackson, was fighting this year to replace Van Buren with Harrison.[44]

However, the Whigs did not discover the central image about which to rally the electorate in 1840. It was given to them. The opposition was supposed to have sneered at Harrison, 'Give him a barrel of hard cider and settle a pension of two thousand a year upon him, and our word for it, he will sit the remainder of his days content in a log cabin.' There is some doubt where this remark originated.

One contemporary attributes it to a disgruntled Clay partisan at the Harrisburg convention, another to the leading newspaper of the Jackson administration.[45] It would be pleasant to establish a Whig origin for the slur which the Whigs turned into victory but, in any event, the campaign of 1840 had with this phrase its central issue. The log cabin, with its evocation of the frontier, the simple life, closeness to nature, and distinctive Americanism, was placed at Harrison's disposal. The accumulated sentiment embodied in the single image of the pioneer's cabin was enough to convince an electorate suffering a depression that William Henry Harrison stood for, and Martin Van Buren perverted, all the virtues Andrew Jackson had represented.

Before the introduction of the log cabin and hard cider motif there had been a chance that Harrison would not succeed. The politicians were lukewarm. Seward says that 'the first feeling among the Whig masses was one of depression rather than exultation.' [46] Weed records how dissatisfied local Whig leaders were with the Harrison-Tyler ticket.[47] But the hysteria over the log cabin turned the election into one great camp-meeting. Supporters of Jackson vainly pointed out that Harrison lived in no log cabin but in a spacious brick dwelling in affluent circumstances; they claimed the Whigs could more appropriately be named the log-rolling rather than the log cabin party.[48] But the Jacksonians should have been the first to recognize that the appeal of the log cabin was not a rational one. The result of the campaign was a classic instance of a party hoist by its own petard.

As the party of 'decency, refinement, wealth and cultivation' became aware of what it had stumbled upon, a
rapid transformation took place in the character of its leaders. 'The young lawyers of Boston made sporadic forays
into the rural districts in cowhide boots, felt hats, and
homespun coats.' [49] The Whigs of Massachusetts found
the homely manner of Henry Wilson, 'the Natick Cobbler,' more effective than the rounded periods of Edward
Everett; in the South the aristocratic Hugh Legaré donned
a coonskin cap and went stumping through the back country.[50] In a campaign of noise and nonsense, 'men of the highest culture did not disdain . . . to go down to the people.' [51]

The climax in this crude patronization of the American
voter came when Daniel Webster returned from his mission to England. The champion of State Street and Nicholas Biddle claimed to be not only a democrat but a Jeffersonian democrat.[52] He camped out with the Green Mountain Boys, ate meals from shingles, and challenged 'at
fisticuffs' anyone who dared to call him an aristocrat.[53] Although Webster chanced not to be born in a log cabin the
fact did not deter him from invoking its aid.

Gentlemen [said Webster in a speech at Saratoga] it
did not happen to me to be born in a log cabin; but
my elder brothers and sisters were born in a log cabin,
raised amid the snowdrifts of New Hampshire, at a
period so early, as that when the smoke first rose from
its rude chimney, and curled over the frozen hills, there
was no similar evidence of a white man's habitation
between it and the settlements on the rivers of Canada.
Its remains still exist. I make to it an annual visit.

I carry my children to it, to inspire like sentiments
in them, and to teach them the hardships endured by
the generations which have gone before them. I love
to dwell on the tender recollections, the kindred ties,
the early affections, and the touching narratives and
incidents, which mingle with all I know of the humble
primitive family abode. I weep to think that none of
those who inhabited it are now among the living;
and if ever I am ashamed of it, or if ever I fail in affectionate veneration for HIM who reared it and defended
it against savage violence and destruction, cherished
all the domestic virtues beneath its roof, and through
the fire and blood of a seven-years Revolutionary War,
shrunk from no danger, no toil, no sacrifice, to serve
his country, and to raise his children to a condition
better than his own, may my name, and the name of
my posterity, be blotted for ever from the memory of
mankind! [54]

Here, in naked parody, are the themes which had served
Andrew Jackson: the rude, humble, log cabin, 'primitive'
yet the outpost of civilization against savagery, symbolizing
the virtue of the founding fathers, to which one must return for moral nourishment.

The Whigs, in presenting Harrison as 'the representative
of the hardy yeomanry,' [55] attached to him not only the log
cabin, which the Jacksonians had established as the seed of
a republican government, but also the still more important
symbol, the plow. Harrison was always denoted as the
'Farmer of the North Bend,' 'The Farmer of Ohio,' or 'The
Ohio Ploughman.' [56] In parades there appeared banners
'on which [were] painted lifelike picture[s] of the Farmer

of the North Bend, with his plow and team halted midway
in the furrow.' ⁵⁷ The cover of *The Harrison Almanac 1841*
presented Harrison in the act of plowing with the spirit of
liberty enshrined in a cloud smiling down upon him.⁵⁸
Representations of the ubiquitous log cabin usually had a
plow near the door and in a cartoon, 'The North Bend
Farmer and His Visitors,' Harrison, with one hand on his
plow, greets Martin Van Buren and other scheming administration members, inviting them to stay with him.
'Gentlemen [says the simple and trusting Harrison] you
seem fatigued. If you will accept the fare of a log cabin,
with a Western farmer's cheer, you are welcome. I have no
champagne but can give you a mug of good cider, with some
ham and eggs, and good clean beds. I am a plain backwoodsman. I have cleared some land, killed some Indians, and
made the Red Coats fly in my time.' ⁵⁹ The contrast between
farmer Harrison's simplicity and the corruption of Van
Buren is made in Van Buren's own words: 'I roll in riches,
and live in splendour, dine with kings, make my sons
princes, enrich my friends, punish my enemies, and laugh
in my sleeve at the dear People whom I gull.' The same
moral is pictorially implicit in the contrast between Van
Buren's conveyance in the background, a coach and four
with two liveried coachmen, and Harrison in buckskin dress
at his plow. Mementos which have come down to us from
the campaign of 1840 constantly repeat the plow motif.
There exists a hexagonal pitcher with Harrison's portrait
on each of the six sides; at the top of each portrait smoke
pours out of a log cabin and the whole is surmounted with
the words, 'The Ohio Ploughman.' ⁶⁰ On a large cotton

handkerchief, printed with the various scenes of Harrison's life, the uppermost view is of Harrison at his plow with a log cabin in the background.[61]

The Democrats had few weapons in a campaign in which the Whigs could sing:

> 'And we'll vote for Tyler, therefore,
> Without a why or wherefore.' [62]

Martin Van Buren in later years found the 'great political whirlwind' of 1840 a cause for even greater reliance on the will of the people since he felt that ninety-nine out of one hundred of 'the soberminded and well informed' had come to regret the 'debaucheries of a political Saturnalia, in which reason and justice had been derided.' [63] Other democrats, however, such as the volatile Orestes Brownson, were completely disillusioned by the fickleness of the voters and fled democracy to find comfort in faiths that offered absolutes in place of the uncomfortable uncertainty of majority opinion.

The election of 1840 should have been a chastening experience for those who believed in the intuitive good sense of the mass of the people. As the editor of the *Democratic Review* pointed out, 'a political phenomenon so unexpected, so astonishing, claims from the philosophical democrat no slight or superficial degree of attention, in the consideration of its causes.' [64] But whatever the causes, the Whigs by unseating the Democrats stamped Q.E.D. on the formula first discovered by the Jacksonians.

PROVIDENCE

But this august dignity I treat of, is not the dignity of kings and robes, but that abounding dignity which has no robed investiture. Thou shalt see it shining in the arm that wields a pick or drives a spike; that democratic dignity which, on all hands, radiates without end from God; Himself! The great God absolute! The centre and circumference of all democracy! His omnipresence, our divine equality!

If, then, to meanest mariners, and renegades, and castaways, I shall hereafter ascribe high qualities, though dark . . . then against all mortal critics bear me out in it, thou just Spirit of Equality, which hast spread one royal mantle of humanity over all my kind! Bear me out in it, thou great democratic God! . . . Thou who didst pick up Andrew Jackson from the pebbles; who didst hurl him upon a war-horse; who didst thunder him higher than a throne! Thou who, in all Thy mighty, earthly marchings, ever cullest Thy selectest champions from the kingly commons; bear me out in it, O God!

Herman Melville, *Moby-Dick*

VI

God's Right-Hand Man

WHEN the carnage of the Battle of New Orleans had passed and it was certain that the British had given up the invasion, the victorious American troops returned to the city to enjoy the plaudits of the people of New Orleans. On January 23, the Abbé Guillaume Dubourg, administrator apostolic of the diocese of Louisiana, celebrated a *Te Deum* in the cathedral of the city in honor of the victory. The occasion was celebrated with appropriate pomp. Troops lined both sides of the streets leading to the church and opposite the entrance to the cathedral a temporary arch was erected. On the right of the arch stood a young lady representing Liberty, on the left another representing Justice; beneath it two children, each on a pedestal, held a crown of laurel.

From the arch in the middle of the square to the church . . . were ranged young ladies . . . all dressed in white, covered with transparent veils, and wearing a silver star on their foreheads. Each of these young ladies held in her right hand a flag, inscribed with the name of the state she represented, and in her left a basket trimmed with blue ribands and full of flowers. Behind each was a shield suspended on a lance struck in the ground, inscribed with the name of a State or territory. The intervals had been so calculated that the shields, linked together with verdant festoons, occupied the distance from the triumphal arch to the church.

General Jackson . . . was requested to proceed to the church by the walk prepared for him. As he passed under the arch he received the crowns of laurel from the two children. . . The General then proceeded to the church, amidst the salutations of the young ladies . . . who strewed his passage with flowers. At the entrance of the church he was received by the Abbé Dubourg, who addressed him.[1]

It had been at Jackson's suggestion that the Abbé decided to chant a Mass in thanks of victory. In a letter of January 19, Jackson requested the Abbé to provide some 'external manifestation' of thanks to *the Ruler of all events.* [2] Jackson's aide, Edward Livingston, suggested the next Sunday as an appropriate day but the Abbé felt that Sunday was too short notice and also that 'setting apart a particular day in the week for the purpose might contribute to give a greater eclat to the solemnity.' The Abbé ended his letter by assuring Jackson that in the celebration 'the brightest ornament will certainly be *yourself,* General.' [3]

As the description given above suggests, éclat was not

lacking, nor did the Abbé fail Jackson in his assurance that
he would be the brightest ornament. In the priest's address,
General Jackson was so blended with the Ruler of all events
that it must have been difficult for a listener to distinguish
between them.

General [the Abbé Dubourg's long salutation began]:
Whilst the state of Louisiana, in the joyful transports
of her gratitude, hails you as her deliverer, and the
asserter of her menaced liberties — whilst grateful
America . . . is now re-echoing from shore to shore
your splendid achievements . . . whilst thus raised by
universal acclamation to the very pinnacle of fame
and ascending clouds of incense, how easy had it been
for you, general, to forget the prime Mover of your
wonderful successes, and to assume to yourself a praise
which must essentially return to that exalted source
whence every sort of merit is derived. But better acquainted with the nature of true glory, and justly placing the summit of your ambitions in approving yourself the worthy instrument of Heaven's merciful designs, the first impulse of your religious heart was to
acknowledge *the signal interposition of Providence*
— your first step is a solemn display of *your humble
sense of His favours.*

Still agitated at the remembrance of those dread-
ful agonies from which we have been so miraculously
rescued, it is our pride also to acknowledge that the
Almighty has truly had the principal hand in our deliverance, and to follow you, general, in attributing to
his infinite goodness the homage of our unfeigned
gratitude. Let the infatuated votary of blind chance

deride our credulous simplicity: let the cold-hearted atheist look up for the explanation of such important events to the mere concatenation of human causes; to us the whole universe is loud in proclaiming a supreme Ruler, who as he holds the hearts of man in his hands, holds also the thread of all contingent occurrences. 'Whatever be His intermediate agents,' says an illustrious prelate, 'still on the secret orders of His all-ruling Providence, depend the rise and prosperity, as well as the decline and downfall of empires. From His lofty throne above he moves every scene below . . . now infusing His own wisdom into the leaders of nations; now confounding their boasted prudence . . . thus executing his uncontrollable judgements on the sons of men, according to the dictates of his own unerring justice.'

To *Him*, therefore, our most fervent thanks are due for our late unexpected rescue, and it is *Him* we chiefly intend to praise, when considering you, general, as *the man of his right hand*, whom he has taken pains to fit out for the important commission of our defence; we extol that fecundity of genius, by which, in an instant of the most discouraging distress, you created unforeseen resources, raised as it were from the ground, hosts of intrepid warriors, and provided every vulnerable point with ample means of defence. To *Him* we trace that instinctive superiority of your mind, which at once rallied around you universal confidence; impressed one irresistible movement to all the jarring elements of which this political machine is composed; aroused their slumbering spirits, and diffused through every rank that noble ardour which glowed in your own bosom.

To *Him* in fine, we address our acknowledgements for that consummate prudence which defeated all the combinations of a sagacious enemy. . . Immortal thanks be to His supreme majesty, for sending us such a gift of his bountiful designs! A gift of that value is the best token of the continuance of his protection — the most solid encouragement to us to sue for new favours. The first which it emboldens us humbly to supplicate as it is the nearer to our throbbing hearts, is that you may long enjoy, general, the honour of your grateful country, of which you will permit us to present you a pledge in this wreath of laurel, the prize of victory, the symbol of immortality.[4]

Jackson accepted the characterization of himself as God's chosen instrument graciously, rejoicing that no cypress was entwined in the emblematic laurel.[5] Jackson could well afford to be gracious. It hardly depreciated his importance at New Orleans to be assigned a secondary role, as long as it was second only to God. As a Jacksonian said later when the Hero of New Orleans was running for the Presidency, 'whether we attribute the victory of New-Orleans to the consummate skill and genius of the American commander, or consider him a chosen instrument of Heaven, to save us in the most gloomy and perilous moment of the war, he is equally entitled to our consideration.'[6]

One expects the ranking prelate of the Catholic hierarchy in Louisiana to see God's hand in daily events but the Abbé was not alone in asserting that it had been God's special care for the United States that had brought victory over the British. As has already been suggested, Jackson's victory was so crushing that it seemed to defy rational explanation. One writer felt that 'were [the account of the battle] transmitted to posterity by tradition, instead of authentic history, it would be ranked among the fabulous, or by those who believed it considered as one of the miracles of *Heaven*.' [7] There was no need to await posterity to ascribe the victory at New Orleans to Heaven. Prior to this very observation a correspondent of the Richmond *Enquirer*, having noted the disparity of the forces engaged, concluded that 'the finger of heaven was in this thing.' [8]

Newspaper editorialists north and south agreed with the *Enquirer's* anonymous correspondent.[9] Contemporary historians of the War of 1812 were no less prone to discover God's hand in the victory and poets were not simply employing the machinery of epic verse when they too saw Heaven in the battle.[10] Perhaps the most famous among the many who published occasional verses on the Battle of New Orleans was Francis Hopkinson, whose 'Lines of An American Poet' were altered expressly for the *National Intelligencer*. After having described the appearance in the sky of Victory, who gave assurance to the American forces, Hopkinson's poem ended:

> But let the few whom reason makes more wise,
> With glowing gratitude uplift their eyes,
> Oh! let their breasts dilate with sober joy,
> Let pious praise their tongues and hearts employ
> To bless our God, with me, let all unite,
> He guides the conq'ring sword, he sways the fight.[11]

Participants in the battle were equally disposed to accept divine intervention as the cause of their victory. With unconscious irony, General Adair, commanding the Kentucky troops, wrote to Governor Shelby that 'history will scarcely furnish us an account of such a battle — may we not rationally conclude that our men were shielded as well as strengthened by that power that rules in war as well as peace.' [12] Jackson himself, in his address to his troops after the battle, referred to the slight American loss as that 'Wonderful interposition of Heaven!' [13] As a student of Jackson's religious views says, during the War of 1812 'Providence . . . must have appeared to him as a sort of an ally that constantly was concerned in his material well-being.' [14] Later in life, Jackson was accustomed to refer to his role in the victory as that of 'the humble instrument of a superintending Providence.' [15]

The widely shared belief that the victory over the British at New Orleans was the result of the intervention of providence is not due simply to the piety of the American people in the early nineteenth century; it is part of the enormous egotism evidenced in Francis Hopkinson's use of the possessive pronoun in referring to God. In a period of intense nationalism, Americans saw themselves as a latter-day chosen race and quite comfortably referred to God as 'ours.' In making the Battle of New Orleans bear witness to God's favor for the United States, Americans were simply extending in time an idea that had been cherished in this country since the Puritans had seen themselves as choice seed sifted by God from the old world for planting in the new. The very phraseology of the Puritans was retained in the headlines of two New York newspapers at the news of the victory: 'Praise Ye the Lord for the avenging of Israel.' [16] Later in the century, under circumstances in which Jackson played an important part, the tradition was to receive its classical name: Manifest Destiny.

In the victory at New Orleans, Jackson was explicitly and directly connected with God, as we have seen in the Abbé Dubourg's address. In the interpretation which assigned the cause of the victory to nature, it was the 'Hunters of Kentucky' that provided the channel through which the power of nature affected the outcome of the battle. Jackson was at one remove, so to speak, and it was not until well after the battle that he was personally linked to nature. But the interpretation which held God responsible for American success recognized Jackson at once as the divine agent. In the edition which followed the extra announcing the victory, the *National Intelligencer* referred editorially to Jackson as 'a General, created almost for the purpose.' [17] A letter to the *Intelligencer* suggested that when Jackson visited the Capitol, his portrait should be painted for the edification and inspiration of future ages. 'This picture of General Jackson [said the correspondent] may be better relied upon for the preservation of our city, than that of a tutelar saint.' [18] Years later, when Jackson was attacked in Congress for his conduct in the Seminole affair, one of his defenders warned his detractors that this was no ordinary man upon whom they were laying their sacrilegious hands.

Surely there must be an overruling Providence [Alexander Smyth reminded the House], who directs the destinies of men and nations . . . [the English] sailed to New Orleans; and there they met the dire avenger. The man appointed by heaven to tread the wine press of Almighty wrath. . . Let me assure you that the American people will not be pleased to see their great defender, their great avenger, sacrificed. . . Had this man lived before Hesiod wrote and Homer sung, temples would have risen to his honor; altars would have blazed — and he would have taken his stand with Hercules and Theseus, among the immortals.[19]

Throughout Jackson's life his supporters were accustomed to refer to his victory at New Orleans to remind the people that God was acting through the leader of the Democratic party.[20] At his death, the conception of Jackson as divine agent received one of its most eloquent statements in the oration of Benjamin F. Butler.

In his command at New Orleans [said Butler in New York City] . . . we seem to follow some heaven-appointed and heaven assisted warrior of the ancient dispensation, rather than a chieftain of modern times. Such superhuman activity . . . such frightful havoc in the troops of the enemy; and such almost miraculous preservation of his own; who in these things does not see the hand of God, the agency of an instrument ordained, prepared, and guided by Himself?[21]

It seemed apparent to contemporaries, as the playwright James Nelson Barker put it, that Jackson was 'stamp'd by the hand of fate.'[22] Rarely did an orator have to make explicit the moral that the victory at New Orleans 'pointed to the Hero who achieved the matchless victory, as an instrument reserved by a munificent Providence to save the political Israel of God.'[23]

— 1 —

In the period under discussion, the people of the United States were predisposed to find God's special favor in nearly every passing event. At the centennial celebration of Washington's anniversary John Quincy Adams found that the sermon 'exalted the character of Washington perhaps too much. There were close approaches to the expression of a belief that there was something supernatural in his existence. There seemed little wanting to bring out a theory that he was a second Saviour of mankind. That he had a charmed life, and was protected by a special Providence, was explicitly avowed as a belief.' [24] We have already seen how one person thought that Jackson's image might serve to protect the city of Washington in the capacity of tutelar saint. At the simultaneous death of Thomas Jefferson and John Adams on the fiftieth anniversary of the Declaration of Independence, a western editor asked, 'Who can reject such evidence . . . such illustrious testimony of divine interposition. And if Providence is for us, who can be against us.' [25] Since the simultaneous death of two leading patriarchs of revolutionary days might just as logically have been taken as a sign of the close of republican freedom, it is apparent that logic is not involved in this 'proof' of God's intentions. The nation, expanding violently, needed confidence to carry on its gigantic task. In its optimism it firmly believed that God had foreordained its success and it therefore saw God's hand in the most unlikely places. There is no sense in protesting the logic of the confident creed of expansion since, in the human process of self-justification, logic has little place.

Perhaps the most durable among the many ideas that have fallen under the generic term, nationalism, is the belief that God will see to it that America will succeed. This vigorous optimism comes down to us in the secularized version that everything will come out all right in the end. It buttresses the anti-intellectual tendencies which are discernible in the celebration of Andrew Jackson as a man of nature. Americans of the nineteenth century, preoccupied with immediate tasks, argued that a self-conscious social philosophy against which all change might be measured was unnecessary because man, in America, would intuitively trod the path of justice. To this was added the belief that the future was inscrutably present in God's mind and was working itself out according to His mysterious and eternal decrees. Since man's intuition was finally God's word mediated through the book of nature, both attitudes implied an acceptance of a higher law which informed and governed each individual action. But this higher law was conveniently beyond the reach of man's conscious mind. The result was that the law of God was comforting rather than critical. Against the troublesome possibility that man's reason might prove unable to validate the promptings of his heart was posed the psychological assurance that all actions were necessarily fragments of a divine mosaic and therefore harmonious, whatever man might think from his limited perspective.

In such a climate of opinion there is little cause for won-

der that the Andrew Jackson who represented the will of
the people should also be taken to represent the will of
God. The victory given Jackson at New Orleans marked
him as one divinely chosen and his entire life was interpreted as proof of the assumption. The fact that Jackson
alone of all his family survived the Revolutionary War
proved that 'the ways of Providence are dark and inscrutable.' [26] Some might think, said a contemporary biographer,
that because he was the sole surviving member of his clan
he was alone, 'like Logan or "The Ancient Mariner" . . .
But he was not alone. There was a God that overruled his
destiny — that set him apart and ordained him as a fit instrument to accomplish His divine purposes in the history
of man.' [27] One eulogist celebrated the memory of Jackson's mother who, for the cause of the Revolution, offered
up her whole family except for her last born son upon the
altar of her country. 'Like Abraham, she would have sacrificed him too, had not her hand been stayed by an invisible
power.' [28] Jackson's first important command in the Southern Division of the Army was remembered by Stephen
Douglas as having come about 'as if by the hand of an overruling Providence.' [29] Even Jackson's momentary setbacks
were used to demonstrate God's far-seeing wisdom. The in-
conclusive engagement of the night of December 23, 1814,
was accounted for by the author of an epic poem on the
Battle of New Orleans as the interposition of Heaven that
Jackson might gain a greater victory later.[30] Appeals were
made to the electorate in 1828 to elect Jackson because he
was the instrument chosen by providence 'to bring back
the republic to the purity and simplicity of the democratic

days of the country.' [31] The Nullification threat was especially propitious for interpretations of Jackson as God's
agent in quieting separatist tendencies. 'The Hero of New-
Orleans was the very man for the times — raised up by
Providence for the crisis.' [32] In Gloucester, Massachusetts,
the same point was made with a certain fitness in a hymn
sung to the tune of 'Old Hundred.' [33] And when Jackson
died eulogists across the nation agreed that his career provided clear proof that he had been the instrument chosen
by providence to guide the American people to the exalted
destiny which God in his wisdom had ordained for the
United States. Jackson was, said Benjamin Butler, the 'instrument of [God's] goodness.' [34] Another insisted that 'his
life affords proof that it was a gift of Providence, being
miraculously preserved until the great object of living had
ceased.' [35] 'Who can say,' aggressively demanded Levi Woodbury, 'that such a man was not raised up by a kind Providence for our national security?' [36]

Such attitudes express the need of the American people
to believe in the success of the historical venture in which
they were engaged. That venture was widely held to be
an experiment in democratic government, and God was
supposed to be guarding the American people in order to
preserve the virtues of republican government for all posterity. Yet the concept of a chosen race contains a violently
anti-democratic assumption. God's solicitude for the American people undermines the democratic creed to which the
people paid allegiance. The acceptance of the leader marked
by God, as Andrew Jackson was at New Orleans, also con-
travenes the normal processes of a democratic society. Al-

though the democratic principle was constantly given divine sanction by making the voice of the people the voice of God, a different inference was always possible: the leader might maintain that as God's select instrument he knew the proper course to be pursued despite the will of the people.[37]

– 2 –

Most of the incidents in Andrew Jackson's life in which the popular mind discovered providence to be playing a role provided little objective support for such imaginative projections. One, however, did. Jackson was the first President upon whose life an attempt was made. In 1835, the President was in the House of Representatives attending funeral services for the late Warren R. Davis, Representative from South Carolina. As Jackson left the House, one Richard Lawrence, a lunatic who later described himself as heir to the British crown, fired two pistols at Jackson not more than six feet away.[38] Fortunately for the life of the President, only the caps exploded, the charges failing to go off. An expert on small arms calculated the odds on two successive misfires of this nature to be about 125,000 to 1.[39]

The nation was shocked and horrified by the attempt upon the life of the President. Davy Crockett, who was present and assisted in overcoming the assailant, said, 'I wanted to see the d-mnd-st villain in this world — and now I have seen him.' [40] Wild rumors circulated as to what lay behind the act. It seems certain that the assailant was a madman but it was believed, at least by Jackson, that Lawrence was a tool of the administration's enemies.[41] On the other hand, Duff Green, editor of the *United States' Telegraph* and at the time alienated from Jackson, suggested that 'the pistols were *prepared* for the occasion, and that the whole matter was a scene got up for effect.' [42] The son of Thomas Ritchie, the Richmond editor, rejected some interpretations of the event for a friend's rational account of the escape of the President.[43] Perhaps one of the accounts rejected by young Ritchie was the explanation given by Francis P. Blair in the *Globe:* 'Providence has ever guarded the life of the man who has been destined to preserve and raise his country's glory and maintain the cause of the people.' [44]

– 3 –

Of the many turbulent episodes connected with Jackson's Presidency one exemplifies neatly America's disposition to see God's agency in its affairs. In this particular controversy both sides wound up with God in their camp. In 1833, as we have seen, Jackson toured the northeastern states and because of his action against South Carolina in the Nullification controversy was welcomed in New England more warmly than might have been expected. To Commodore Jesse D. Elliott, Commandant of the Boston Navy Yard at Charlestown, the moment seemed propitious for an overt gesture of New England's good will toward the President. Elliott had just been appointed to his command at Boston in the spring of 1833. His previous assignment had been as senior officer of the federal fleet stationed off Charleston, South Carolina, during the threat of secession. Perhaps it was because Jackson's action had saved the Constitution then, or because it had been under Jackson's administration that the frigate *Constitution,* 'Old Ironsides,' had been preserved, but whatever the reason, Commodore Elliott suggested to the Navy Department that a figurehead of Andrew Jackson be placed on the prow of the *Constitution* which was then undergoing repairs in the Boston Navy Yard.

Elliott was, it seems, an enthusiastic admirer of Jackson. It was he who in 1845 offered Jackson as a tomb the sarcophagus of a Roman emperor which Elliott had procured in Palestine. Jackson declined in a famous letter which pointed out that it did not befit the republican simplicity of the United States to have a President buried in an Emperor's tomb.[45] Elliott thought so highly of Jackson that he carried a lock of Old Hickory's hair in his wallet as a relic.[46] Besides Elliott's personal admiration for Jackson, however, there was good precedent for putting the figurehead of a President on the prow of a naval vessel. Jackson's defense of the Constitution of the United States and his relation with the ship, *Constitution,* added to the good feeling at that time in New England, made the gesture seem particularly appropriate. Elliott had the further wish that by this act he might soften western hostility toward the Navy. He thought that 'to place the image of the most popular man of the West upon the favorite ship of the East, would present the navy to the Western people with associations of a new and friendly character.' [47]

While the figurehead was being carved, however, Jackson signed the executive order to withdraw the deposits of the Treasury from the Second Bank of the United States.

What momentary grace had been his in New England vanished immediately. Those who had been able to find kind words for the President because of his Nullification Proclamation relapsed into the customary New England habit of vituperating the tyrant in the White House. Elliott might have succeeded in putting Andrew Jackson on the prow of New England's storied ship before the withdrawal of the deposits; afterward he had no chance at all.

The outburst was so violent in Boston against the 'desecration' of the *Constitution* that Elliott decided to order a stoppage of work on the carving of the figurehead and suggested to the Navy Department that it might appropriately be transferred to another ship. Before the Department acted on this cautious suggestion, however, ugly handbills appeared in Boston. One bill, signed 'A NORTH ENDER,' called on the Freemen of Boston to awake lest the *Constitution* should sink.

> It is a fact [went the body of the handbill] that the old 'Glory President,' has issued his special orders for a Colossean Figure of his *Royal Self* in Roman Costume, to be placed as figurehead on OLD IRONSIDES!!! Where is the spirit of '76 — where the brave tars who fought and conquered in the glorious ship, where the Mechanics, and where the Bostonians who have rejoiced in her achievements? Will they see the Figure of a Land Lubber at her bows? No, let the cry be 'all hands on deck' and save the ship by a timely remonstrance expressing our indignation in a voice of thunder!
>
> Let us assemble in the 'Cradle of Liberty,' all hands up for the Constitution — let the figure head (if mor-

tal man be worthy) be that of the brave HULL, the immortal DECATUR, or the valiant PORTER, and not that of
a Tyrant. Let us not give up the ship, but nail the flag
of the Union to the mast, and let her ride the mountain
wave triumphant, with none aboard but the Sons of
Liberty, and flesh and blood, having the hearts and
souls of Freemen.

North-enders! shall this Boston built ship be thus dis-
graced without remonstrance. Let this *Wooden God*,
this Old Roman, building at the expense of 300 dollars
of the People's money, be presented to the *Office Holders* who glory in such worship, but for God's sake SAVE
THE SHIP from this foul disgrace.[48]

Not all the handbills appealed simply for an assembly
in Faneuil Hall, the 'Cradle of Liberty.' Another, signed
'Tea Party,' ended with a reminder to the 'BOSTON BOYS'
that 'in the days of '74–'75, when the minions of despotic
power dared to insult and outrage the feelings of the people, by wanton acts and threats of petty tyranny, they received at the hands of our fathers such brief and summary
punishment as their conduct merited — A COAT OF TAR AND
FEATHERS, was then considered a suitable emblem and ornament for such contemptible fools.' [49] Elliott also received
an anonymous note recommending that the next time he
walked Boston streets he should wear a tar and feather
proof coat.[50] The result was predictable. Commodore Elliott felt he could not now back down with grace and therefore proceeded because of the opposition.[51]

It quickly became apparent that Boston was not going
to allow the act to go unchallenged. A bribe of $1000 is

supposed to have been offered the carver of the figurehead if he would allow it to be removed from his shop. When this was reported to Elliott he had the figurehead removed to the Navy Yard and completed there. But after the figurehead had been placed on the bow of the *Constitution*, some unknown person, on the night of July 2, 1834, during a violent thunder and rain storm, sawed off the head of the figure. Elliott immediately offered a reward of $1000 for the apprehension of the culprit.[52] The offender was never discovered, and the authorities finally took the *Constitution* to New York and there fitted her out with a new figurehead of Jackson. Commodore Elliott was not without imagination. When the *Constitution* sailed from Boston, the mutilated figure at its bow was draped with a five striped flag, the emblem of New England's separation from the rest of the United States during the War of 1812.[53]

The incident of the figurehead provided a perfect opportunity for the anti-Jacksonians. Philip Hone had visited the Navy Yard in Boston, where he saw 'Old Ironsides' being prepared to receive the figurehead. In his diary, the aristocratic Hone noted that the ship 'has that which disfigures her and disgraces Commodore Elliot [sic], the commandant of the yard, who has placed it there: the full length figure at her bows of Gen. Jackson, white hat, cloak, pantaloons and all.' However, Hone added philosophically, it was appropriate, since the effigy 'cannot but run *ahead* of the *Constitution*, as the original is wont to do.'[54]

After its removal, the missing head seems to have become ubiquitous. Russell Jarvis, the biographer of Commodore Elliott, related in his version of the affair that 'a few weeks after the figure was mutilated, the president of the national bank visited Boston.' This, presumably, meant Nicholas Biddle.

> While he was there [wrote Jarvis], some of the most leading, the most active 'Whig' politicians, particularly those connected with the monied institutions, to the number of forty-four, invited him to an evening entertainment at one of the Boston coffee-houses. After the cloth was removed, the servants were sent from the room, the doors locked, and, — Bostonians! blush while the revolting story is told! THE HEAD OF THE IMAGE WAS BROUGHT IN, LAID UPON THE TABLE AND BACCHANALIAN ORGIES WERE HELD OVER IT!!! [55]

One would like to believe this story in order to linger over the spectacle of a bacchanalian orgy held by the proper Bostonians of State Street. Unfortunately, the same story was told by an old New Yorker except this time the setting was Philadelphia, the home of the bank, and there the head was served on a salver.[56] In Jarvis's version, the dastardly forty-four demolished the head, preserving bits of it which were passed about State Street, although not in the fashion of fragments of the true cross. In another version, the head remained intact. Ben: Perley Poore claimed to have known the man who did the act, a Cape-Codder named Dewey, who, again having dined over the head with friends, afterward presented it to the Secretary of the Navy.[57] Mahlon Dickerson, who was then Secretary of the Navy, did record in his diary a visit from Dewey and receipt of the mutilated figurehead from him. Dewey claimed he had intended to deliver the figurehead earlier but that he had been prevented by some Whigs who seized him and had him confined eighty-one days in New York as a madman.[58] Those days in a New York madhouse raise some doubt about Mr. Dewey but none about the fact that he had somehow got hold of the head, whether or not he was the culprit that first obtained it. The mutilated head remained in possession of the Dickerson estate until 1854.

Ben: Perley Poore's account also had Dewey dining over the head, which Dewey denied to the Secretary of the Navy. Poore's account further elaborated the story by having the Secretary of the Navy show the head to Jackson, who so appreciated the humor of the whole affair that he rewarded Dewey with a postmastership for having destroyed such an infernal image of himself. Dewey, later in life, was supposed to have made for himself a calling card with the figure of a saw, inscribed 'I came, I saw, I conquered.' [59]

These delightful stories surely contain apocryphal elements but there remain two artistic conceptions of the figurehead of Andrew Jackson which finally bring us back to the role of providence in the matter. A cartoon appeared, probably in New York, entitled 'The Decapitation of a Great Blockhead by the Mysterious agency of the Claret coloured Coat' (Pl. IV).[60] In the cartoon, the *Constitution* is pictured with a sleeping sentinel beside it on the dock. A large coat, enwrapped in an amorphous cloud, is bearing off the head of Andrew Jackson. A ship is next to the *Constitution*, named the *Independence*, and on it a sentinel is sounding 'All's Well.' The whole scene is lit by a burst of lightning overhead. The important thing to be observed is that the beheading of Andrew Jackson is effected by the lightning; a long bolt of lightning passes clearly through the neck of the figurehead. The artist seems to be implying that God in his eternal justice has intervened directly to wreak a just vengeance on Andrew Jackson.[61]

The second graphic portrayal of the figurehead of Andrew Jackson appeared in a magazine. The Library of Congress has a clipping of the woodcut but unfortunately no reference to the source from which it was taken (Pl. V). The clipping can, however, be dated with respect to the cartoon already discussed. In the magazine version, the artist has simply reproduced the figurehead without reference to the *Constitution* affair. The perspective is from slightly to the left and below the figure. The drawing is a literal reproduction: Jackson gazes sternly off to his right front and stands with his left hand plunged into a tightly fitted military jacket in a pose that is decidedly Napoleonic. The artist was not, however, content with his literal statement. He added a symbolic device to round out his treatment. In the right background is a long jagged streak of lightning.

The two cartoons present us with a problem in Jacksonian iconography. Although neither can be dated exactly, they can be dated with reference to each other. It will be remembered that after the *Constitution* left Boston it went to New York to be fitted out with a new figurehead. So there were two figureheads of Andrew Jackson. Reference to the cartoon and to the drawing will show that the two figureheads were markedly different. In the cartoon, Jackson is represented with his hat in his left hand (the white hat which Hone saw in Boston) and with the Constitution (presumably) in his extended right hand. In the magazine woodcut, the Constitution is still in the right hand, but held closely to the body, and there is no hat, the left hand being placed within the opening of a short military jacket. The figurehead with the hat, according to Philip Hone's description and the probable accuracy of the cartoon description of the disseverance of the head, was then the first figurehead; the Napoleonic figurehead was the second.[62]

What has clearly happened is that the lightning has been abstracted in the second picture and used to connote Jackson's affiliation with the primal force of the universe. It also should be remembered that in the popular mind Napoleon, too, was a man of destiny. The coming together of these two symbolic devices testifies strongly to the popular identification of Andrew Jackson with an inevitable providence.[63] Just as with the figure of the jackass, the symbol of lightning was taken from an anti-Jacksonian context and put to work in behalf of the hero of New Orleans.

— 4 —

The address of the Abbé Dubourg with which this chapter began embodies a distinct attitude toward the manner in which God intervenes in the world of human affairs. The Abbé suggests that at New Orleans providence operated indirectly, through secondary causes. It is not made clear whether the 'instinctive superiority' of Jackson's mind is an independent second cause or is one of a long sequence of other causes. In either event, God is the 'prime Mover' who acts through Andrew Jackson. Another account of God's role in the victory at New Orleans, a poem in the *National Intelligencer,* shared the Abbé's conviction that God acts indirectly in human affairs. According to the poem, the moral of the British defeat was:

> To shew the vanity of human trust,
> To shew them that a *hand unseen*
> Directs and guides the whole machine.[64]

This poem ignores the possibility that the American people might themselves need to learn the lesson of the 'vanity of human trust,' but it does bear witness to the currency in America of the Newtonian world view in which God and his world are described in the language of celestial mechanics. The Abbé Dubourg, on the other hand, as a high-ranking Catholic prelate, probably has in mind an Aristotelian universe when he speaks of the 'prime Mover.' In 1819, one of Jackson's early biographers, in recounting the Battle of New Orleans, described Jackson as the *'first motion* of every movement,' and drew the conclusion that the victory was 'the necessary effect produced by a known cause.' [65] Although the language could derive from either world view, neither the deistic Newtonian nor the catholic Aristotelian could accept this account since, in stressing Jackson as the first motion, the writer heretically dismisses God from the whole scheme of things.

The important point is that no matter how sophisticated or whence derived one's cosmology might be, it was always possible to interpret Jackson's success as a mark of divine favor. Although by 1815 Newtonian physics had penetrated nearly every area of American thought, there were many,

like Jackson himself, to whom God meant the avenging
God of the Old Testament who was not averse to rending
the fabric of time to demonstrate his power over man.[66]
The more sophisticated might feel it necessary to place
God off-stage, so to speak, but there were still Americans
to whom God was Jehovah, a personal deity, whose anger
was likely at any moment to blaze into temporal manifestation. A goodly number of them seems to have been
with Jackson at New Orleans.

In 1937, an aged gentleman, Mr. Martin G. Fowler,
sang for the benefit of a student of American folklore
a song which had been composed and sung by the soldiers who had fought under Jackson. Mr. Fowler had
'learned the song orally from [his] father and coppied
[sic] it down — words and music.' [67] The song had come
into the Fowler family with Mr. Fowler's grandfather.
The account of the battle, passed down by word of mouth
through three generations, is important here for one of
the stanzas which were communally composed by the fighters at New Orleans.

> With rockets and with bombshells,
> like comets we let fly;
> Like lions they advanced us,
> the fate of war to try.
> Large streams of firey vengence
> upon them we let pour
> While many a brave commander
> lay withering in his gore.

Beside the militia's conception of themselves as 'comets'
raining 'streams of firey vengeance' upon the British, I
should like to place the similar imagery that a poet found

appropriate for Andrew Jackson in the Battle of New Orleans. In a poem, 'The Mississippi River,' printed in the *National Intelligencer* shortly after the battle, an anonymous versifier wrote:

> In future days a monument shall rise
> High on thy bank, to greet the patriot's eyes,
> Where JACKSON, hero of the western world,
> Against Columbia's foes destruction hurl'd;
> Where, like a comet blazing from afar,
> He shone portentous thro' the ranks of war.[68]

In the other providential accounts we have examined, in the description of God as a 'prime Mover' or of the world as a 'machine,' the intention has been to prevent God from tampering with the immutable order of cause and effect which in his divine wisdom he had set up for eternity at the moment of creation. One might still attribute good fortune to God's favor, but the ultimate intent was to remove God from the world of nature. One of the chief obstacles to such an intention was the superstition that comets and meteors were divine agents, 'fireballs flung by an angry God.' [69] Putting God at the beginning of an infinite series of events was less dramatic and less satisfying to the imagination than having God right at one's side. By likening themselves to comets bent on vengeance, the militia are drawing upon an ancient set of assumptions to express covertly the lingering belief that God acts directly in man's affairs, that they are the chosen instruments of God's wrath visited upon the British. Whether one was an Aristotelian, a Newtonian, or a staunch Fundamentalist, the relation of God to nature could be made to work in Jackson's behalf.

It is understandable that at a time when Americans liked to believe that God was overwatching their destiny, they would seek analogies to describe their hero suggestive of his affiliation with heaven. Metaphors which attempt to establish Jackson as some sort of cosmic force recur constantly. We have already seen how the bolt of lightning used to attack Jackson could be transformed to support him. Lightning came naturally to the minds of those who attempted to assess Jackson's power. While traveling the western states with President Monroe in 1819, he was toasted at Louisville, Kentucky, in this fashion: 'Gen. Jackson: The veteran troops of England fled before the lightning of his sword.' [70] Jackson was described as the 'swift son of lightning' and at New Orleans he was supposed to have fallen upon the British 'like a flash of lightning.' [71] Amos Kendall found the image useful to describe Jackson's intellectual powers: 'his lightning mind'; 'His reason was like lightning and his action like a thunderbolt.' [72] The thunderbolt analogy was used by another to describe Jackson's thrusts against the Indians: 'he fell among the enemy almost literally as the thunderbolt of war.' [73] Just as his fighters used catastrophic astronomy to describe themselves, supporters of Jackson used comets and meteors to suggest his importance: 'It was in his dauntless exposure and individual prowess, in the midst and indeed in every part of the battle, that we realize all that we read of in heroic stories, of the warrior streaming like a meteor through the fight, and working wonders by his presence and single arm.' [74]

And an early biographical sketch of Jackson said, 'We know little more of this luminary than by what we can behold while dazzled with its effulgence pouring from its excentric orbit.' [75] In addition to the lightning, thunderbolt, and comet images, one poet writing an epic on the Battle of New Orleans compared Jackson to a 'whirlwind' and his line of riflemen to 'heaven on fire.' [76] George Ripley, appraising Jackson's career at its end in 1845, also found the 'whirlwind' image appropriate.[77] At one of the innumerable electioneering banquets in 1828, one Missouri Jacksonian offered the toast, 'Henry Clay at Baltimore. The genius of war, pestilence, famine and any other scourges. Is there not some bolt in the magazine of Heaven, reddened with peculiar wrath, to blast the man who builds his greatness on his country's ruin?' [78] Every Jacksonian present knew the answer to that rhetorical question.

It was the desire to believe that 'the preservation of New-Orleans was as great a miracle as the falling down of the walls of Jericho' which led the American imagination to reach out for symbols of cosmic power to describe their leader.[79] The same impulse eventually fashioned a story that was eagerly accepted as proof of the fact that God had all the while been guarding America's destiny. In the politically strategic year of 1828, the Jacksonians held rousing celebrations on the eighth of January in the major cities of the country. A young lady recalled for James Parton that in Nashville 'on that triumphant night the band played the hymn familiar to all, beginning "Blow ye the trumpet, blow," and ending "The year of Jubilee is come, return ye ransomed people home." ' She remembered that it 'certainly seemed like deifying the man whom they delighted to honor . . . it seemed very wicked.'[80] In Washington on the same day Edward Livingston, then United States Senator from Louisiana, who had worked closely with Jackson at New Orleans, delivered the major address to the assembled banqueters. Livingston reminded those present of the nature of Jackson's glorious victory and, by way of demonstrating the cause of the American success, he related an incident which he felt contained a sublime moral. There was a nunnery at New Orleans, remembered Livingston, in which 'the pious sisterhood were awakened from their rest, or disturbed in their holy vigils, before the dawn of the 8th of January, by the roar of cannon and volleys of musketry. The calendar which pointed out the prayers of the day was hastily opened, and indicated the auspicious name of ST. VICTORIA! They hailed the omen . . . and while they daily offer up their thanks to that Power to whose aid they ascribed their deliverance, they have not been unmindful of him who was chosen as the instrument to effect it.'[81]

According to a reporter present, wild applause greeted this story. More than fifteen years later, at the Carlton House in New York, Ralph Waldo Emerson, who in 1829 had thought that the country had 'fallen on evil days' with the advent of Jackson to power, heard the same story in a slightly different form from Major Davezac, an ardent Jacksonian and expansionist Democrat, who had also been at New Orleans. Emerson recorded in his journal that Davezac told him the story of the 'Abbess of the Ursuline Convent and her bell of Ste. Victoire.'

A vow [continued Emerson's journal notes] of a bell of
one thousand pounds' weight, not if the victory, but
because the victory. The book opened of itself to the
prayer of the day, it was the prayer to Ste. Victoire. [Af-
ter the battle Davezac told Jackson of this incident.]
General Jackson said, 'This was very extraordinary,
Major Davezac, and I tell you, sir, that something very
remarkable has attended this campaign. Ever since the
battle of the night of the 23d, until the retreat of the
British, I have had the sense that these things occurred
to me before, and had been obliterated; and when I observed it, I was sure of success, for I knew that God
would not give me previsions of disaster, but signs of
victory. He said this ditch can never be passed. It cannot be done.' [82]

Emerson did not record his own reaction to this story
and there seems to have been no caviller present at the
Washington banquet to suggest that, barring a stalemate,
victory for one side or the other was the necessary conclusion to the Battle of New Orleans; the fact that it was
fought on St. Victoria's day provided no logical basis for
inferring the triumph of one army rather than the other. It
will be noted, however, that Davezac's version of the story
contains two items in proof of God's solicitude for the
American side where Livingston's has only one. The main
point of both accounts is that the Battle fell on St. Victoria's
day, which was an omen that Jackson was fated to win.
Now, to suspend our disbelief for a moment, this would
mean that God had planned victory for the American side
so that its moment in history coincided with the revolutions
of the seasons which brought the calendar to St. Victoria's

day. Now obviously the story was directed to the realm of the imagination which was not concerned with critical considerations. But if such literal objections were introduced, either the Abbé Dubourg or the anonymous *Intelligencer* poet, had they been present, might have answered by asserting that all history was a gradual unfolding of the divine plan and that coincidence played no part in the world; that the coincidence had been planned for all eternity. But Davezac's account contains another element. There is not only the date but the suggestion that Jackson had direct assurance from God of his success. The God who interrupts his divine scheme to provide for his favorites is not the creator of a universe moving toward some far-off divine event. He is an unlimited God free to penetrate history at any moment. The real point of the story is not, however, concerned with theology or the realm of logical consistency. The point of both versions is that, though they knew quite well that they were God's chosen people, Americans preferred that God should now and then give them some objective verification of their election. This is underlined by the fact that the eighth of January falls within the octave of the Epiphany (in 1815 as well as today) and is, therefore, assigned to no particular saint in the martyrology of the Catholic Church. It was impossible for the calendar of the Mass to ascribe the day of the Battle of New Orleans to St. Victoria, but the delight Americans found in the story prevented a literal test of its imaginative appropriateness.

In the long run, however, the personal God of the Old Testament proved less amenable to the support of American nationalism than the God who worked at some removes through secondary causes. This was not simply because of passion for 'truth' but also because the discovery of God's will in nature proved particularly congenial to the American environment. God's special care could then be demonstrated to a people self-conscious of their destiny through the unique advantages America had in its relation to nature. A solicitous God and an empowering nature were blended in the minds of a nation which saw its destiny written by providence in the configurations of new world geography.

VII

Extending the Area of Freedom

In the election of 1824 Andrew Jackson received a plurality of the popular vote but he did not have a majority in the electoral college, so the selection of the President devolved upon the House of Representatives. There, John Quincy Adams was elected President of the United States. *The Illinois Gazette,* which had supported Jackson, called on the people after the election to lay aside their party grievances and to remember they were still one nation. To submerge domestic political differences did not seem too great a sacrifice to the editor of the *Gazette.*

Who is there among us [he asked] that is not capable of making it for such a country as ours? A country *manifestly called by the Almighty to a destiny* which Greece and Rome, in the days of their pride, might have envied — the destiny of holding up to a benighted and struggling world the great example of *a government of the people by the people* themselves — the illustrious example of a free government; — the destiny of regenerating, by our example, a fallen world, and 'restoring to man his long lost rights.' Who is there that would put aside from his country this proud destiny. . . These confederated states have risen above the horizon like a constellation of suns, and the world has started up from the slumber of ages to admire the splendid phenomenon — to watch and to imitate.[1]

This editorial has a general and a particular interest for us. Here, in embryo in a single paragraph, are two of the most famous phrases in American history. In addition to a definition of republican government to which an Illinois lawyer was to give classic enunciation some years later, we have what seems to be the earliest conjunction of the two words which were to provide the rationale of American expansion throughout the nineteenth century. The phrase, 'manifest destiny,' has been ascribed to John L. O'Sullivan, editor of the *Democratic Review,* who first used the words in an editorial in 1845. In 1839, O'Sullivan (presumably) had used the phrase 'destined to manifest itself' which is thought to be the forerunner of the terser phrase and the first usage of the two words together.[2] But in 1825, fourteen years earlier, in a western editorial, one discovers the sentiment expressed in very nearly its final form. What is of general interest here is the double demonstration that the famous slogan can emerge only as the final expression of a sentiment already long present in the society.[3]

The particular interest of the editorial in the *Illinois*

Gazette is that in it the concept of manifest destiny has connotations radically different from those carried by the phrase when O'Sullivan came to use it twenty years later. O'Sullivan invoked the manifest destiny of the American people to lend an aura of morality to American expansion into the Southwest and Northwest, into Texas and Oregon country. O'Sullivan's concern was to point out that foreign nations were intruding themselves into the question of the annexation of Texas, thus 'limiting our greatness and checking the fulfillment of our manifest destiny to overspread the continent allotted by Providence for our yearly multiplying millions.' ⁴ Applied to the Texas question, the phrase at first gained no widespread notice. Five months later, however, in a discussion of the Oregon question, the slogan was attacked by opponents of expansion in Congress and thus quickly gained currency. In response, O'Sullivan spelled out the significance of our country's manifest destiny. Because providence had assigned the cause of freedom to the American people, legal decisions, precedents of international law, and merely logical objections to the expansion of the United States were, he maintained, quite beside the point. In an editorial in the *New-York Morning News*, O'Sullivan, having reviewed the legal ground of America's right to Oregon, concluded:

And yet after all, unanswerable as is the demonstration of our legal title to Oregon — and the whole of Oregon, if a rood! — we have a still better title than any that can ever be constructed out of all these antiquated materials of old black-letter international law. Away, away with all these cobweb tissues of rights of discovery, exploration, settlement, continuity, etc. To state the truth at once in its neglected simplicity, we are free to say that were the respective cases and arguments of the two parties, as to all the points of history and law, re- versed — had England all ours, and we nothing but hers — our claim to Oregon would still be best and strongest. And that claim is by the right of our manifest destiny to overspread and possess the whole of the con- tinent which Providence has given us for the develop- ment of the great experiment of liberty and federated self government entrusted to us . . . The God of na- ture and of nations has marked it for our own; and with his blessing, we will firmly maintain the incontestable rights He has given, and fearlessly perform the high Duties he has imposed.[5]

The destiny that the editor of the *Democratic Review* foresaw was an aggressive, activistic destiny. But the destiny that the editor of the *Illinois Gazette* had seen some years before had been passive, quietistic. In 1825, Americans were to save the world by example; in 1845, Americans were to save the world by absorbing it. Both schemes, al- though differing radically in emphasis, were based upon belief in God's special favor for America. Andrew Jackson was not only involved as an actor in the historical move- ment of expansion, he symbolized the underlying as- sumption which made expansion seem necessary and right. When in 1843 he so felicitously described expansion as 'extending the area of freedom,' Jackson not only pro- vided a convenient rationalization for American imperial- ism, he also represented in his own person the living proof that God *was* on our side, that expansion could not be wrong.[6]

– 1 –

The idea that America was destined to extend the area of freedom represents a union under the aegis of providence of two separate ideas, democracy and expansion. In the eighteenth century no organic connection was perceived between democracy and the government of the United States; democracy as a way of life was considered to be a universal ideal, not the special property of the new nation.[7] Although America was generally held to be an example to the rest of the world, it was not felt that democracy could prosper under American auspices alone nor that, as a corollary, the spread of freedom necessarily entailed the territorial expansion of the United States. In addition to the absence of a logical connection between democracy and American expansion, a further obstacle blocked the union of the two ideas. From Montesquieu, political theorists in the United States derived the belief that democratic government could thrive only in small states and that by centrifugal force large states would disintegrate politically.[8] The fear of extended territory was quieted by stressing the representative character of American democracy and by asserting that the creation of many sectional interests would result in their counterbalancing one another, thus extending in an unforeseen direction Montesquieu's famous balance of power scheme for maintaining republican government. The image of 'a constellation of suns,' used by the editor of the *Illinois Gazette* to convey the idea of the light spread by the American example, easily allowed the inclusion of more suns to increase the radiance spread by the new world. The tragedian (and Jacksonian), Edwin Forrest, in his Fourth of July Oration at New York in 1838, said that the experience of our fathers now stands as 'the mark and model of the world. . . New stars [i.e. new states], from year to year, emerging with perfect radiance in the western horizon, have increased the benignant splendor of that constellation which now shines the political guiding light of the world.' [9] The additional wattage which Forrest's simile makes possible is the imaginative equivalent of O'Sullivan's flat assertion that since America has been chosen by God to be the depository of freedom nothing must stand in the way of its development.

From the time John Winthrop aboard the *Arabella* told his fellow voyagers that 'wee must Consider that we shall be as a City vpon a Hill, the eies of all people are vppon vs,' Americans were intensely aware of the universal import of their experiment in the new world.[10] In 1828, William Plumer echoed the Puritan phrase, saying that 'our American Republic exists not for herself alone. She is a city set upon a hill which cannot be hid, a beacon kindled upon a mountain top.' [11]

The United States, in its experiment of republican freedom, was constantly compared to a city or a column set upon a hill, a beacon or a guiding light, a constellation of stars or suns in the west.[12] The connotations of such metaphors are, of course, the same as the cosmic imagery which so abundantly clustered about the symbol of Andrew Jackson. Felix Grundy, in a speech in 1840, demonstrated quite clearly how Andrew Jackson was used to implement a belief long part of the American tradition.

> I *have* seen [said Grundy] a light arise in the West; and so brilliant was it, that it dimmed and obscured all the lesser lights around it; it ascended higher and higher, until it reached the meridian; there it remained stationary for a time [!]; so effulgent was it, that it irradiated this whole continent; its rays crossed the Atlantic and penetrated the courts and palaces of kings, and influenced their councils; it was seen and felt wherever civilized man dwelt. But that light is fast descending in the West; it has almost reached the horizon, and will soon be beyond the sight of mortals. Mr. President, you and I shall never see its like again; we are too old. Such lights do not visit our earth but at rare and long intervals. I need not say to the Senate, or to this audience, that the individual I have described . . . is Andrew Jackson, the pride and glory of our country.[13]

— 2 —

The idea of America as example served a developing nationalism in two ways. It made American isolation morally acceptable. It supported nearly any self-seeking national program by phrasing it in terms of the highest international altruism. Andrew Jackson represented both aspects in his own proper person. He symbolized the special concern of providence for America which is the basic assumption of the various ideas grouped under the term, manifest destiny. Also, as we have seen, the presentation of Jackson as a child of nature embodied the concept which made it seem feasible and even necessary that America cut itself off from Europe. Lastly, it was Jackson himself who pointed out to his contemporaries how they could justify their acquisitiveness by subsuming it under the divine plan of providence manifestly indicated for all to see in the configurations of new world geography, so that nature and providence were intertwined at every turn. God was, as O'Sullivan reminded his readers, the 'God of nature and of nations.'

As America turned, after the War of 1812, to its own development it was not willing to conceive of its isolationist ideal in egoistic terms. The Republic was still regarded as an international force by virtue of its influence. When a Fourth of July orator described his audience to themselves as 'but the favoured instruments of Heaven' he also made clear that 'we are responsible not only to our own country . . . but to every other country of this globe, and all its present and all its future inhabitants.' [14] Echoing Jefferson, who had said, 'It is impossible not to be sensible that we are acting for all mankind,' a less literate American wrote to his son in Congress, 'You must not loose sight that you are ligislating for a great Nation whose Decisions may be a president [precedent] for ages to come.' [15] By a neat dialectic, isolationism took on the aura of internationalism by the leavening influence America's example was to have in the world. An editorial in the *National Intelligencer* made the point by drawing upon classical mechanics:

' "Give me a place to stand on," said the ancient Mathematician, "and I will move the World." This place, in the ideal world of politics, the founders of the United States discovered.' [16]

The belief that America existed as an example for the rest of the world not only provided an account of America's place in the community of nations but made it possible for Americans to perceive national selfishness as international good will. In 1825 it was pointed out that America 'has left to other empires to do but half what she has done — and with a selfishness that may be forgiven, she has reserved to herself the reward of her valour and her toils, while to all mankind she has given, freely given, the benefit of her example.' [17] In the 'thirties, the *New-York American* closed an editorial called 'The Influence and Example of the United States' with the assertion that 'it is in this way, by her moral influence and example . . . that America may and does repay her debt to Europe.' [18] In the 'forties, a literal minded Iowa editor even made the concrete proposal that America repudiate its debts to Europe on the ground that Europe was sufficiently recompensed by having been allowed to assist in the spread of the American example.[19] Even as a debtor nation, the United States had no sense that it might be other than first in the world community.

The special mission assigned America by providence to show the way to the rest of the world not only supported a repudiation of debts owed Europe, it supported a repudiation of Europe itself. If America was elected to point the way for the unregenerate to political salvation, then it

behooved her to preserve her purity by avoiding the con-
tamination of Europe, which was after all, as the *Illinois
Gazette* had observed, a 'fallen world.' Richard B. Lee, in
an address in which he traced the whole course of American history, ended by alluding to the inland empire, 'equal
in extent to that of imperial Rome.'

> We shall need [said Lee] little or no connection, even
> in commerce, with foreign countries, if we improve the
> vast resources of our own. . . And is it not worthy of
> consideration, whether the diminution of our inter-
> course with foreign nations, whose modes and notions
> of government, and whose manners are so different
> from our own, would not have the most salutary tend-
> ency in preserving untainted the industrious habits,
> and the pure and manly virtues of our citizens, and
> thereby perpetuating to the most remote future ages
> the happiness and freedom which we possess. . . "Oh,
> yet happiest, if we seek no happier state / And know to
> know no more." [20]

Lee's address presents a clear statement of the economic
basis of America's self-absorption. Present also is the article of faith, observed already in characterizations of Jackson, which made it possible to dispense with the old world.
Europe was corrupt and could contribute nothing of value
to the United States. Nature, as raw material, made economic isolation seem possible; nature, as the fount of wisdom, made intellectual isolation seem acceptable. As one
orator put it, America had rescued 'that vestal fire of liberty
. . . from the sickening depravity of the Stuarts, to be rekindled amid the primeval forests' and it was her duty to

nurse the flame which 'is yet to illumine every region of the world.' [21] The stress was on the present and future; the past was rejected as a fallen world of sickening depravity. The rejection of the past was an integral part of the concept of manifest destiny and was implicit in the care providence bestowed on America. When John L. O'Sullivan first hit upon the slogan of manifest destiny, he wrote:

> What friend of human liberty, civilization, and refinement, can cast his view over the past history of the monarchies and aristocracies of antiquity, and not deplore that they ever existed. . .
>
> America is destined for better deeds. . . We have no interest in the scenes of antiquity, only as lessons of avoidance of nearly all their examples. The expansive future is our arena, and for our history. We are entering on its untrodden space with the truths of God in our minds, beneficent objects in our hearts, and with a clear conscience unsullied by the past. . .

O'Sullivan's next paragraph states that the United States is 'destined to manifest' the design of providence in the world and deplores the vestigial remains of European habits that still persist in this country.

> But [he continues] with all the retrograde tendencies of our laws, our judicature, our colleges, our literature, still they are compelled to follow the mighty impulse of the age; they are carried onward by the increasing tide of progress; and though they cast many a longing look behind, they cannot stay the glorious movement of the masses, nor induce them to venerate the rubbish, the prejudices, the superstitions of other

times and other lands, the theocracy of priests, the divine right of kings, the aristocracy of blood, the metaphysics of colleges, the irrational stuff of law libraries. Already the brightest hopes of philanthropy, the most enlarged speculations of true philosophy, are inspired by the indications perceptible amongst the mechanical and agricultural population. There, with predominating influence, beats the vigorous national heart of America, propelling onward the march of the multitude, propagating and extending, through the present and the future, the powerful purpose of soul, which in the seventeenth century, sought a refuge among savages, and reared in the wilderness the sacred altars of intellectual freedom. This was the seed that produced individual equality, and political liberty, as its natural fruit; and this is our true nationality.[22]

For a people who believed that they had been chosen by God for the preservation of liberty and that the hut in the primitive forest was the seed of republican government, Andrew Jackson provided one conjunction that wedded the two ideas. God and nature watched over the unique course of America's destiny; both were symbolized in the figure of Andrew Jackson.

– 3 –

Manifest Destiny was Janus-faced, however. As America looked toward Europe, its destiny was passive; facing eastward, America's role was confined to the presentation of an example. It was rarely suggested that to extend the area of freedom America should actively intervene in the affairs of Europe. John Quincy Adams, in a Fourth of July address at Washington in 1821, having pointed out how America had served the world by demonstrating the feasibility of republican government, added that America 'has abstained from interference in the concerns of others, even when the conflict has been for principles to which she clings, as to the last vital drop that visits the heart. . . she goes not abroad . . . she is the champion and vindicator only of her own. She will recommend the general cause by the countenance of her voice, and the benignant sympathy of her example.' [23] This mild view of America's international role was made even milder when President Monroe delivered the message that is now called his 'doctrine.' America retreated to the lone ground of an example to the rest of the world, denying to the struggling Greeks so much as the countenance of her voice.[24] The country was little interested in world developments which did not impinge directly upon the western hemisphere.

But as the United States fronted westward, Manifest Destiny dropped its quietistic character. The aggressive nature of America's destiny, always present in the treatment of the Indians, was characteristic of the western advance. The two attitudes, one isolationist, one expansionist, could be yoked, as we have seen, by arguing that to preserve the lustre of the example, America should prosper. But if 'the vestal fire of liberty' was rekindled amid the 'primeval forests,' the United States faced the same dilemma it faced in asserting the superiority of nature over civilization. Lee's speech, quoted above, recognizes this dilemma. The primitivistic statement slightly misquoted from *Paradise Lost* ('Oh, yet happiest, if we seek no happier state, / And know to know no more') suggests that America, as the unfallen world, must not only avoid the touch of degenerate Europe but must put off the temptations that led to Europe's corruption.

The dilemma can be illustrated further by examining the meaning of Jackson's famous phrase at the time of the Texas question, 'extending the area of freedom,' in the context within which it was made. When Jackson died, a eulogist, having described his Indian removal policy as 'most humane,' said:

> His constant aim was to enlarge the area of Christianity and civilization, to diffuse the blessings of our liberties and laws throughout the western wilderness. During his time, much was accomplished — nor shall we stop here.
>
> Westward we have pressed — westward still is our destiny.
>
> The keen and piercing eye of the sagacious patriot did not fail to discover through the dim vista of the future, that nothing short of the Pacific shore could stop our progress; and he often predicted that the influence of our institutions, in its western march, would yet agonize the eastern portions of the old world, arouse from their immemorial lethargy the worshippers of men and idols, and fire their hearts with the enthusiasm of civil and religious liberty.[25]

Westward was freedom; eastward was the immemorial lethargy of Europe. Between these the United States must find its future. The equation was permissible, perhaps, so long as the West equalled the wilderness (even with Indians in the woods). But one will observe that Jackson's eulogist paraphrased the old hero while describing a state of affairs somewhat different than that in which Jackson used the famous phrase. It was not the wilderness which was under consideration when Jackson wrote, 'I thought with the ancient Romans, that it was right never to cede any land or boundary of the Republic, but always to add to it by honorable treaty, thus extending the area of freedom . . . the annexation of Texas to the United States promises to enlarge the circle of free institutions.' [26] From the context, Jackson obviously intends to equate freedom with the Republic, that is, the United States, not with the republican form of government. Texas was at that time a republican state, so recognized by the United States during Jackson's own administration, as well as by the major European powers, England and France. Jackson's famous phrase, with its nationalistic illogic, proved so appealing, however, that it provided the battle-cry for 'Young Hickory,' the expansionist James K. Polk.[27] Americans had arrived at the position where freedom followed the American flag.

It is true that expansion into the Southwest gained popular support only when it seemed that England or France might gain a foothold in the new world and thus revive the traditional policy of containing the United States. It could then be maintained that absorption of Texas into the American system was vital to the maintenance of American freedom. But such a view only focuses more sharply American self-centeredness. Moreover, a nation which believes itself to be the ark of the covenant of republican freedom is not the best judge of what represents a threat to freedom's complete development. In the case of Texas, the real irony in the phrase, 'extend the area of freedom,' was the underlying fear of southern slave-owners that through England's agency Texas might actually become an area of freedom and provide a threat to the peculiar institution of the republican South.

Since Andrew Jackson, as God's right-hand man, represents the rationalization of American imperialism, his own course of action might well stand for the unsavory reality that underlay the idealistic protestations of the United States as it expanded westward. To gain Texas, Jackson countenanced attempts at bribery by his special emissary to Mexico, Anthony Butler, until an actual revolution by Texas made further dealings with corrupt Mexican officials fruitless.[28] Despite his public disavowal of Sam Houston's filibustering activities in the Southwest, Jackson tried in the most practical fashion to support Houston.[29] Through the 'thirties, however, Jackson was running ahead of national sentiment. Not until the 'forties, spurred on in part by Jackson's own phrase-making, were the majority of Americans ready to accept the proposition that it was their destiny to spread freedom by spreading the United States across the western continent. Whether he recognized it or not, Jackson was quicker to act on the assumption that underlay the popular conception of him than were the people themselves. If God demonstrated his care for a nation by equipping its leader, it was not too much to expect that He would also sanctify that nation's material ambitions.

Major Davezac, who told Emerson the story of the Bell

of Ste. Victoire, neatly provides the end to the train of thought which began with providence at the Battle of New Orleans. Davezac remembered Jackson's glorious victory as proof of the grace of God and, in 1844, he naïvely exposed the land hunger which gave Manifest Destiny its emotional force.

> Land enough — land enough [said Davezac to the New Jersey Democratic State Convention]. Make way, I say, for the young American Buffalo — he has not got land enough; he wants more land as his cool shelter in summer — he wants more land for his beautiful pasture grounds. I tell you, we will give him Oregon for his summer shade, and the region of Texas as his winter pasture. (Applause.) Like all of his race, he wants salt, too. Well, he shall have use of two oceans — the mighty Pacific and the turbulent Atlantic shall be his. . . He shall not stop his career until he slakes his thirst in the frozen ocean. (Cheers.)[30]

The buffalo, whose shaggy wildness made it an appropriate symbol of the rejection of Europe as Americans moved westward into the wilderness of the new world, calls to mind also the exploitation of nature which lay at the heart of American expansion. Andrew Jackson symbolizes the philosophy of nature which sanctioned the rejection of Europe. He also stands for the special favor of God which consecrated American expansion. As we shall see in the next section he further represents the ideal of self-sufficient individualism which was the inevitable rationalization of America's disorganized development.

WILL

The reason why this or that man is fortunate is not to be told. It lies in the man; that is all anybody can tell you about it. See him and you will know as easily why he succeeds, as, if you see Napoleon, you would comprehend his fortune.

Ralph Waldo Emerson, 'Character.'

VIII

The Man of Iron

In the two versions of the Battle of New Orleans that attributed American success to nature or to God, Andrew Jackson, although important, was not quite at the center of attention; he functioned as the representative of a more basic force. Thus, in the Abbé Dubourg's address quoted before, when the Abbé says to Jackson, 'we extol that fecundity of genius, by which, in an instant of the most discouraging distress, you created unforeseen resources, raised as it were from the ground, hosts of intrepid warriors, and provided every vulnerable point with ample means of defence,' the significant point of reference is '*Him*' who outfitted Jackson as '*the man of his right hand.*' There was a third explanation, however, of the American victory that was ready to make Jackson himself the center of focus, dispensing with the beneficence of nature or the providence of God. The shift in emphasis may be observed by comparing the Abbé's speech with one at Jackson's death by a eulogist who lifted the Abbé's words but in doing so left God behind. 'Not one in a whole generation could be found [said Hugh A. Garland] with [Jackson's] powers of command, that fecundity of genius, by which, under the most trying circumstances, he created unforeseen resources — raised, as it were, from the ground, hosts of intrepid warriors, and provided every vulnerable point with ample means of defence.' [1] In the Abbé's address, the next words are: 'To *Him* we trace that instinctive superiority of your mind, which at once rallied around you universal confidence.' But in Garland's eulogy, the following words are: 'that instinctive superiority, self-reliance, and impulsive energy, which at once rallied around him universal confidence.' Although the priest's language with its suggestion of the miraculous is retained, the thought is radically different. Andrew Jackson, as the self-reliant man, had no need of God.

— 1 —

From the day of the Battle of New Orleans, the idea that the victory was due to Jackson alone was widely entertained. *The Enquirer* printed a letter from New Orleans to a gentleman in Congress which held that 'to Jackson every credit is due, for inspiring general confidence, uniting our scattered efforts, for calling forth our dormant strength.' [2] A more widely printed letter said, 'the glorious result is principally attributable to the wisdom, prudence, decision and personal example of General Jackson, which really seemed to instil into every breast his own patriotism and heroic courage. He is truly the great man.'[3] As Major Latour, Jackson's engineer, expressed it: 'Although his body was ready to sink under the weight of sickness, fatigue and continued watching, his mind nevertheless, never lost for a moment that energy which he knew well how to communicate to all that surrounded him. . . the energy manifested by General Jackson spread, as it were, by contagion, and communicated itself to the whole army.'[4] Latour dedicated his study of the Battle of New Orleans to Jackson, saying, 'The voice of the whole nation has spared me the task of showing how much of these important results are due to the energy, ability and courage of a single man.'

In making Jackson the cause of victory, the ground taken was that he communicated his own will to win to his comrades in arms. As one said, 'his master-spirit pervaded every bosom.'[5] A contemporary history of the United States recorded that 'undismayed by the difficulties which surrounded him, General Jackson . . . mingled with the citizens and infused into the greater part his own spirit and energy.'[6] Biographers of Jackson borrowed the sentiment from one another. With only minor variations, three separate works on Jackson carried the words: '*Before him was an army proud of its name, and distinguished for its deeds of valour* — an army, the finest that ever appeared on our shores, — one that had driven the warriors of France, the conquerors of continental Europe, from the pillars of Hercules to the Pyrenees. *Opposed to this was his own unbending spirit, and an inferior, undisciplined, and half-armed force.*'[7] The militia victory at New Orleans was compared to the militia disaster at Washington by pointing out that 'there was unmistakeable evidence of the presence [at New Orleans] of a chief, who inspired confidence, courage and determination in all under his command.' [8] The difference made by a resolute commander was emphasized by the *New-York Evening Post*: 'If we had a Jackson everywhere we should succeed everywhere.' [9] Charles Jared Ingersoll deduced a general law from Jackson's victory at New Orleans. Quoting Voltaire, Ingersoll remarked that 'seldom . . . is anything great done in the world, except by the genius and firmness of some one man, contending with the prejudices of the multitude, and overcoming them.' [10]

As the years passed, the thesis which held Jackson's master-spirit to be the cause of victory was more clearly defined. In 1827, a poet wrote of Jackson at New Orleans:

> His eye shows openness and seems to speak,
> But nothing's there that shows a woman's freak,
> His *will* chains every nerve — none durst betray
> The secret feeling he would hide from day —
> But when he *wills*, his every look takes fire
> And flames to view the hidden soul's desire.[11]

Against seemingly insuperable obstacles, upon which every chronicler of the Battle of New Orleans loved to dwell, Jackson's will was sufficient.[12] It was said of Jackson at New Orleans, 'In an instant he resolved; and his resolutions, let me tell you were as firm as the decrees of Heaven . . . never were the words of the poet more applicable, than to him —

From orbs convulsed, should all the planets fly,
World crush on world, and ocean mix with sky;
He, unconcerned, would view the falling whole,
And still maintain the purpose of his soul.' [13]

Finally, an account of the battle published in a magazine just before Jackson's death said, 'Nothing was ready except the General — Andrew Jackson. . . he had already evinced that iron energy, indomitable perseverance and ceaseless activity, so necessary. . . Not one of the wavering, but a man who could keep his object as steadily before him as the mariner his port, and trample them down and crush without remorse whoever barred the path.' [14]

As used in the last quotation, 'iron' was the key word in most appraisals of Andrew Jackson. Throughout his career, Jackson was lauded as a man of iron; his iron will was central to innumerable descriptions of his character. Even before the news of his victory at New Orleans reached the northern cities, the word 'iron' had been applied to him. In *The Enquirer* of January 28, 1815, one week before the *National Intelligencer, Extra* announced the outcome of the battle of January 8, a writer offered a curious nation some notice 'of the life and character of . . . a man whose life will constitute, and has constituted already, an important epoch in the history of our country.' After describing the bare biographical items of Jackson's career up to 1815, the account took notice of his person: 'He is tall, thin and spare, but muscular and hardy, with an eye quick and penetrating — I have frequently seen Gen. Jackson, and such was the impression his appearance made on my mind, that I have said to myself he is a man of Iron. Adversity can make no impression on a bosom braced by such decision and firmness as is visible in his face and manners.' [15] Their appetite further whetted by the news of Jackson's glorious victory, the people eagerly read this account which was copied by nearly every newspaper in the nation.[16] It proved so popular that when Jackson entered the political scene it appeared as campaign literature and was even reprinted in eulogy at his death.[17]

– 2 –

From the time of his victory in 1815 to his death in 1845, Jackson was constantly before the American imagination as the embodiment of the success that awaits the man of iron will, the man who can overcome insuperable opposition simply by determination. At the end of Jackson's life, eulogists across the nation reminded the American people of his 'inflexibility of purpose, the indomitable will,' the character 'run in that iron mould.' [18] One recalled the compliment paid by the French to the ' "*tete de fer,*" the iron will of the stern old man.' [19] During his life, visitors to Jackson came away and recorded that they 'had seen and scanned the Man of Iron will.' [20] Not only was there general agreement that Jackson's 'well known inflexibility of purpose was, unquestionably, one of his most remarkable characteristics,' [21] but nearly every commentator on Andrew Jackson sought the adjective 'Iron' to describe his self-reliance.[22]

As did the description in the *Enquirer,* which noted Jackson's 'quick and penetrating' eye, accounts which dwelt on Jackson's extraordinary will power usually noted his flashing eye, which was, of course, the physical sign of the spirit within, or as the anonymous poet quoted above put it, 'But when he *wills*, his every look takes fire / And flames to view the hidden soul's desire.' An historian of the Battle of New Orleans described Jackson's entry into the city in this fashion: 'The chief of the party . . . was a tall, gaunt man, of very erect carriage, with a countenance full of stern decision and fearless energy, but furrowed with care and anxiety. His complexion was sallow and unhealthy; his hair was iron grey, and his body thin and emaciated. . . But the fierce glare of his bright and hawk-like grey eye, betrayed a soul and a spirit which triumphed over all the infirmities of the body.' [23] Jackson's infirmity some years later caused young Josiah Quincy in Boston to make a similar observation: 'But the spirit in Jackson was resolute to conquer physical infirmity. His eyes seemed brighter than ever, and all aglow with the mighty will which can compel the body to execute his behests.' The President nearly collapsed on his tour of New England and Quincy elaborated his remark: 'No person who had seen the collapsed condition in which the President was deposited at the hotel would have imagined that he could resume his travels the next day; and it was, undoubtedly, by an exertion of the will of which only the exceptional man is capable that he was able to do so. But the art of mastering the physical nature was familiar to Jackson. . . An immaterial something flashed through his eye as he greeted us in the breakfast room, and it was evident that the faltering body was again held in subjection.' [24] The belief that the spirit of man was to be apprehended in the expression of the eye led Clark Mills in a wood carving of Jackson's head to accentuate the eyes so that the sculpture verges toward caricature.[25]

Andrew Jackson's constant ill-health provided admirers of his will power many opportunities to elaborate upon the superiority of mind over matter. As one biographer wrote of Jackson during the Creek War, 'his mind arose in majesty as his body was emaciated by toil.'[26] Alexander Walker observed that at New Orleans 'his body was sustained alone by the spirit within.'[27] Now there was, to be sure, greater justification for lauding Jackson's will power in the matter of his physical condition than (say) in his victory over the British at New Orleans,[28] but Jackson's contemporaries were more concerned with proving the efficacy of the will than with making valid descriptive statements. In the important struggle against the Second Bank of the United States, which occupied so much of Jackson's political life, the social and economic complexity of the problem was naïvely reduced to a dramatic struggle between the Hero and the Monster. George Lippard remembered that when the proponents of the bank suggested that rebellion might follow if the bank was crushed old Andrew Jackson rose from his seat in anger.

> I can see him yet [wrote Lippard]. 'Come!' he shouted in a voice of thunder, as his clutched hand was raised above his white hairs, 'come with bayonets in your hands instead of petitions, surround the White House with your legions. I am ready for you all! With the people at my back, whom your gold can neither buy nor awe, I will swing you up around the capitol, each rebel of you — on a gibbet — high as Haman's!'

When I think . . . of that ONE MAN, standing there at Washington, battling with all the powers of Bank and panic combined, betrayed . . . assailed . . . when I think of that one man placing his back against the rock, and folding his arms for the blow, while he uttered his vow, 'I will not swerve one inch from the course I have chosen!' I must confess that the records of Greece and Rome — nay, the proudest days of Napoleon, cannot furnish an instance of a WILL like that of ANDREW JACKSON.[29]

Still another said that in the bank controversy it required Andrew Jackson's 'amazing inflexibility of will' to put down the monster of corruption.[30] George Bancroft made the point with greater flourish:

The storm [against Jackson] rose with unexampled vehemence . . . the impetuous swelling wave rolled on, without one sufficient obstacle, till it reached his presence; but as it dashed in its highest fury at his feet, it broke before his firmness. The commanding majesty of his will appalled his opponents and revived his friends. He, himself, had a proud consciousness that his will was indomitable. . . he stood erect, like a massive column, which the heaps of falling ruins could not break, nor bend, nor sway from its fixed foundation.[31]

The belief that Andrew Jackson was able to put down the Second Bank of the United States solely because he willed its destruction was so widespread that when James Parton assembled materials for the first scholarly (and still the best) biography of Jackson he concluded the description of the bank crisis with the observation that 'never was there exhibited so striking an illustration of the maxim, that WILL, not talent, governs the world. The will of one man, Andrew Jackson . . . carried the day against the assembled talent and the interested capital of the country.' [32] The degree of Jackson's appeal to the imagination of his contemporaries as the embodiment of the power of the will is suggested by the motto that Parton found appropriate for his three-volume study: 'Desperate Courage Makes One a Majority.'

In other controversies besides the bank fight Jackson's opponents, as well as his supporters, testified to the esteem in which the self-reliant man was held in the United States. The testimony of the opposition was, of course, negative. They attacked Jackson on the ground that he was weak-willed. During the struggle over the bank, the anti-Jacksonians castigated the President as a weakling led by 'advisers who are goading him on.' [33] The same accusation was made in connection with the removal of office-holders. It was said that Jackson was 'scarcely a free agent,' that 'he has been ruled, against his better judgment, by a combination of interest and prejudice, by which he was surrounded from the moment of reaching the seat of government.' [34] In the election of 1824, the editor of the *Richmond Enquirer*, then in opposition to Jackson, had written that he would be too much exposed to other men, shrewder statesmen than himself. '*They* will probably govern more than he will — they will generally be the power behind the throne greater than the throne itself.' [35] In similar vein, Duff Green was represented as 'the Dictator at Washington,' with Jackson as his pliant tool.[36] It was admiration for the self-reliant man that gave emotional force to the characterization of Martin

Van Buren as the 'little magician' and that informed the attacks on Jackson's 'Kitchen Cabinet.' In both cases Jackson was made to appear as the object of manipulation; stress on the roles of the foxy Vice-President and the backstairs politicians made Jackson seem to be the will-less leader. Americans agreed with Fanny Kemble who, knowing nothing of Jackson's measures, asserted that 'firmness, determination, decision, I respect above all things; and if the old general is, as they say, very obstinate, why obstinacy is so far more estimable than weakness, *especially* in a ruler, that I think he sins on the right side of the question.' [37] The majority of Americans seemed to agree, and the importance of will power is suggested by the attempt of Jackson's opponents to strip him of that attribute.

– 3 –

Of the many incidents in Jackson's life that provided material for the glorification of the man of iron will, the most notorious was, perhaps, Andrew Jackson's famous duel with Charles Dickinson. Jackson's quarrel with Dickinson was of long standing and its origin does not concern us here as much as its result.[38] The result was a duel with pistols at twenty-four feet. Dickinson was a skilled pistol shot. Tradition has it that on the way to the site of the duel he delighted those who accompanied him by placing four shots from a distance of twenty-four feet into an area that could be covered by a silver dollar. He was even supposed to have cut a string at that distance and left it as mute evidence for Jackson of the fate that was in store for him.[39] Because of Dickinson's excellence as a duelist Andrew Jackson decided that his only course was to allow Dickinson to fire first; then Jackson, if not dead, would be able to place his shot unhurriedly. However, there was a good chance that Jackson would be dead. To shorten the odds against such a possibility, Jackson dressed himself in a loose-fitting cloak which disguised his extremely slender figure hoping to deceive Dickinson and mislead his aim.

On the dueling ground John Overton, Jackson's friend, gave the command to fire. Jackson deliberately took Dickinson's shot which hit him in the breast. Then, calmly and decidedly, he waited until Dickinson was brought back to the mark from which he had recoiled in horror at the thought he had missed. Jackson levelled his pistol and fired; the pistol stopped at half-cock. Under the rules of the occasion, this was not considered a fire. Jackson recocked his pistol, aimed, and shot Dickinson fatally through the groin.

In the company of Overton, Jackson left the field without disclosing the fact that he had been seriously wounded himself. A friend of the general wrote later to Parton that Jackson did not want the dying Dickinson to have even the gratification of knowing that he had not missed.[40] Dickinson's bullet had lodged near Jackson's heart; it pained and troubled him all his life and was probably the source of the pulmonary disorders which Jackson usually attributed to tuberculosis.[41]

One must admit that Jackson's conduct in the duel provides an example of animal courage of an intense degree. But in telling the story, admirers added the final touch: 'His astonishing self-command appeared almost superhuman to his friends who witnessed the scene; to one of whom he declared, that so fixed was his resolution, that he should have killed his antagonist, had he himself been shot through the brain.' [42] In this embellishment, Jackson is presented as able to put aside death itself until his object is achieved. Another anecdote to the same end concerns a conversation supposed to have occurred in a New York omnibus between a merchant and a broker, whose speculative occupation makes him an appropriate adversary of Jackson.

> MERCHANT (with a sigh): 'Well, the old General is dead.'
> BROKER (with a shrug): 'Yes, he's gone at last.'
> MERCHANT (not appreciating the shrug): 'Well, sir, he was a good man.'
> BROKER (with a shrug more pronounced): 'I don't know about that.'
> MERCHANT (energetically): 'He was a good man, sir. If any man has gone to heaven, General Jackson has gone to heaven.'
> BROKER (doggedly): 'I don't know about that.'
> MERCHANT: 'Well, sir, I tell you that if Andrew Jackson has made up his mind to go to heaven, you may depend upon it he's there.' [43]

The tradition that glorified Jackson as the man of iron will not only found God to be unnecessary, it asserted that the intensity of Jackson's determination was sufficient to set aside the very judgment of God. As we shall see, this was not a typical attitude, but it represents the extreme of the admiration for Jackson as a symbol of the success that inevitably awaits the man of sufficient determination.

IX

The Self-made Man

In 1845 when Andrew Jackson died, Andrew Stevenson pointed out for the benefit of the citizens of Richmond, Virginia, the moral implicit in Jackson's life.

I shall say nothing [asserted Stevenson] of his ancestors. Virtue and greatness have no need of birth. Born a simple citizen, of poor but respectable parents, he became great by no other means than the energy of his own character, and being, as he seems to have been, the favourite of nature and Heaven! Had he been born to wealth and influence, he might probably have lived and died, an obscure and ordinary man!

Severe discipline and poverty, inured him, in early life, to great hardship and industry, and it has been justly said of him that he seems to have been an orphan from the plough to the presidency. He must, therefore, be regarded as the architect of his own fortunes! [1]

Andrew Jackson's rise from humble circumstances gave substance to the idea that man is the master of his own fate. 'Of all the men I have known,' Francis P. Blair told James Parton, 'Andrew Jackson was the one most entirely sufficient for himself.' To Blair's remark Parton added that 'not only had [Jackson] no such word as *fail,* but no belief, not the slightest, that he could fail in anything seriously undertaken by him. And he never did.' [2] Thus, after more than 2000 pages of narrative, James Parton found Jackson's life to illustrate the fact that 'what man supremely admires in man is manhood.'

> Every great career [wrote Parton], whether of a nation or of an individual, dates from an heroic action, and every downfall from a cowardly one. To dare, to dare again, and always to dare, is the inexorable condition of every signal and worthy success, from founding a cobbler's stall to promulgating a nobler faith.

> It is not for nothing that nature has implanted in her darling the instinct of honoring courage before all other qualities. What a delicate creature was man to be tossed upon this planet . . . compelled instantly to to [sic] begin the 'struggle for life.' [3]

The phrase, 'struggle for life,' leads one's imagination to the period after Jackson, to the end of the nineteenth century rather than to its beginning. This only reminds us that history is a development. In the social situation of the late nineteenth century, it may have seemed that the great man needed only 'the energy of his own character,' but as Stevenson's eulogy reminds us, in the America of Andrew Jackson, he needed more than daring. It helped to be the 'favourite of nature and Heaven!'

— 1 —

The idea that every man is the architect of his own fortunes
has its roots deep in the American past, although the years of
Jacksonian democracy, according to one student, contain
the first important enunciation of the cult of the self-made
man.⁴ One thinks immediately of Franklin in connection
with the theme of self-help and contemporaries of Jackson
linked their Hero with the sage of Philadelphia in order to
state explicitly what Jackson's whole career was held to
demonstrate implicitly: 'He had, like Franklin, to establish his name without the patronage of a single relative or
friend; if he had not talents and virtues, would he not have
remained in obscurity?' ⁵ Franklin suggests the long history
which belongs to the idea of success. The same pattern which
one discovers in examining the concepts of nature and
providence emerges when one scrutinizes Jackson's relation to the idea of the self-made man. The concept of will,
which is at the base of the idea of self-help, did not suddenly
come to be valued because of Andrew Jackson's career. The
idea that man is the architect of his own fortunes had long
been present in the society. Jackson simply lent further support to an article of faith already subscribed to in America.

Central to the idea that man is the master of his own fate
is the belief in the efficacy of the human will. If one is believed to succeed through personal determination, the will
must be exalted and the limitations of environment and
heredity must be denied. As a social type the man of efficient
will power, the man capable of self-direction, comes to be
valued when society, because of social and economic fluidity,

presents its members with a variety of choices and demands a great amount of initiative.[6] Such a social period is, of course, a period of change, a period of transition. Transition is a pallid word for what was happening to America in the period 1815 to 1845. Change was the ruling characteristic. Movement was not only westward geographically, it was upward socially. Expansion was extensive, measured by land mass, and intensive, measured by economic development. But as America faced its future, less attention was paid to the material basis which made that future seem so promising than to the quality of American character. The material endowment of the new continent was not denied; it was asserted to be secondary. 'The character of the American people,' said a Fourth of July orator, 'has been the sole cause of their growth and prosperity. Natural advantages have been elsewhere wasted.' This speech echoes that of Representative Troup with which we began. America has been given its opportunity to succeed, but it must have the will power to seize and improve that opportunity. Sixteen years after Troup, the Fourth of July orator arrives at the same conclusion as the Congressman from Georgia: 'A nation that wills to be free, is free.' [7]

The idea that character is more important than extrinsic advantage received full development by another Fourth of July orator for the edification of the mechanics of Troy, New York.

It too often happens [said O. L. Holley] . . . that the practical value of character, even in private life is underrated, and an undue importance is attached to external condition. . . But, though external circumstances and the accidents of birth and connexion, are not to be disregarded. . . It is plainly character alone, that can lift a man above accident — it is that alone, which, if based upon good principles and cultivated with care, can render him triumphant over vicissitudes and prosperous even in adversity; and it is that alone, which, if neglected and suffered to degenerate, will defeat the most benevolent designs of Providence; will render a man weak, though surrounded by wealth, and unsuccessful, though backed by numbers. The Almighty may, indeed, if it so please him, give the race to the slow and the victory to the feeble; but he has indicated by the ordinary course of his dispensations to mankind, that he does not often choose to do so; that he prefers, as an enticement to exertion and for the reward of prudence, to permit effects to follow their appropriate causes — to give the race to the swift and the battle to the strong.[8]

The importance of character was insisted upon throughout the period. In 1817, 'Decision of Character' was offered as the key to the future success of the individual and the nation: 'And what is this great secret which we are anxious to be put in possession of, this talisman that dissolves difficulties into air, this magic wand which disperses every opposing obstacle, and seems to command surrounding events? Nothing more nor less than a firm, decisive mind.' [9] A newspaper urged in 1828 that 'it was the great duty of man to be active. . . It is that firmness of purpose — that ardour of soul, which shrinks at no discouragement, startles at no false alarm, but with an eye steadily fixed on the object of pursuit, makes its way with resistless energy to attainment. It is *this* that elevates the character of man.' [10] And at the end of the period, in 1842, it was pronounced as obvious that every great man is marked by a 'hearty self-reliance' and that every failure is due to self-distrust.[11]

From beginning to end, the period 1815 to 1845 is dominated by the belief that the cause of man's success lies within himself.[12] It was no accident that the people attributed Andrew Jackson's victory over the British to his superior will power, or that they selected as their leader a man in whom they saw living proof that success inevitably awaits the man of iron will.

– 2 –

Andrew Stevenson, in the quotation with which this chapter began, said of Jackson that 'he seems to have been an orphan from the plough to the presidency.' For another, who was trying to get Jackson into the world without any parents at all, the sentiment seemed so hackneyed that he apologetically enclosed it in quotation marks: 'he was almost born an orphan, and won his way "from the plough to the presidency." ' [13] Jackson's father died before Andrew was born; when Jackson was fourteen his mother went to an unknown grave, from a disease contracted while caring for prisoners of the Revolutionary army aboard a British prison ship in Charles Town harbor.[14]

Jackson's orphaned youth made various appeals to the American imagination. First, of course, was the one of simple sentiment. It was also suggested that because he had no personal family Jackson took for his family the democracy, that is, the people of the country. But the most persistent attitude derived from the circumstances of Jackson's childhood was the one stressed by Stevenson: 'He must, therefore, be regarded as the architect of his own fortunes.' Jackson was the self-made man *par excellence* because, alone in the world from the very beginning, he must have created his own future beyond any possible doubt.

A highly fluid society, such as the United States in the early years of the nineteenth century, faces the problem of insuring social conformity and establishing social direction without the aid of traditional institutions which implement such purposes. The most obvious institution which makes for conformity and direction is the family. Jackson, without a family almost from birth, is the epitome of the self-directed man. As one of his many admirers said, 'There was no one to counsel or guide him; no one to inculcate lessons of prudence; no one to lead him into the paths of useful industry and of restored tranquility — but Jackson wanted no one. At this, perhaps the most critical period of his life, the *"iron will"* subsequently attributed to his treatment of others, was nobly exercised in governing himself.' [15]

A society in flux solves the problem of social direction by the development of a new character type. Instead of relying upon tradition, which would be impossible since tradition is what is changing, an expanding society internalizes its goals within each of its members, creating what the sociologist, David Riesman, calls the 'inner-directed' character.[16] 'Inner-directed' more precisely describes the type I have been calling 'self-directed.' 'Self-directed has honorific overtones; it suggests that one creates one's own standards of conduct from within, it creates a sharp antithesis between the individual and the society. What actually seems to happen is that the individual incorporates society's demands into his own consciousness and thereby is led to strive even harder because the demands of the society seem to be the demands of one's own self. The wide horizon of possibilities before the member of a society which is economically and socially open requires the goals of society to be defined in generalized terms. Thus, 'work,' or 'power,' or 'wealth' are designated as goals, goals which are by their nature almost infinitely expansive.

But abstractions are not generally effective instruments of persuasion. It is for this reason that society creates its symbols. Symbols make abstract ideals concrete. One of the functions of the popular image of Andrew Jackson was to give substance to the abstraction, will. For the early nineteenth century Jackson objectified the belief that man was not the creature of circumstance but the master of his own destiny. As President, he seemed to prove that man could overcome all obstacles and rise from obscurity to greatness. As an orphan he underlined the moral implicit in the myth of the self-made man: man is 'self-supported by the innate energy of his own master-spirit.' [17] The history of Andrew Jackson, it was said, established 'beyond disputation . . . that true merit, sooner or later, meets a suitable reward. . . Connected with his life history, there is a moral lesson, imposing as it is grand. To the youth of the country, it is a volume written in letters of gold, and establishes a precedent for imitation, that is beyond price. . .

In this land of equal rights, the humblest youth, with honesty, talents and perseverance to recommend him, enjoys the same opportunities with the high-born and wealthy . . . An orphan child, unprotected, without friends, without influence [became President]. . . The American presidents were all "self-made men." ' [18]

The statement that all American Presidents were 'self-made' discloses the psychological rather than the factual basis of the myth of the self-made man. It also reminds us that Jackson was only one among a number of men whose careers were interpreted to support the myth.[19] An essay, 'Representative Men,' in the *Southern Literary Messenger* maintained that the two men who stood for the political divisions of the nation, Andrew Jackson and Henry Clay, also represented the basic unity of the nation: 'Both were denied the advantage of education. . . Both were dependent only upon their own exertions and equally independent of adventitious aid. Both were the architects of their own fortunes . . . Both displayed from the start the same enterprizing spirit — the same obduracy and vehemence of will — the same almost arrogant defiance of opposition — the same tenacity and continuity of purpose.' [20] There is a certain ironic appropriateness that Henry Clay, the proponent of Whig economics, should be credited with coining the phrase, 'self-made man,' in a speech on behalf of a paternalistic tariff.[21] But the fact testifies to the universal acceptance of the cult of self-help in America. Clay may have found the phrase that described the belief that man succeeds to the degree of his own will power; Andrew Jackson embodied that belief.

– 3 –

After the Revolution 'our orphan hero,' as Bancroft called Jackson, 'was alone in the world, with no kindred to cherish him, and little inheritance but his own untried powers.' [22] This was sufficient to support the assertion, in the words of still another, that Jackson 'owed to himself, and himself alone, both his education and his fortune.' [23] However, Jackson's youth was not outstanding for the exemplification of 'labour, temperance, and perseverance and virtue,' which was ascribed to it by one biographer.[24] On the contrary, he gambled away what little inheritance he had from his family and was remembered by those who knew him in his early years as a cock-fighting, horse-racing, swaggering young blade.[25] Rather than a depressant, however, Jackson's wastrel youth provided a stimulus to those who were intent on objectifying through him the myth of the self-made man.

> Bereft of the guardianship of father or mother, or friends, with the idle and dissolute habits contracted in times of confusion and civil war, he soon squandered the little patrimony that was left him. And to all discerning eyes, the lad, Andrew Jackson, was destined to wander a vagabond through the world, and doomed to a life of want and profligacy. But the divine fire that burned in his bosom, kindled up an energy that enabled him to make his greatest conquest — the conquest of himself. He fled from the country in which he was born — forsook the companions that led him astray; and in a strange land threw away his habits and commenced a new life.[26]

Although this admirer of Jackson has to invoke the divine
fire of God (who as we shall see has an important role in
the myth of the self-made man) and transport Jackson to
a new environment before he can find success, the sense
of the statement is that self-control is the final requisite of
a man of strong will.

Only to one who assumes that myth-making is a logical
process will it seem strange that Jackson's youth could
support the belief that the deserving alone find success.
The reason such awkward material suited the myth of self-
reliance lies in a sentence quoted before. When Jackson
was compared to Franklin, it was said that he had 'to establish his name without the patronage of a single relative or
friend.' The next clause is the important one: 'if he had
not talents and virtues, would he not have remained in obscurity?' Behind that 'if' lies the assumption that the world
is a world of justice, an ordered world in which, as we have
seen another maintain, God permits 'effects to follow their
appropriate causes.' Because they did not doubt that virtue
does receive its own reward, believers in the myth of the
self-made man were not arguing from cause to effect,
they were arguing from effect back to cause; if Jackson
succeeded he *had* to deserve success, particularly since 'he
entered the stage of life entirely alone . . . [and] received
no aid but what he commanded by his own energy.' [27] In
taking Jackson as the example of the self-made man, the
popular mind was not arguing from his youth to his success; it was arguing from his success to his youth. If the
youth were dissolute, it made little difference. The fact
only proved he must have been doubly victorious; he must

have conquered himself as well as adverse circumstances.

The orator who was quoted before as saying that 'the character of the American people has been the sole cause of their growth and prosperity,' also observed that the early settlers 'built no alms-houses; (for they tolerated no paupers).' [28] One who tolerates no paupers can justify his lack of charity only on the grounds that paupers deserve their poverty. This is the obverse of the belief that man succeeds because of himself; he also fails because of himself. When, under the guidance of Robert Hartley, the New York Association for Improving the Condition of the Poor attempted in 1843 a city-wide plan of social service it sent volunteers into the homes of the poor. The function of each social service worker was to combine material aid with exhortations to thrift, diligence, and temperance, and to help the needy to 'discover those hidden springs of virtue within themselves from which *alone* their prosperity might flow.' [29] One patriot put it succinctly: 'Plenty overspreads the land. There may be, it is true, much poverty and even suffering; but these, to some extent, spring necessarily from the condition of human society, from the dispensations of Providence, and in no small degree from the vices of mankind.' [30] The tentative tone, 'there may be' and 'to some extent,' vanishes when it comes to the vices of mankind.

When the editor of the *Democratic Review* reviewed 'The Course of Civilization' he felt that the culmination of progress would come when 'all ranks of men would begin life on a fair field, "the world before them where to choose, and Providence their guide." Inclination and sagacity would select the sphere, and dictate the mode and measure of exertion. Frugality and vigilance would compel success, and defeat and ruin be felt only as the requital of ill-desert; or, if such things be, as vicissitudes inflicted by Heaven among its inscrutable designs.' [31] The uneasy qualification at the end is lessened first by the doubt that such things as unmerited adversity do exist, and then dismissed with the assurance that vicissitudes are incorporated in the divine scheme, anyway, and not to be questioned by man.

Andrew Jackson was felt to symbolize the fact that the time had already come when all Americans could begin life on a fair field. The first lesson for posterity that Levi Woodbury found in Jackson's life was the fact that 'without wealth or powerful connections, which even in republics are sometimes passports to fame, he first appeared on the theatre of public action as an orphan. . . he soon displayed an energy and perseverance . . . which are full of encouragement to the most lowly and unfriended.' [32] Another observed that 'when we see the humble orphan boy become a mighty ruler, we feel increased attachment to our form of government, which secures alike to high and low its blessings and its honours.' [33] The success of the self-made man in the United States was due to 'the actions of institutions . . . which throw open to the humblest individual the avenues to wealth and distinction.' [34]

Belief in the self-made man was a source of national pride to Americans, since the American system was supposed to establish conditions which made individual worthiness the only means to success. In the United States an inauspicious beginning in life was a boon; it proved that one deserved whatever success one achieved. 'The greatest merit of our system is that it cooperates with providence to execute the primeval curse, "In the sweat of thy face shalt thou eat bread, till thou return unto the ground." No individual among us can arrive at any high degree of respectability and influence, except by his own efforts.' [35] The primeval curse is transmuted in America into a blessing. As Andrew Stevenson observed in the quotation which began this chapter, 'had [Jackson] been born to wealth and influence, he might probably have lived and died, an obscure and ordinary man!' Although wealth and powerful connections might sometimes, even in republics, bring success, they more often brought the impotence of indolence; poverty is the breeding ground of success. By a geological rather than a biological metaphor, a contemporary admirer ascribed Jackson's success to poverty.

His origin was humble; and the poorest may learn from his career, that poverty is no insuperable bar to the soarings and triumphs of the free spirit. Nay! Let us rather say, as we remember how the soil of poverty has sent up its harvest of great men, our Franklin, our Adams, our Henry, and our Jackson; let us rather say, that, as in *the kingdom of geology* the everlasting granite, the underlying basis of all other formations is found in the deepest gulf, yet ever bursting upward from the abyss, towering aloft into highest hills, and crowning the very pinnacles of the world; so in *the kingdom of man,* the primitive rock, the granite formation, is poverty; found deepest in the abyss, borne down, buried thousand-fathom deep, overlaid, crushed to the very centre, yet everywhere forcing its way upward, towering aloft and claiming kindred with the sky! [36]

Although nearly obscured, there was always present in the worship of success the dogma that America *is* an open field. Otherwise it made little sense to compliment the dispossessed of society on their high good fortune.

X

The Man of (*Malleable*) Iron

After the Battle of New Orleans, an obscure American artist named Wheeler did a portrait of Andrew Jackson. This portrait became widely known in America in engraved form as the frontispiece to the Reid and Eaton biography published in 1817. About 1819 it received the dubious compliment of being copied by the much better known painter, John Wesley Jarvis. Jarvis's more graceful version was in turn given general circulation in a fine stipple engraving by Charles Phillips, an Englishman who had come to this country to practice his craft. The inscription of Phillips's engraving (Pl. VI) has led to the mistaken belief that Jarvis did his portrait from life in 1815. But the interest of this widely duplicated likeness lies only partly in its confused history. The portrait is important because it demonstrates how subjective attitudes can distort ob-

jective fact, how, in this case, the image of the victorious
general present in the artist's imagination caused him to
distort the physical features of his sitter, Andrew Jackson.
One of the most distinctive of Jackson's physical characteristics was his bristling gray hair, which even until his old
age rose straight back from his high forehead. The hair of
the general painted by Wheeler and Jarvis belongs to Napoleon, not to Andrew Jackson.[1] Parton, in his life of Jackson, describes Jarvis's portrait in detail and says that Jackson later presented it to the daughter of Edward Livingston. Parton recognized the literal inaccuracy of the portrait.
He wrote that 'not a man in the United States would recognize in it the features of General Jackson.' Although he
failed to see Napoleon in the portrait, Parton did not miss
its symbolic truth; in the face of Jackson he saw a 'still, set
countenance' which wore what he described as a '*Presbyterian* expression.'[2]

Shortly after Andrew Jackson's victory at New Orleans,
Napoleon's sudden return from exile and his dash to Paris
with his guard of six hundred filled the columns of the
American press. But America's interest in Napoleon was
not simply of the moment. He was more than passing news.
A scholar, examining McGuffey's readers to see what has
gone into the making of the American mind, believes that
an 'inappropriate' amount of attention was paid Napoleon
by a democratic nation. In the McGuffey readers, says this
student, 'the lesson of Napoleon runs from the earliest editions throughout the whole series; but the explanation of
this popularity remains, for us, a closely guarded secret.'[3]
The secret does not seem so closely guarded. It was Na-

poleon's energy and daring that captured the American imagination. Albert Guerard in his study of the Napoleonic legend has insisted that 'what America admires in Napoleon is the typical American. . . Napoleon is the type of the self-made man.' [4] Contemporaries of Jackson recognized this; Emerson pointed it out clearly in his essay on Napoleon in *Representative Men*. Napoleon combined the man of energy with the man of fate. In America this was the function of Andrew Jackson. It was almost inevitable that the two symbols should fuse, to the extent that a painter setting down the features of the American general should see in him the French emperor.

Comparisons were often made between Andrew Jackson and Napoleon. As we have seen before, the second figure-head of Jackson on the *Constitution* is decidedly Napoleonic in pose. In John Frost's *Pictorial Life*, the young boy who is sabered for defying the British officer's command to clean his boots stands straddle-legged, one hand plunged into his tunic, and the hair style, although not clearly defined, suggests the curling locks so prominent in Jarvis's portrait.[5] Verbal comparisons were, for obvious reasons, more common. Because Jackson's victory was over the British troops who under Wellington had defeated Napoleon, Americans asserted that their general was the equal of Bonaparte or the Iron Duke.[6] It was a stock rhetorical device to refer to New Orleans as a victory over the conquerors of the conquerors of Europe. When the Spanish Minister expostulated about Jackson's actions in Florida during the Seminole War, the French Minister, Hyde de Neauville, said he could not support Spain's claims, but neither did he condone the actions of Jackson, whom he called that 'Napoleon des bois.'[7]

But the comparison of Jackson with Napoleon in the context of the Battle of New Orleans is a comparison on the level of military ability; the characterization of Jackson as a 'backwoods Napoleon' has even something of the slur in it. Other comparisons were more honorific and involved more than military capacities.[8] As we have seen, George Lippard felt, with no sense that the comparison might be derogatory, that 'the proudest days of Napoleon, cannot furnish an instance of a will like that of ANDREW JACKSON.' The reason why Napoleon Bonaparte could appear in a favorable light to Americans was that he seemed, as a contemporary of Jackson's put it, 'the child and champion of democracy.'[9] Napoleon was a king-breaker. For a moment in history he appeared as the champion of the people. Calhoun studying law at Litchfield under Tapping Reeve watched the rising fortunes of Napoleon with keen interest,[10] and Jackson, while Senator in 1798, wrote home to Tennessee that a Napoleonic invasion of England could be a victory for republicanism.[11] Jackson's deep interest in Napoleon is evidenced by no less than five lives of Napoleon in his library.[12] When Napoleon was exiled to St. Helena, the *National Intelligencer* copied a long article from Europe which bemoaned Napoleon's passing because he had wished only for the happiness of France.[13] There even seems to have been no sense of incongruity in picturing Napoleon with Washington 'in the center of the American stars of freedom' in one of the popular dioramas of the day.[14]

America's admiration for Napoleon is not hard to account for. He was, as Albert Guerard has said, 'the type of the self-made man.' Like Jackson, he had risen from the ruck to world eminence. As Jackson believed in his destiny, Napoleon followed his star. Both were men of great personal magnetism and were driven by a tremendous will to power. America admired these qualities in the person of Andrew Jackson; Napoleon, however, spelled the danger implicit in the man of iron will. Will, Napoleon's career proved, might lead to one man's success but to society's disaster.

The man of will, such as Napoleon, might prove to be a man of unbridled egotism. There was always the danger that the man who was entirely self-sufficient might be beyond the control of society. The fear that the man of will might also be a man of lawlessness was at the base of the charge most widely pressed against Andrew Jackson during his public life, the charge that he was a 'military chieftain.' The epithet embodied two distinct ideas. The first was that, as a military man, Jackson was insufficiently prepared to serve as chief executive. This objection was met in two ways. Negatively, it was asserted, as we have seen in the section on Nature, that formal training was not the measure of a man's worth. Positively, it was maintained that in the troubled state of the world, a military man would make an ideal chief executive since he could take command of the armies in time of sudden danger.[15] The second charge implied in the characterization of Jackson as a military chieftain was more difficult to get around since it involved one of the themes upon which the symbol of

Jackson was built, his dominating will power and self-sufficiency. Political adversaries often maintained that, as a military man, Jackson was a menace to republican freedom. Henry Clay, in a speech during the Seminole controversy, gave this charge its most famous statement. Clay's speech was on the motion before the House of Representatives to censure Jackson's actions in Florida. Clay reviewed the course of events, strongly emphasizing the arbitrariness of Jackson's command.

Recal [sic] to your recollection [Clay said to the House in closing his long speech,] the free nations which have gone before us. Where are they now, and how have they lost their liberties? If we could transport ourselves back to the ages when Greece and Rome flourished in their greatest prosperity, and, mingling in the throng, ask a Grecian if he did not fear some daring military chieftain, covered with glory, some Philip or Alexander, would one day overthrow his liberties? No! No! the confident and indignant Grecian would exclaim, we have nothing to fear from our heroes; our liberties will be eternal. If a Roman citizen had been asked, if he did not fear the conqueror of Gaul might establish a throne upon the ruins of public liberty, he would instantly have repelled the unjust insinuation. The celebrated Madame de Stael, in her last and perhaps best work, has said, that in the very year, almost the very month, when the President of the Directory declared that monarchy would never more show its frightful head in France, Bonaparte, with his grenadiers, entered the palace of St. Cloud, and dispersing with his bayonet, the deputies of the people, deliberating on the affairs of the state, laid the foundations of that vast fabric of despotism which overshadowed all Europe.[16]

As he neared the end of his peroration, Clay asserted he meant no slur on the motives of General Jackson, a remark which must have seemed somewhat anti-climactic to the House. Rather, Clay bewailed the unconstitutional precedent Jackson's action set for the future. Warming up to his close, Clay warned the representatives of the people, 'Beware how you give a fatal sanction, in this infant period of our republic, scarcely yet two score years old, to a military insubordination.'

> Remember that Greece had her Alexander, Rome her Caesar, England her Cromwell, France her Bonaparte, and that, if we would escape the rock on which they split, we must avoid their errors. . . He hoped gentlemen would deliberately survey the awful position on which we stand. They may bear down all opposition; they may even vote the general the public thanks; they may even carry him triumphantly through this house. But, if they do, in my humble judgment, it will be a triumph of the principles of insubordination — a triumph of the military over the civil authorities — a triumph over the powers of this house — a triumph over the constitution of the land. And he prayed most devoutly to Heaven, that it might not prove, in its ultimate effects and consequences, a triumph over the liberties of the people.[17]

The core of Clay's charge involves the threat that the man of iron will presents to society. The charge of 'military chieftain' is, at bottom, the charge that Andrew Jack-

son placed his own will above majority opinion or constitutional law. Jackson was arraigned for violating the law of
the land not only by Congress after the Florida affair but
by a Federal court after the Battle of New Orleans when
under the aegis of martial law Jackson had refused to honor
a writ of *habeas corpus* issued by the court. Both instances
suggested that the self-determined man, if his tremendous
will power were not enlisted in the disinterested service of
his country, might destroy the fabric of society by his ego-
tistically determined course. When, at Jackson's death, the
New-York Historical Society proposed a eulogistic resolution in his honor, one intransigent member protested that
'truth should come from societies like this' and opposed
the resolution. This bitter enemy of Jackson's said, 'Well
may they call him "the man of iron will"; for he was determined to make it the sole arbiter of truth and false-
hood.' [18] It was this fear, mixed with admiration for the
man of determined will, that Clay's speech tapped.

There were many ways by which the Jacksonians could
quiet the fear of the anarchic individualism that was always
implicit in the symbol of the man of iron will. One was to
deny that Jackson had passed beyond the bounds of law,
to assert that *this* man of will finally respected the rights
of society. Jackson's actions in Florida were defended as
completely consonant with the law of nations.[19] Arbitrary
actions during the defense of New Orleans were excused
on the ground of military necessity. Following the restora-
tion of civil law in New Orleans, Jackson willingly submitted to a fine for contempt of court imposed by the judge
whose writ he had denied under martial law. When a pop-

ular demonstration threatened in his behalf, Jackson even lectured the people of New Orleans on the necessity of obedience to magistrates. His actions supported a favorable view of his character rather than the imputation of his political opponents.[20]

A second, and less direct, method of countering the 'military chieftain' charge was to compare Jackson to the nation's first 'military chieftain,' George Washington. Public toasts linked the two: ' "Military Chieftains" / As WASHINGTON, first President, / No Tyrant proved to be, / so JACKSON, our next President, / Will leave his country free.' [21] As Jackson's friend, John Henry Eaton, observed of the election of a President after the Revolution: 'One flushed with success, and at the head of a victorious army, was called to take charge of the government. He was a military man, and the nation, so far from apprehending a capacity or disposition on his part, to subvert the liberty he had acquired for his country, confided with one voice her destinies to his hands. Then it was not an inquiry, who could write a paragraph with the greatest classical purity; or who, the most finished veteran at intrigue; the question was, who is he that, fearless of consequences, and regardless of danger, has breasted the storm in the hour of peril, and risked himself for his country.' [22] The name of Lafayette was invoked as well as that of Washington, to remove any stigma that might attach to the 'military chieftain.' [23]

Neither of the two answers, however, quite meets the charge that the man of iron will is a potential threat to society. The first simply denies that Jackson is completely self-determined; it says that his self-reliance operates only

up to the limits defined by society. The second is an evasion of the issue. Despite Clay's speech there was no basis
for the fear that Jackson might engineer a *coup* in Washington. But the question how society was to harness for
its own good the will of the self-determined individual did
loom large in the context of contemporary history. The
symbol of Jackson as the man of iron will posed an important problem for a democratic ideology.

— 1 —

The ambivalent attitude of Americans toward the man of
iron will can be detected in the very first account that attributed this character to Jackson, the brief sketch by
Nathaniel Claiborne which has been quoted before. Claiborne wrote that Jackson struck him as 'a man of Iron.
Adversity can make no impression on a bosom braced by
such decision and firmness as is visible in his face and manners.' We have explored some of the reasons why Jackson's contemporaries admired the man who is sufficient
unto himself, but for those same contemporaries Claiborne
felt the need to qualify his statement. He warned, 'Let not
the reader conclude from this that he is haughty, distant
and imperious — quite the contrary.' Claiborne recognized
a repellent element, something cold and inhuman, in the
character who recognizes no obligation outside himself. He
went on to say, 'If in the field and at the head of armies in
battle, we admire the dauntless soldier; we love the man
who at home, and in retirement, is hospitable and friendly,
and in this particular the General is preeminently conspicu-
ous.' It may be more than an accident that Claiborne chose

the verb, 'admire,' for the grandly isolated man, the verb, 'love,' for the social man. The potentiality for danger, explicit in the comparison of Jackson to Napoleon, is implicit in Claiborne's description of Jackson as a man of iron will. To circumvent the objection that the man who is beyond society might also be against society, Claiborne asserts that Jackson is open to the softer sentiments, that the iron in his system is fairly malleable stuff.

Claiborne's solution, to describe Jackson as the stern, unbending man of will and at the same time to aver that he was an example of the softer, social virtues, was one that was not followed so much as separately discovered by others who also presented Jackson as the symbol of the self-sufficient man. Compare the pattern of Claiborne's description of Jackson, written, it will be remembered, before the Battle of New Orleans, with that of an address delivered thirty years later on the occasion of Jackson's death:

> He who had occupied so important a page in his country's history, who had possessed a popularity and influence exceeded only by Washington's, who had filled every station of dignity and trust which his country could confer, both civil and military, became when in the domestic circle and around the social hearth, as simple as a child. . . Although, in character marked by such strength of features, the lineaments of the softer virtues could scarcely be expected to mix; yet those who knew him best in private life, and in the unbendings of retirement, knew the genuine indications of their existence, and the childlike simplicity and tenderness of his nature.[24]

Nicholas Trist, in his reminiscences of Jackson published in the *New-York Evening Post,* succinctly expressed the train of thought developed in this eulogist's oration when he wrote, 'There was more of the woman in [Jackson's] nature than in that of any man I ever knew — more of woman's tenderness.' [25] Bancroft, when he recommended 'the commanding majesty of Jackson's will' to the American people, repeated the formula originally set by Claiborne by going on to say, 'To the majestic energy of an indomitable will, he joined a heart capable of the purest and most devoted love, rich in the tenderest affections.' [26]

Of all the images offered by Andrew Jackson to the imagination of his contemporaries, perhaps the one least present to the modern mind is Jackson in the role of the sentimental hero, the man so attuned to the promptings of the heart that he is moved to tears on the slightest provocation. Since the period 1815 to 1845 contains the earliest of 'the sentimental years,' it is not surprising that evidences of sentimentalism should be detected in characterizations of Andrew Jackson. The presence of the pervasive sentimentality of the age is not, however, accidental; it is not merely the addition of an incongruous element to the popular conception of Jackson. In the symbol of Jackson, the element of sentimentality is functional; it operates to soften the hard outlines of the character of the man of iron. Jackson, the sentimental hero, blurs the threatening implications of Jackson, the stern man of implacable will.

The two chief means of identifying Jackson with the softer virtues are suggested in the quotations already given. On the one hand it was said that Jackson was 'as simple as a child'; on the other that he had 'more of the woman' in him than any other man. Contrast the latter comparison with the words of the poet we have read before: 'His eye shows openness and seems to speak, / But nothing's there that shows a woman's freak. / His *will* chains every nerve.' Perhaps the most severe condemnation that can be made of nineteenth-century America is that it equated charity and love with a lack of manhood. With the symbol of Jackson we are in the midst of the tradition which would divide life into two parts, one the province of the home, the other that of the practical world. By making the women and children of the society the guardians of virtue, the male was released to act amorally in the world outside the home, but at a large price. The male became simply an adjunct to the home. He was relegated to a function in which virtue, appreciation of the arts, or leisure time had no organic part. The woman also paid a price although at first, being enthroned, she seemed to be favored.

Except for metaphorical purposes, however, it was not suitable to make a child or a woman of Andrew Jackson. The more effective way to suggest that there was not so much iron in him that it could not be softened by love was to display Jackson in the melting presence of the woman or child. Such a ritual served two purposes: it proved that Jackson was open to the impulses of the heart; it also proved that virtue, personified by the woman or child, was somehow ultimately more powerful, that good was transcendent in the universe.

At the very outset of his career, Jackson was aligned on the side of womanhood by protecting the 'beauty' of New

Orleans from the lust of a savage British soldiery. A memori-
alist of Jackson asked the women of America:

> And you, too, my fair and beloved countrywomen,
> whose first honour is in the gentleness of your nature,
> will you not unite your sympathies and tears over the
> grave of that man, who, above all others, was the most
> devoted friend and admirer, might I not say romantic,
> that woman ever had?
>
> Who so prompt to defend and protect her rights, or
> guard her from injury and insult?
>
> Who ever cherished or exalted more the purity of the
> domestic and social virtues, so infinitely more impor-
> tant to human happiness than all others? Whose valour
> was it that protected our mothers, and wives, and
> daughters, from the savage tomahawk, and a licentious
> soldiery, and one of our finest cities, with its 'Beauty
> and booty,' from ruthless invaders?
>
> Whose, but Andrew Jackson's? [27]

The 'beauty and booty' theme of the song, 'The Hunters
of Kentucky,' asserted, as we have seen before, that the
Americans were fighting on the side of civilization, which
is the side of society rather than the side of the solitary man.
The uncivilized man is also the 'unfeeling' man, as Poindexter characterized the British in his letter that first made
the 'beauty and booty' charge. The anonymous poet who
recounted Packenham's purpose in tempting his troops
by offering them the fair of New Orleans has the British
officer say, 'By that, at Hampton I the fight acquir'd —
/ Maddening the blood *as though* the heart were fir'd.' [28]
The British officer must urge on his troops by evil prom-

ises because their hearts are closed to normal feeling; unlike the American defenders they are insensible to the demands of the nobler virtues and can hope to find success only through the stimulation of animal desire, a corrupt opposite of true sentiment. The man of feeling is the true representative of civilization.

Jackson was, however, only one among many who proved their moral worth by preserving the women of New Orleans. Jackson was more directly connected with the springs of virtue through the women in his own life, his mother and his wife. Despite his mother's early death, biographers insisted on making her good counsel the source of Jackson's later greatness.[29] In an oration at the tomb of Washington's mother, Jackson lent his testimony to such a moral by ascribing Washington's public glory to the early offices of his mother.[30] It was, however, Jackson's wife, Rachel, who best filled the role of the symbolic woman, the 'pilot [as one described her] in pious woman's form, who showed him the way to gain victory over self.' [31]

The controversy which arose, during Jackson's political life, over the circumstances of his marriage provides sufficient evidence that the woman was considered the source of morality in America and that one means of identification with the social virtues was through a good woman. Jackson had married the wife of Lewis Robards believing her at the time to be divorced. Two years later it became known that Robards had not actually divorced his wife. In those days divorces were granted by legislative act, but Robard's petition to the Virginia legislature resulted not in a divorce but in an enabling act which allowed him to

bring suit for divorce through the courts. Robards, however, had not instituted court proceedings, and the report
that Rachel was free had been false. After Rachel's marriage to Jackson, Robards did receive a divorce on the
grounds that Rachel was living in adultery with another
man, one Andrew Jackson. With much personal embarrass-
ment, Jackson had his marriage re-performed to avert possible legal consequences.[32] Jackson was notoriously touchy
on the subject of the irregularity of his marriage, and it
took the utmost efforts of his friends to control him during
the vicious campaign of 1828 in which Rachel was likened
to a 'black wench' and branded as a 'profligate woman.' [33]
In a period when 'one of the customs and courtesies of the
time was to refrain from discussing women individually in
the newspapers,' it seems hard to believe that the opponents
of Jackson could have blundered so badly as to malign his
wife.[34] Led on by Charles Hammond, editor of the Cincinnati *Liberty Hall*, they obviously hoped to place Jackson outside the pale of society. What better way to prove
the anti-social character of a man than to convict him of
showing contempt for the one institution which lay at the
very basis of civilization? But the effective defense of Jackson made him seem a champion rather than a despoiler of
womanhood.[35] As the Peggy Eaton affair proved later, it
was better to err on the side of quixotism than to be found
arraigned against a woman. Then when Rachel died, sup-
posedly of a heart broken by the slanders against her, Andrew Jackson achieved a vicarious martyrdom and became
a fit object for the sentimental outpourings of the nation.
General Sam Dale remembered visiting Jackson during

the Nullification controversy and finding the President
alone. Jackson remarked on the loss of Rachel and then,
wrote Dale, 'the iron man trembled with emotion, and for
some time covered his face with his hands, and tears dropped
on his knee.' [36] Nicholas Trist went one night to Jackson's
room in the White House: 'He was sitting at the little table,
with his wife's miniature . . . before him, propped up
against some books; and between him and the picture lay
an open book, which bore the marks of long use. This book,
I afterward learned, was *her* prayer book.' [37] Jackson's defense of his wife and his devotion to her after her death
established 'another trait in his private character, not un-
usual in vigorous intellects, though apparently so opposite
to the current of their ordinary feelings, respect and attachment to female worth.' [38]

Although Jackson had no children of his own, his supporters took many opportunities to record his gentle sympathy for children. Thomas Hart Benton loved to tell how
he arrived at Jackson's home 'one wet chilly evening, in
February, and came upon him in the twilight, sitting alone
before the fire, a lamb and a child between his knees.'

> He started a little [Benton remembered], called a serv-
> ant to remove the two innocents to another room, and
> explained to me how it was. The child had cried be-
> cause the lamb was out in the cold, and begged him to
> bring it in — which he had done to please the child,
> his adopted son, then not two years old. The ferocious
> man does not do that! and though Jackson had his pas-
> sions and his violence, they were for men and enemies
> — those who stood up against him — and not for

women and children, or the weak and helpless: for all whom his feelings were those of protection and support.[39]

The child in Benton's story provided still another superb opportunity for those who wished to display the man of sentiment beneath the man of iron. The child was an Indian, orphaned by one of Jackson's own campaigns. After the battle of Tohopeka some Indian women were discovered about to kill an infant whose parents had died in the battle. Jackson took it under his own care in order to protect it from the forthright solution of its troubles intended by its own people. The Indian boy's name was Lincoyer and Jackson made him his ward. The story of Lincoyer was widely told to point the obvious moral. One biographer said that 'American hearts shall throb with tearful pleasure' at such a story.[40] Jackson's action was described as 'a garland of roses around the iron helmet of the warrior,' [41] and it was said that 'this touching incident reflects more honour on the heart of the general than the entire glory of the Creek War.' [42] Jackson's adoption of the orphan Indian boy was so appealing that it moved Henry Lee to write a poem on the incident.[43]

The sentimental spirit of the age can be grasped to perfection in a tableau, involving Jackson, described by Andrew Ewing at the inauguration of a bust of Jackson in Memphis, Tennessee. Ewing told his audience how as a child he was called upon to say a speech of welcome to Andrew Jackson upon his return to Nashville after retirement from public office. Ewing remembered his greeting had 'wound up by saying, "that the children of his old soldiers and friends welcomed him home, and were ready to serve under his banner." His frame shook, he bowed down his head and whilst the tears rolled down his aged cheeks, he replied, "I could have stood all but this, it is too much, too much!" The crowd gathered around and for a few moments there was a general outburst of sympathy and tears.' [44] The meaning of the iron man's tears, of course, lies in the fact that all those present would join in the watery effusion, the real function of which was to prove the moral worth of the sentimental personality. Jackson's role as the sentimental hero was clear to his contemporaries: '. . . friends and foes have bestowed on him another characteristic — of being a man of iron will. When this is meant to imply hardness of heart, nothing could be further from the truth; since no child, at the sight of suffering, overflowed quicker with the milk of human kindness than the stern-visaged warrior.' [45]

When Andrew Jackson died, the Reverend Mr. George W. Bethune, minister of the Third Reformed Dutch Church in Philadelphia, extolled Jackson's patriotic example for the edification of his congregation. Having reviewed Jackson's career and attributed it to 'the iron will, whose upright strength never quivered amidst the lightning storms that crashed around it,' Mr. Bethune continued:

Remarkable as the contrast is, there were traits in the temper of the indomitable old man, tender simple and touching. With what faithful affection he honoured her while living, whose dear dust made the hope of his last resting place more sweet, that he might sleep again at her side! And if his heart seemed sometimes steeled against the weakness of mercy, when crime was to be punished, or mutiny controlled, or danger annihilated; he could also stoop in his career of bloody conquest, to take a wailing, new-made orphan to his pitying heart; with the same hand, that had just struck down invading foes, he steadied the judgment-seat shaken with the tremors of him who sat upon it, to pronounce sentence against him for law violated in martial necessity; and at the height of authority, the poor man found him a brother and a friend.[46]

In one paragraph, the minister has compressed the two main lines of defense against the charge that Jackson's iron-willed self-sufficiency embodied a potential threat: he was not iron-hearted, really, and he was not anarchically self-reliant since he respected the rule of law.

— 2 —

It was, however, quite beside the point to prove that Jackson was not completely self-willed or to blur the image of the man of will by imposing upon it the image of the sentimental hero. The age admired the self-reliant man. To deny Jackson's self-reliance .or to soften his will did not solve the real problem; it only testifies to the mixture of attraction and repulsion the self-contained man had for the American mind. What was needed was not a denial of the self-reliant man, but assurance that the self-reliant man was on the side of society and not against society. At the last, no less an authority than God had to settle the problem how society and the self-willed individual could harmoniously co-exist.

We have seen earlier how God functioned in the myth of the self-made man by providing certainty that success went only to the virtuous. For the unbeliever who still had qualms it was then demonstrated that Jackson's heart *was* good. If it were possible for the man of great will to be a man of great evil, then a society of self-reliant men might be a society of mutual warfare. To avoid the uncomfortable conclusion of this syllogism the society turned to the belief that will, no matter how powerful, was efficient only when it found its place in God's eternal plan.[47]

The image of Jackson as the man of iron will was meant to prove that man succeeds because of himself. There was even the possibility, as we saw in the conversation between the broker and the merchant, that a man of Jackson's willpower could storm Heaven itself. Promethean defiance was a possibility because Jackson did not comfortably fit the requirement that only the virtuous find success. Jackson was not markedly of God; he was not a church-member.

Five years after Jackson's death, Herman Melville explored the problem of the man of will with an intensity that doomed him to neglect in his own time. Melville created Ahab who, defiant of even the gods in his terrible self-reliance, brought ruin to his world, the *Pequod,* which is the world in microcosm. Only one was saved, one who came to the recognition that the world was a joint-stock enterprise and that in love, not pride, lay human salvation. Ahab, unlike Jackson, had turned his back on home, wife, and child; Ahab was the man of will who excluded all human sympathy from his heart. The whole drama of *Moby-Dick* is an enactment of Ahab's defiance of the power that rules the universe. Melville's most terrifying insight is the suggestion that at the center of the universe there is nothing; that blind chance, not God, rules; that there is no meaning.

Melville's contemporaries did not read *Moby-Dick*. In more obscure fashion, however, in their creation of the symbol of Andrew Jackson they grappled with the same problem so dramatically present in Ahab's career. Unlike Melville, they could not bring themselves to a clear statement of the problem. They would not allow Jackson to be completely the man of will and, finally, they never lost trust that God was at the center, that there was a meaning in the universe and that the meaning was good.

The shapers of the myth always insisted on the goodness of Jackson's course; his iron will, unlike Napoleon's, was disinterested.[48] When the young Democrats of New York spoke of the man 'whose iron will and inflexible integrity and purity of purpose bore him triumphantly through to the last,' the integrity and purity of purpose were quite as important as the iron will.[49] And Jackson's biographers qualified the respect paid to his will in the same fashion: 'The several actions in Jackson's life . . . show the irresistible strength which heaven has granted to an honest purpose. They show the homage which men pay to an iron will, based upon the consciousness of right intentions.'[50] The wishful thinking of these sentiments attained the semblance of fact when at the end of his public career in retirement at 'The Hermitage,' Andrew Jackson joined the Presbyterian Church.

Except in the terms I have been suggesting, it is difficult

to account for the extraordinary attention paid at Jackson's death to the matter of his conversion. One cannot help but detect a sense of relief in memorials which praising his self-reliance always come to the somber conclusion that 'his iron constitution, and vigorous, undaunted mind, could not ward off the blow of death.' [51] No eulogist allowed the opportunity to pass to remind his audience that the man of iron had finally succumbed to God. A clergyman in Alabama said, 'To bend that will of iron was reserved alone for the grace of God'; [52] in Ohio it was pointed out that the 'man of iron [had] laid himself down at the foot of the cross.' [53] Benjamin Butler in New York told how Jackson applied himself after his conversion, 'with child-like docility, to the duties and privileges of the Christian life.' [54] The degree of national interest in Jackson's death can be measured by the existence of at least six lithographs picturing the moment of his passing. Currier and Ives published no less than four different versions of this one scene.[55] In all that still exist (see Pl. VII), Jackson's right hand rests upon an open Bible and a curly-haired child (sometimes two) weeps at the bedside; a doctor on the farther side of the bed holds up his watch so the exact moment of death is told; women are there to mourn the passing of the hero. Death attended by the tears of the woman and the tenderness of the child, the moral of it all indicated by the open Bible — what more could a sentimental age ask of its hero?

When Jackson had been converted newspapers told the nation that 'to see this aged veteran, whose head had stood erect in battle, and through scenes of fearful bearing, bend-ing that head in humble and adoring reverence at the table of his divine Master, while tears of penitence and joy trickled down his careworn cheeks, was indeed a spectacle of most intense moral interest.' [56] The interest in Jackson's conversion and Christian death was not due solely to the public attention given the movements of any national figure. Jackson's death was, as the newspaper account said of his conversion, 'a spectacle of most intense moral interest.' The universal stress on the fact that the man of iron will had in the end bowed to God proved that in the last analysis God ruled the universe, that the man of iron will offered no threat to society because he too had his master. In the end, the man whose will-power was great enough to put him beyond social restraint could be tolerated because, subject to God's infinite wisdom, he had his place in the divinely ordered development of society. Jackson's final turn toward God disproved the fears of those of little faith: *'He was great because he was good!'* [57]

SYMBOL

. . . what [the historian] finds at the very beginning
of his research is not a world of physical objects but
a symbolic universe — a world of symbols.

Ernst Cassirer

XI

Coda

In the preceding sections three concepts — Nature, Providence, and Will — have been examined separately. These three ideas with their individual connotations do not exhaust the meaning that Andrew Jackson had for the imagination of his contemporaries, but they do provide the main structural elements about which his appeal took shape. They are, to use a violent metaphor, the ideational skeleton of the ideal Andrew Jackson.

Two things are to be observed about the total significance of the concepts, nature, providence, and will. First, they possess a dramatic unity; that is, all three achieve realization through one figure, Andrew Jackson, who was the age's hero in a wider sense than has commonly been recognized. Any student of American culture will quickly be able to point to other manifestations at the time of these

three ideas, either singly or in conjunction with one another. This is necessarily so and is the best proof of the
point I wish to make: that the symbolic Andrew Jackson
is the creation of his time. Through the age's leading figure
were projected the age's leading ideas. Of Andrew Jackson
the people made a mirror for themselves. Now obviously
Andrew Jackson, the man, offered more tractable material
for the construction of a symbol that carried the meanings
we have discovered in the ideal Jackson than (say) John
Quincy Adams could offer. But this is less important than
the obvious fact that historical actuality imposed little re-
striction on the creation of the symbolic role the people demanded Andrew Jackson to play. Without attempting to
explore the significance of his remark, Richard Hofstadter
has observed that 'the making of a democratic leader is not
a simple process. . . Andrew Jackson . . . has often been
set down as typical of the democratic frontiersman; but
many patent facts about his life fit poorly with the stereo-
type.' [1] This is most obviously the case with the relation of
Jackson to nature, as Hofstadter sees. It is no less true, as
we have seen, with the ideas of providence and will. But
this is only to prove what Carlton J. H. Hayes pointed out
some years ago: 'Nationalist mythology is not in every detail strictly accurate and literally true — no mythology ever
is — but after all its main purpose is didactic, "for example
of life and instruction of manners," and didacticism need
not depend slavishly upon historical or scientific fact. It
claims and deserves the wider range of imagination and
emotion.' [2]

The second point to be made about the ideas, nature,

providence, and will, is that in addition to their dramatic unity they possess a logical unity. If only the former were true, if these three ideas had in common only a mode of presentation, one would be quite justified in disentangling them and regarding each by itself as I have done. But the process of examining each idea in isolation is artificial; it is carried out for the purpose of analysis. The concepts, nature, providence, and will, are organically inter-related; they possess a logical coherence which makes a whole and it is their total configuration that determines the symbol, Andrew Jackson.

As can be seen in most of the quotations already presented in this essay, each concept drew strength from one or both of the other two. In addition each idea usually suggests one or both of the others. For example, the idea of providence is implicit in the tutelary power of nature; the glorification of the will is permissible because providence guarantees that the world is oriented toward good; the anti-traditional aspect of nature nourishes the idea that every man has the making of his own greatness within his own determination. As we saw, the ideas of providence and will co-existed least easily; the idea that the future is your own creation is difficult to reconcile with the idea that the future has been prescribed by God. But it is not surprising that a process of the mind which can dispose of brute fact can likewise ignore the demands of internal logic. It was under the auspices of nature and providence that the cult of the self-made man prospered in America. By making God's favor depend upon each man's exertion, the people of the Age of Jackson easily reconciled personal striving with cosmic determinism, as determinists have done from Puritanism to Communism. It is perhaps possible that an age may have ideals which are mutually destructive but the ideas we have discovered in the image of Andrew Jackson are not. In their integration they make a whole stronger than any constituent part.

It is in their broad tendency, however, that the three concepts, nature, providence, and will, most fully coincide. To whatever degree each idea bolstered the others, they were all oriented in a single direction. In an age of widening horizons all three ideas sanctioned a violently activistic social philosophy. In 1815, the year in which Andrew Jackson entered upon a stage already furnished by the American imagination, *Niles' Weekly Register* observed that America was marked by the 'almost *universal ambition to get forward.*' [3] The unchecked development of the individual was the chief implication of the ideas of nature, providence, and will. It is in this respect that the figure of Andrew Jackson most completely embodies the spirit of his age.

As representative of the idea of nature, Andrew Jackson acted out the belief that training was unnecessary, that traditional learning was no more than an adornment to native sense. The theoretical result of such an attitude was the depreciation of acquired learning and the appreciation of intuitive wisdom. The practical result was a release of energy. Thought was made subordinate to action. Although it need not have done so, the theme of will tended in the same direction. The belief that man's future was his own creation could logically have led to an emphasis on the training of the individual to assure that he wrought wisely.

Actually, however, the glorification of the will minimized
the value of learning and training. The reason why Jackson's success was used to prove action more important than
thought can be inferred from such articles as one called
'Self-Cultivation' (subtitled, 'Every Man is the Architect
of His Own Fortunes'), in which formal education was
maintained to be 'but a mere drop in the sea, when compared with that which is obtained in the everyday journey-
ings of life.' [4] The bias of such a point of view is echoed
in the statement that 'in the wilds of the West [Jackson]
acquired that practical form of thought which led him to
look to results, and to what was to be done, rather than to
matters of speculation.' [5] The argument was the same as
the one that made environment subordinate to character:
'all the instructions of others can do nothing for a man who
does not aid himself and proceed with a fixed purpose.' [6]
Thus, Jackson was described as 'starting in life with a few
strong natural endowments, everything besides was, with
him, self made. It was he himself that improved what God
had bestowed or placed near him.' [7] This eulogist had more
trouble with the place of providence in the theme of the
self-made man than did the person who wrote ecstatically
of Jackson's first inauguration that 'here, the dignity of
man stood forth in bold relief, — man, free and enlightened man — owing nothing to the adventitious circumstances, of birth, or wealth, or extrinsic ornaments — but
ennobled by nature — bold in conscious liberty.' [8]

The doctrine of nature which relegated the precedents
of the past to the ash-heap of history released Americans
to act in the present for their glorious future. No people,

declared a western editor, 'are so ready to make experiments respecting social relations and domestic arrangements, as those of the western country, — none . . . are so little fettered by established habits, or . . . are less disposed to consider hereditary prejudice and heirlooms which cannot be parted with.' [9] For an age eager to claim its future the past was no more than accumulated prejudice and sentimental trinkets. The future of America was in the interior because 'foreign influences . . . cannot reach the heart of the continent where all that lives and moves is American.' [10]

The theme of the will more specifically relegated extrinsic circumstances to a place of minor importance. Joseph G. Baldwin extolled Jackson as 'one of the Ironsides. He was built of Cromwell's stuff. . . He was incredulous of impossibilities. . . He had no thought of failure . . . there was no such word as fail. Accordingly [!] there was no such thing as failure in his history.' [11] Another asserted there was no failure because Jackson was 'a Hercules of action, without learning, except that which was self-taught . . . taking [the stakes of life] by main force and commanding success by seizing the prize he sought.' [12] A society that held up for emulation this type as its ideal placed a tremendous burden on the individual. It further increased the individual's personal responsibility by implying, through the theme of nature, that the figuratively new man in America stood at the beginning of time. Both the theme of nature and the theme of will demanded tremendous exertion of the isolated man.

For the weak who might take fright at such a limitless prospect, or for the tender who might recoil from the buccaneering overtones of the theme of self-help, there was always the idea of providence. Man in America could commit himself violently to a course of action because in the final analysis he was not responsible; God was in control. Because it was believed that America had a glorious destiny, a mission, which had been ordained by divine providence, the immensity of the task facing the nation and each citizen was bathed in a glorious optimism.

The massive emotions and psychological sanctions of all three of these ideas, nature, providence, and will, converged in the image of Andrew Jackson. The result was a symbolic figure. The symbol was not the creation of Andrew Jackson from Tennessee, or of the Democratic party. The symbol was the creation of the times. To describe the early nineteenth century as the age of Jackson misstates the matter. The age was not his. He was the age's.

NOTES

I   IN THE BEGINNING WAS NEW ORLEANS

1. S[amuel] G. Goodrich, *Recollections of a Lifetime, or Men and Things I Have Seen, in a Series of Familiar Letters to a Friend, Historical, Biographical, Anecdotical, and Descriptive* (New York, 1857), I, 505.

2. George Dangerfield, *The Era of Good Feelings* (New York, 1952), pp. 15–91, has a good discussion of the contrast between the war message and the message accompanying the treaty of peace with an analysis of the reasons underlying the shift in tone.

3. Some sense of the foreboding that gripped the country just before the announcement of the victory at New Orleans and of the peace can be grasped by reading the doleful article, 'The Prospect Before Us,' *The Enquirer*, January 3, 1815. The *National Intelligencer*, October 4, 1814, reported that money lenders in New Orleans would not advance funds or extend a loan for as much as sixty days for fear of a change in government within that time. The *Salem Gazette*, September 23, 1814, was arguing whether the union was not 'virtually dissolved,' and as late as February 3, 1815, the *Boston Daily Advertiser*, although taking issue with its correspondents, could record views that a British victory at New Orleans would be a boon to the country because it would expose the weakness of the administration and rid the union of Louisiana which was 'a curse to the nation' anyway.

4. *Boston Patriot*, January 28, 1815; *National Intelligencer*, cited by James Parton, *Life of Andrew Jackson*, 3 vols. (Boston, n.d.), II, 244.

5. *New-York Evening Post*, January 20, 25, 1815.

6. *Washington Republican*, February 3, 1815.

7. Wilson McCandless, 'Eulogy Delivered at Pittsburgh, July 17, 1845,' *Monument to the Memory of General Andrew Jackson: Containing Twenty-five Eulogies and Sermons Delivered on the Occasion of His Death,* comp. B[enjamin] M. Dusenbery (Philadelphia, 1848), p. 116.

8. In order, these captions are taken from the *National Intelligencer, Extra,* February 4, 1815, the Cincinnati, Ohio, *Spirit of the West,* February 5, 1815, the New London *Connecticut Gazette,* February 8, 1815, and the *Boston Patriot,* February 11, 1815. The news traveled by two channels: east by mail from New Orleans to Washington so that the *National Intelligencer* had most of its accounts from the postmaster in New Orleans or from private letters from people on the scene; west by mail to Kentucky and then *via* copies of the *Frankfort Palladium,* January 30, 1815, to the Northwest so that extras were out in Cincinnati (by the *Liberty Hall*) and in Washington, D.C., on the same day, February 4, 1815.

9. Peace was 'officially' announced in the *National Intelligencer,* February 15, 1815, although rumors of it had been circulating in the eastern papers for a week.

10. *National Advocate* in *The Albany Argus,* February 21, 1815; *The Enquirer,* March 1, 1815.

11. *National Intelligencer,* February 23, 1815.

12. *The Enquirer,* February 18, 1815; *Eastern Argus,* March 9, 1815.

13. *National Intelligencer,* February 21, 1815 (my emphasis).

14. Epes Sargent, *The Life and Public Services of Henry Clay,* rev. ed. (New York, 1848), p. 19.

15. *New-Hampshire Patriot,* February 21, 1814.

16. *National Intelligencer,* February 17, 1815. This speech was widely reprinted; for example, *The Enquirer,* February 22, 1815, *The Albany Argus,* February 21, 1815.

II 'THE HUNTERS OF KENTUCKY'

1. Noah M. Ludlow, *Dramatic Life As I Found It: A Record of Personal Experience* (St. Louis, 1880), pp. 237–8. Ludlow's account is not entirely correct. He remembered that his brother had seen 'The Hunters of Kentucky' in the *New-York Mirror.* There was, however, no *Mirror* published in New York in 1822, nor in any year near that date.

Samuel Woodworth's poem, which was to be transmuted into the lyrics
of the song, 'The Hunters of Kentucky,' seems to have circulated first
in broadside form. Ludlow's account of the origin of 'The Hunters
of Kentucky' suggests that the song is a 'folk-song' only in the sense
that its popularity was so great it was eventually taken over by the
folk. Following is the version of the song to be found on a broadside
in the Library of Congress (Pl. VIII):

1. Ye gentlemen and ladies fair,
    Who grace this famous city,
   Just listen if you've time to spare,
    While I rehearse a ditty;
   And for the opportunity
    Conceive yourselves quite lucky,
   For 'tis not often that you see
    A hunter from Kentucky
   O Kentucky, the hunters of Kentucky!
   O Kentucky, the hunters of Kentucky!

2. We are a hardy, free-born race,
    Each man to fear a stranger;
   Whate'er the game we join in chase,
    Despising toil and danger,
   And if a daring foe annoys,
    Whate'er his strength and forces,
   We'll show him that Kentucky boys
    Are alligator horses.
         Oh Kentucky, &c.

3. I s'pose you've read it in the prints,
    How Packenham attempted
   To make old Hickory Jackson wince,
    But soon his scheme repented;
   For we with rifles ready cock'd,
    Thought such occasion lucky,
   And soon around the gen'ral flock'd
    The Hunters of Kentucky.
         Oh Kentucky, &c.

4. You've heard, I s'pose how New-Orleans
    Is fam'd for wealth and beauty,
   There's girls of ev'ry hue it seems,
    From snowy white to sooty.
   So Packenham he made his brags,
    If he in fight was lucky,

He'd have their girls and cotton bags,
    In spite of old Kentucky.
        Oh Kentucky, &c.

5. But Jackson he was wide awake,
    And was not scar'd at trifles,
For well he knew what aim we take
    With our Kentucky rifles.
So he led us down to Cypress swamp,
    The ground was low and mucky,
There stood John Bull in martial pomp
    And here was old Kentucky.
        Oh Kentucky, &c.

6. A bank was rais'd to hide our breasts,
    Not that we thought of dying,
But that we always like to rest,
    Unless the game is flying.
Behind it stood our little force,
    None wished it to be greater,
For ev'ry man was half a horse,
    And half an alligator.
        Oh Kentucky, &c.

7. They did not let our patience tire,
    Before they showed their faces;
We did not choose to waste our fire,
    So snugly kept our places.
But when so near we saw them wink,
    We thought it time to stop 'em,
And 'twould have done you good I think,
    To see Kentuckians drop 'em.
        Oh Kentucky, &c.

8. They found, at last, 'twas vain to fight,
    Where *lead* was all the *booty*,
And so they wisely took to flight,
    And left *us* all our *beauty*.
And now if danger e'er annoys,
    Remember what our trade is,
Just send for us Kentucky boys,
    And we'll protect ye, ladies.
        Oh Kentucky, &c.

2. Ludlow, *Dramatic Life*, p. 250.

3. Ben: Perley Poore, *Perley's Reminiscences of Sixty Years in the National Metropolis* (Philadelphia, 1886), p. 90.

4. Thomas Low Nichols, *Forty Years of American Life, 1821–1861*, second ed. (New York, 1937), p. 309.

5. *New-Hampshire Patriot and State Gazette*, January 14, 1828.

6. Anon., 'Campaign Songs of Past Years,' *The Antiquarian*, III (October 1924), 25.

7. Anon., *Republican Campaign Songster* (New York, 1868), 'Preface.'

8. The earliest political use of the song that I have been able to discover is not in connection with Jackson but in behalf of General Joseph Desha's candidacy for the governorship of Kentucky. An article including the song, addressed to the 'Hunters of Kentucky' by 'Daniel Boone,' appeared in the *Argus of Western America*, June 9, 1824. Noah Ludlow did not give the song to the press until he was in Huntsville, Alabama, at the end of the summer season of 1822 (Ludlow, *Dramatic Life*, pp. 241–2), but since the words were not original with him they may have received general circulation before.

As the political use of the song increased, 'The Hunters' became 'The Voters of Kentucky':

> We are a hardy free born race,
>   Who always fight for glory;
> And never gave our votes to place,
>   As President, a *tory;*
>
> And we will not consent to be,
>   Like hirelings bought and sold, sirs;
> We'll rise and show the world we're free —
>   Above the reach of gold, sirs!
>   O Kentucky, The Voters of Kentucky!

This version refers to Henry Clay's 'sale' of Kentucky's electoral votes in the election of 1824. It first appeared in the Jackson organ, *U. S. Telegraph*, and was copied in the *Argus of Western America*, July 16, 1828.

9. An anonymous poet tried his best to render the numerical superiority of the British force:

As leaves, innumerous, quiver on the trees —
As swarming multitudes of clustering bees —
As stars in heaven, as sands upon the shore,
So seem the invaders from the deep to pour.

Anon., *An Epick Poem in Commemoration of Gen Andrew Jackson's Victory on the eighth of January, 1815* (Boston, 1827), p. 17.

10. Americans estimated the British loss at over 3000, but the official British report (in A. Lacarriere Latour, *Historical Memoir of the War in West Florida and Louisiana in 1814–1815. With an Atlas*, trans. H. P. Nugent [Philadelphia, 1816], Appendix, pp. cliii–cliv) gave 2,037, of which 291 were killed, 1,262 were wounded, and 484 were missing.

11. Report of Adjutant-General Robert Butler to the War Department, January 16, 1815 (in Latour, *Historical Memoir*, Appendix, pp. lviii–lx), gives the American losses on *both* sides of the river as 13 killed, 39 wounded, and 19 missing; Patron (*Life*, ii, 209) gives the figure of 8 killed and 13 wounded. After the battle the Americans were less fortunate. The troops under Coffee and Adair that had been stationed in the Cypress Swamp incurred fever and dysentery; over 500 died as a result (Latour, *Historical Memoir*, p. 225).

12. The only attempt I have seen in a contemporary account to explain the disparity of loss in some logical manner was in *The Albany Argus*, February 10, 1815. Since the American force suffered so slightly, the editor surmised that the British must have charged without flints, planning a bayonet assault, and thus never brought fire to bear on the American line.

13. Nearly every biography of Andrew Jackson deals at length with the Battle of New Orleans. The best account is still Latour, *Historical Memoir*. Henry Adams's excellent account gives a great deal more weight to the English background (*History of the United States of America During the Second Administration of James Madison* [New York, 1921], ii, 311–85).

14. [George Robert Gleig], *A Subaltern in America: Comprising His Narrative of the Campaign of the British Army, at Baltimore, Washington, &c. &c. During the Late War* (Philadelphia, 1833), p. 219; see also pp. 220–27 for a good account of the engagement of the night of December 23, 1814.

15. Latour, *Historical Memoir*, p. 112.

16. Latour, *Historical Memoir*, p. 146; Anon., 'A Contemporary Account of the Battle of New Orleans,' p. 11.

17. Latour, *Historical Memoir*, pp. 145–52, has a detailed description of Jackson's lines on the morning of the eighth.

18. The assignment of the 44th to this dangerous task seems to have been one of many British blunders. The 44th was not well considered as a regiment ([Gleig], *Subaltern in America*, p. 257), although opinion to this effect had the advantage of looking back upon the 44th's failure.

19. For a graphic account of the confusion that followed the discovery of the failure of the 44th to bring up the fascines and ladders see R. S., 'Battle of New Orleans, 8th January, 1815,' *Museum of Foreign Literature and Science*, XIII (December 1828), 749–51 [extracted from *Blackwood's*].

20. Lt.-Col. Mullins was cashiered for his part in the Battle of New Orleans. He was tried on three charges: '1st — For having on the 8th January, 1815, shamefully neglected and disobeyed the Orders he had received from the late Major General Gibbs, commanding the 2d Brigade, to collect the Facines and Ladders, and to be formed with them at the Head of the Column of Attack at the time directed, and in disobedience of said Orders, suffering the regiment under his Command to pass the Redoubt where the Facines and Ladders were lodged, and remaining at the Head of the Column for half an hour or upwards, without taking any steps to put the 44th Regiment in possession of the Facines and Ladders, in conformity with the said Orders, knowing the period of Attack to be momently approaching, in consequences of which disobedience and neglect, the 44th Regiment on being sent back to the Redoubt, and returning hurriedly with the Facines, &c. &c. was thrown into confusion, and moved off to the attack in an irregular and unconnected manner leading to the fire and disorder which ensued in the attacking Column, and the disasters attending it.'

'2d. — For scandalous and infamous misbehavior before the enemy, near New Orleans, on the 8th January, 1815, in not leading and conducting the 44th Regiment under his Command up to the Enemy's Works; in not placing the Ladders and Facines in the Ditch as he was ordered to do; and in not setting that Example of Gallantry to the Soldiers, so indispensably requisite, a part of an Officer's Duty, to insure the success of an Attack, in consequence of which misbehavior, the 44th Regiment did not perform the Service allotted to them, never

having made an attempt to place the Facines in the Ditch, and thereby
leading to the Cause of the failure of the attack.'

'3d. — For scandalous Conduct in having said to an Officer of his Regiment, on the 7th January, 1815, when informed the 44th was destined
to carry the Facines, &c. 'It is a forlorn hope, and the Regiment must
be sacrificed,' or words to that effect, such an expression being calculated to dispirit those under his Command, to render them discon-
tented with the Service allotted to them, demonstrative of the feeling
with which he undertook the enterprise, and infamous and disgraceful
to the character of a Commanding Officer of a British Regiment.'
*General Court Martial Held at the Royal Barracks, For the Trial of
Brevet Lieutenant-Colonel Hon. Thomas Mullins, Captain of the
44th Regiment of Foot, The Court Assembled on the 11th of July,
1815, and continued by Adjournments to the 1st of August following,
on the Annex'd Charges* (Dublin: William Espy, 1815), reprinted in
its entirety in *Louisiana Historical Quarterly*, IX (January 1926), 34–
110. The Espy pamphlet is not an official record but a pamphlet version which, as the editor of the *Louisiana Historical Quarterly* observes, seems to have been prepared under editorial supervision somewhat friendly to Mullins. Mullins was found guilty on the first two
specifications but acquitted on the third.

21. *New-York Evening Post*, February 8, 1815. Latour, *Historical
Memoir*, p. 155, records the British halt and the movement to the left
to make way for the 44th, but he thought that the maneuver was to
evade the fire of Battery No. 7.

22. *National Intelligencer*, February 7, 1815.

23. Anon., 'A Contemporary Account of the Battle of New Orleans
by a Soldier in the Ranks,' *Louisiana Historical Quarterly*, IX (January 1926), 11.

24. *National Intelligencer, Extra*, February 4, 1815.

25. *Kentucky Palladium*, January 30, 1815; *Liberty Hall*, February
4, 1815.

26. Latour, *Historical Memoir*, pp. clxxxii–clxxxv; Williams,
Sketches of the War, p. 473; *The Enquirer*, February 22, 1815; *National
Intelligencer*, February 27, 1815.

27. *The Albany Argus*, February 10, 1815 (my emphasis).

28. *National Intelligencer*, February 7, 1815. It should perhaps also
be pointed out that none of the batteries were manned by frontier

militia; they were all worked by Barratarians, Navy men, or regular U. S. Army artillerists (Latour, *Historical Memoir,* pp. 147–8).

29. *Liberty Hall,* March 11, 1815; *Spirit of the West,* March 25, 1815, attributed the story to a New Orleans paper; *The Albany Argus,* March 21, 1815, had the shot in the left eye rather than below it, and copied it from the *National Intelligencer.*

30. R. S., 'Battle of New Orleans,' p. 750.

31. *National Intelligencer,* June 29, 1815.

32. Alexander Walker, *Jackson and New Orleans. An Authentic Narrative of the Memorable Achievements of the American Army Under Andrew Jackson Before New Orleans in the Winter of 1814–'15* (New York, 1856), pp. 369–70.

33. Anon., *An Epick Poem,* p. 5.

34. *The Jackson Wreath, or National Souvenir* (Philadelphia, 1829), p. 34.

35. Above, pp. 7–9.

36. John Spencer Bassett, ed., *Correspondence of Andrew Jackson,* 6 vols. (Washington, 1926–33), II, 118.

37. As most of Jackson's addresses at New Orleans, this was probably written by Robert Livingston; Parton (*Life,* II, 63n) claims to have seen the original in Livingston's hand but it is no longer extant. Scholars generally agree that the substance of all of Jackson's communications is his, although the phrasing may be someone else's. I have chosen to use the word 'thought' in order to anticipate any objections on this score, but I should like to point out that for this study it matters little whose words these are since my purpose is to demonstrate the currency of the idea rather than its uniqueness.

38. In 1848, Bernard Marigny published his *Reflections on the Campaign of General Andrew Jackson in 1814 and '15* in order to controvert the 'general impression that it is only due to the Anglo-Saxon race that we owe the glorious results of 1814–'15.' There is some ground for attributing the neglect of the part played by the French at New Orleans (see pp. 73–5 in Marigny's work for an impressive summing-up of that part) to Anglo-Saxon pride; for example, S. Putnam Waldo (*Memoirs of Andrew Jackson,* third ed. [Hartford, 1819], pp. 12, 181–2, 185) attributes the victory to Anglo-Saxon strength. Also such a view is suggested by the statement in the *Boston Patriot,* February 11, 1815, accounting for the American defeat on the left bank, that the Creoles

'would not stand.' In view of the fact that the British were providing the opposition, it must have required some ingenuity to attribute the American victory to the racial prowess of the Anglo-Saxon. Although such a position may account for some of the neglect of the French Creoles, I believe that the chief reason was the Creoles, as residents of the city of New Orleans, did not fit the more popular version of the battle as the victory of the frontiersman.

39. Latour, *Historical Memoir*, pp. 150–52.

40. Latour, *Historical Memoir*, p. 141.

41. Andrew Jackson to Secretary Monroe, January 3, 1815, quoted in Latour, *Historical Memoir*, p. 142; Bassett, *Correspondence*, II, 130, has a slightly different reading: 'not more than one third of them are armed, and those very indifferently.' Jackson did not have arms to give the Kentucky troops either. The arms which Jackson ordered to be sent to New Orleans in the mid-summer of 1814 arrived after January 8, 1815.

42. Walker, *Jackson and New Orleans*, p. 158.

43. Walker, *Jackson and New Orleans*, p. 159.

44. Waldo, *Memoirs of Andrew Jackson*, p. 12; see also *Civil and Military History* (1825), p. 14, which is nothing more than Waldo's biography of 1819.

45. Nathaniel H. Claiborne, *Notes on the War in the South* (Richmond, 1819), p. 60.

46. Claiborne, *Notes on the War in the South*, p. 69. I would like to call passing attention here to Claiborne's use of the word 'cultivated.' In opposing the country to the city, Nature to Civilization, Claiborne has introduced an ambiguous element into the equation by the word, 'cultivated.' I mention the matter here to indicate my awareness of the fact that the problem is not as simple as a topical treatment at first makes it seem.

47. *The Western Spy*, July 7, 1815.

48. *Niles' Weekly Register*, VIII (March 4, 1815), 417.

49. Asher Ware, *An Oration Delivered Before the Washington Society in Boston on the Fourth of July, 1816* (Boston, 1816), p. 12.

50. Anon., *An Epick Poem*, p. 23.

51. Henry D. Gilpin, *A Speech Delivered at the Union and Harmony Celebration . . . of the Twenty-first Anniversary of the Victory of New Orleans* (Philadelphia, 1836), p. 4.

52. For a general discussion of the theme of Nature in American thought, see Smith, *Virgin Land,* to which this chapter is heavily in debt.

III   NATURE'S NOBLEMAN

1. Francis J. Grund, *Aristocracy in America,* 2 vols. (London, 1839), II, 306.

2. Jacksonian philosophy is here exhibiting a trait that characterizes much of American thought: reacting to native stresses and strains the American thinker reaches out to the older and denser culture of Europe for suitable concepts, but in transmission the ideas of Europe become altered to fit American needs and American conditions.

3. George Bancroft, Manuscript Notebook, Jackson Papers, New York Public Library, p. [13]. Thomas Hart Benton, after reading Parton's *Life of Jackson,* had suggested that a 'democratic' biography needed to be written and suggested that Bancroft was the man for the job. Bancroft's notes may be the rudimentary beginnings of a life of Jackson or, more probably, the preparation for Bancroft's funeral oration on the occasion of Jackson's death. The notebook is homemade and consists of lined paper, stitched along the left hand edge. There is no interior evidence for a precise attribution.

4. Speech of Francis Boylies, *The Western Sun and General Advertiser,* September 20, 1828.

5. *Richmond Enquirer,* January 18, 1827. For further expressions of the same sentiment, see: Nathaniel B. Felton, *Addresses of Messrs. Hill, Thornton, Felton and Harper, January 8, 1828* (Concord, N. H., 1828), pp. 42–3; *Jackson Wreath,* p. 56; *Argus of Western America,* February 6, 1828; *Richmond Enquirer,* January 3, 1828; *The Illinois Gazette,* January 15, 1825.

6. The originals of both cartoons are to be found in the Jackson papers at the Tennessee State Library, Nashville, Tennessee.

7. These lines are slightly misquoted. Compare Lord Byron, 'Childe Harold's Pilgrimage,' Canto IV, Verse CXVI (Ernest Hartley Coleridge, ed., *The Works of Lord Byron,* rev. ed. [London, 1904], Poetry: II, 400–401).

8. The persistence of the conflict in these terms may be seen in the examination of a modern cartoon by Henry Nash Smith in his article,

'The West as an Image of the American Past,' *University of Kansas City Review*, XVIII (Autumn, 1951), 29–40.

9. *Mississippi Republican, Extra,* January 20, 1815. This letter was reprinted in nearly every paper in the nation: *National Intelligencer, Extra,* February 11, 1815; *National Intelligencer,* February 13, 1815; *New-York Evening Post,* February 14, 1815; *The Enquirer,* February 18, 1815; *Spirit of the West,* February 18, 1815; *Liberty Hall,* February 18, 1815; *The Albany Argus,* February 21, 1815. The 'Beauty and Booty' story was accepted as truthful in nearly every contemporary account of the War of 1812 or of Jackson's career. The British government refused to take notice of a charge made through the press so the incident was never officially disproved; neither does it seem to have been proved. Eighteen years after the Battle of New Orleans, five British officers wrote a joint letter to James Stuart repudiating the 'Beauty and Booty' story which he had recounted in *Three Years in the United States.* In their letter, the officers 'most unequivocally den[ied] that any such promise was ever held out to the army.' (*Niles' Weekly Register,* XLV [October 19, 1833], 121.) The American papers found it curious that it had taken the officers eighteen years to hear a charge that had received wide circulation in American books and newspapers ever since the alleged incident had occurred. Even when the letter of the British statement was accepted, some commented that the promise of 'Beauty and Booty' may not have been 'publicly or explicitly made to the troops, but that it was tacitly understood.' (*Philadelphia Gazette,* in *Niles' Weekly Register,* XLV [November 23, 1833], 203.) The Duke of Wellington had arrived at the same conclusion; although he disbelieved the actuality of such a countersign, he thought that it was probably true that rapine and pillage would have followed a British victory. (Duke of Wellington to Lord Longford, Brussels, May 22, 1815, *Louisiana Historical Quarterly,* IX [January 1926], 8.)

10. *Spirit of the West,* February 18, 1815.

11. 'A Card from the Ladies of New Orleans,' January 3, 1815, The Jackson Papers, Library of Congress.

12. Bassett, ed., *Correspondence,* II, 118. For other representations of the British as vandals, barbarians, or savages, see: *Niles' Weekly Register,* VIII (March 4, 1815), 417; Latour, *Historical Memoir,* pp. viii, 5, 164; Ellis Lewis, 'Eulogy Delivered at Lancaster, Pa., June 26, 1845,' Dusenbery, comp., *Monument,* p. 161; *The Louisiana Gazette,*

February 2, 1815; *National Intelligencer,* March 6, 1815; Reid and Eaton, *Life,* p. 352; C. E. Grice, *The Battle of New Orleans, or Glory, Love, and Loyalty; An Historical and National Drama in Five Acts* (Georgetown, 1816), p. 29.

13. Walker, *Jackson and New Orleans,* p. 244.

14. [Gleig], *Subaltern in America,* p. 220.

15. Walker, *Jackson and New Orleans,* p. 221. For similar qualms about the American style of fighting see Fr. Flaneur, 'The Battle of New Orleans,' *New England Family Magazine; For the Diffusion of Useful Knowledge,* I (March 1845), 71–2.

16. Above, pp. 28, 224 (n46).

17. The OED attributes the first use of the word to Joseph Glanvill (*Scepsis Scientifica,* p. 81) in 1665. In the literal sense of improving the soil, the OED attributes the word to the period 1620–55, so it seems that the figurative usage was adopted almost as soon as the word appeared. However, the word 'cultive,' meaning roughly to air the ground, dates from 1483, and Hobbes speaks of children's education in *Leviathan* as 'a culture of their minds.'

18. Chester E. Eisinger, 'The Freehold Concept in Eighteenth Century American Letters,' *William and Mary Quarterly,* 3d series, IV (January 1947), 42–59.

19. Agnew D. Roorbach, *The Development of Social Studies in American Secondary Education Before 1861* (Philadelphia, 1937), pp. 113–14.

20. Charles A. Goodrich, *A History of the United States of America* (New York, 1829), p. 399.

21. Bassett, *Correspondence,* I, 494–5.

22. Above, pp. 34–5.

23. *National Intelligencer,* December 24, 1814; [Rev. Samuel Williams], *Sketches of the War Between the United States and the British Isles Intended as a Faithful History* (Rutland, Vt., 1815), p. 454.

24. Jesse Denson, *The Chronicles of Andrew: Containing an Accurate and Brief Account of General Jackson's Victories in the South, Over the Creeks. Also His Victory over the British at New Orleans, With a Biographical Sketch of His Life* (Lexington, Ky., 1815), pp. 22–3.

25. George M. Dallas, 'Eulogy Delivered at Philadelphia, June 26, 1845,' Dusenbery, comp., *Monument,* p. 55.

26. William Foster Otis, *An Oration Delivered Before the 'Young Men of Boston,' on the Fourth of July, MDCCCXXXI* (Boston, 1831), p. 33.

27. The legislative history of the removal of the American Indians is told in Annie Heloise Abel, 'The History of Events Resulting in Indian Consolidation West of the Mississippi,' *Annual Report of the American Historical Association for the Year 1906* (Washington, 1908), I, 233–450.

28. James D. Richardson, ed., *A Compilation of the Messages and Papers of the Presidents, 1789–1908* (n.p., 1909), III, 294. For an even more explicit statement of the destructive influences of civilization on the Indians, see Jackson's 'Seventh Annual Message,' Richardson, *Messages and Papers*, III, 171–3. The same ambivalence is discernible in Noah Webster's dictionary: 'CIVILIZATION, n. The act of civilizing, or the state of being civilized; the state of being refined in manners, from the grossness of savage life, and improved in arts and learning. SAVAGE, n. A human being in his native state of rudeness, one who is untaught, uncivilized, or without cultivation of mind or manners. The *savages* of America, when uncorrupted by the vices of civilized men . . .' *An American Dictionary of the English Language* (1828). Webster's definitions were brought to my attention by Roy Harvey Pearce, *The Savages of America: A Study of the Indian and the Idea of Civilization* (Baltimore, 1953), p. [2]. I think Professor Pearce too quickly concludes there was allegiance to the idea of civilization because of a rejection of savagism. His study contains much evidence to support my point here: that America was trying to establish a middle-ground between savage nature and effete civilization. See, e.g., the long quotation from Thomas Farnham on p. 65 of his study.

29. Anon., *The Tennessee Farmer; or, Farmer Jackson in New York* (n.p., n.d.), p. [3]. Although Sabin (Biblio. No. 35391) dates this pamphlet 1824, it is obvious from interior evidence that it belongs to the election of 1828. On page [3] the writer refers to the support of *The Albany Argus* for Jackson. In 1824, the Argus was a Crawford organ; not until the election of 1828 did it come out for Jackson.

30. Anon., *The Life of Andrew Jackson, President of the United States . . . By Major Jack Downing of the Dowiningville Militia* (Philadelphia, 1834), pp. 147–8. The reference to 'hosses, chickens and

niggurs' is to suggest Jackson's fondness for horse-racing and cock-fighting as well as his position as slave-owner.

31. Arthur M. Schlesinger, Jr., 'The Pattern of Democratic Change in the United States: Andrew Jackson and Franklin D. Roosevelt,' *The Democratic Process: Lectures on the American Liberal Tradition* (New London, Conn., 1948), pp. 3–16.

32. *Register of Pennsylvania,* IV (August 1829), 80.

33. Andrew Jackson to General Francis Preston, January 27, 1824, Avery O. Craven, ed., *Huntington Library Bulletin,* No. 3 (February 1933), 124–5.

34. [Margaret Bayard Smith], *The First Forty Years of Washington Society,* ed. Gaillard Hunt (New York, 1906), p. 283.

35. Mitford M. Mathews (*A Dictionary of Americanisms on Historical Principles* [Chicago, 1951], I, 896) gives an example of just such usage. The following sentence was recorded in *American Speech,* XVIII (1842), 126: 'Away with the wild Kentuckian. . . Take this barbarian from my sight! This Jacksonist — away!'

36. Andrew Jackson to Samuel Swartout, December 14, 1824, Henry F. DePuy, ed., 'Some Letters of Andrew Jackson,' *American Antiquarian Society Proceedings,* n.s., XXXI (1921), 76, 78, and compare 86.

37. *Columbian Observer,* quoted *National Intelligencer,* November 14, 1823. The introduction of the Cincinnatus theme here might logically raise an objection in the mind of the reader. One of the points of this chapter is that the United States rejected Europe by stressing the superiority of nature over civilization, that is America over Europe. The Roman imagery in which the period of this study is saturated seems, however, to imply an obeisance to European tradition rather than an alienation from it. I suggest, however, that Americans were so fond of classical imagery because they imagined themselves to constitute a return to the uncorrupted state of the past, before the fall, so to speak, while contemporary Europe seemed a corruption of the virtues of *its own* past. The significant point, particularly in regard to the image of Cincinnatus, is that the classical world was thought to draw its vigor from its historical position, from being the earliest stage of civilization, that is from its recent (and with Cincinnatus still continuing) contact with nature. Thus, a contemporary periodical, in a panegyric on 'The Life of the Husbandman,' compared the American farmer to the Romans because 'the ancient Ro-

mans venerated the plough, and at the earliest purest time of the Republic, the greatest praise which could be given to an illustrious character was a judicious and industrious husbandman.' (*The Rough-Hewer*, 1 [March 26, 1840], 43.) Now it might have been logically possible for Americans in their rejection of Europe as degenerate to have become antiquarians and to have exemplified Europe's present fall from grace by reference to the golden past; whatever the logical possibilities, it was psychologically improbable. A dramatist, using the Battle of New Orleans as his theme, stated the matter succinctly when he put in the mouth of General Coffee the words: 'Our western wilds preserve the ancient glory.' (Grice, *The Battle of New Orleans*, pp. 44–5.) If nature nourished the classical past, there was no need to seek out the past; it was only necessary to recognize the source of its greatness. Nature was plentifully at hand.

This is a suggestion which I have not had time to explore to my own satisfaction and I offer it tentatively. It does fit the cyclical course of history which lies back of Thomas Cole's famous series of paintings, 'The Course of Empire,' done in this period. It is undeniably present in the words of the playwright quoted above. In any event, the image of Cincinnatus, which introduced this digression, is intimately associated with the power of nature. Cincinnatus comes down to us out of the shadowy past of 458 B.C. as Roman, yes, but plowman first.

38. *Knoxville Register*, February 6, 1824.

39. *Argus of Western America*, July 9, 1828.

40. *Argus of Western America*, September 17, 1828.

41. [John Henry Eaton], *The Letters of Wyoming, to the People of the United States on the Presidential Election and in favor of Andrew Jackson* (Philadelphia, 1824), p. 103. These letters first appeared individually in the *Columbian Observer*.

42. *New-Hampshire Patriot and State Gazette*, February 12, 1827.

43. Samuel A. Cartwright, 'Eulogy Delivered at Natchez, Miss., July 12, 1845,' Dusenbery, comp., *Monument*, p. 302.

IV   THE PLOWMAN AND THE PROFESSOR

1. Andrew Jackson, 'Address to his Troops,' January 21, 1815, *The Enquirer*, February 22, 1815; also in *National Intelligencer*, Febru-

ary 27, 1815, *The Albany Argus*, February 28, 1815. Reprinted in Latour, *Historical Memoir*, pp. clxxxii–clxxxv.

2. Latour, *Historical Memoir*, p. 107.

3. Walker, *Jackson and New Orleans*, pp. 154–5.

4. Walker, *Jackson and New Orleans*, p. 244.

5. *National Intelligencer*, February 25, 1815; *Niles' Weekly Register*, VIII (March 11, 1815), 30–31.

6. See Troup's speech, above p. 8; Ware, *An Oration*, p. 12; Walker, *Jackson and New Orleans*, p. 152; *An Epick Poem*, p. 13; 'Address of the Mayor of New York to Andrew Jackson, February, 1819,' *Niles' Weekly Register*, XVI (March 6, 1819), 29; 'Address of the Officers of the 14th Brigade, Maryland Militia,' *Niles' Weekly Register*, XVI (March 6, 1819), 32–3; Edward Livingston, 'Unpublished Notes,' *United States Magazine and Democratic Review*, VIII (October 1840), 379; McCandless, 'Eulogy,' Dusenbery, comp., *Monument*, p. 115; Lewis, 'Eulogy,' Dusenbery, comp., *Monument*, p. 163; George W. Bethune, 'A Discourse on the Duty of a Patriot, with some allusions on the Life and Death of Andrew Jackson, pronounced July 6, 1845,' Dusenbery, comp., *Monument*, p. 352; Pliny Merrick, 'Eulogy Delivered at Boston, Mass., July 9, 1845,' Dusenbery, comp., *Monument*, pp. 171–2; Francis R. Shunk, 'Eulogy Delivered at Harrisburg, Pa., July 24, 1845,' Dusenbery, comp., *Monument*, p. 148; Thomas L. Smith, 'Eulogy Delivered at Louisville, Ky., July 3, 1845,' Dusenbery, comp., *Monument*, p. 276; Andrew Stevenson, 'Eulogy Delivered at Richmond, Va., June 28, 1845,' Dusenbery, comp., *Monument*, p. 258.

7. James Russell Lowell, 'Thoreau,' *My Study Windows*, The Complete Writings of James Russell Lowell, 16 vols. (Cambridge, Mass., 1904), II, 134.

8. Daniel J. Boorstin, *The Lost World of Thomas Jefferson* (New York, 1948), p. 169; Harry H. Clark, 'The Influence of Science on American Ideas, from 1775 to 1809,' *Transactions of the Wisconsin Academy of Science, Arts, and Letters*, XXV (1943), 305.

9. Ernst Cassirer, *The Philosophy of the Enlightenment*, trans. Fritz C. A. Koelln and James P. Pettegrove (Princeton, 1951), p. 5 and *passim*.

10. Rush Welter, 'The Adams-Jefferson Correspondence 1812–1826,' *American Quarterly*, II (Fall 1950), 234–50.

11. Thomas Jefferson to Peter Carr, August 10, 1787, *The Works of Thomas Jefferson*, Federal Edition, ed., Paul Leicester Ford, 12 vols. (New York, 1904), v, 323.

12. 'Address of the Herkimer Convention,' *Jackson Republican*, October 4, 1828.

13. Although not intending the volume as an aid to the incipient Transcendentalist movement, James Marsh, by editing Coleridge's *Aids to Reflection* (Burlington, Vt., 1829) made these categories available to Emerson and others. For a more thorough exposition of the distinction between the Reason and the Understanding, see Emerson to Edward Bliss Emerson, May 31, 1834, *The Letters of Ralph Waldo Emerson*, ed. Ralph L. Rusk, 6 vols. (New York, 1939), I, 412–13.

14. *The Illinois Gazette*, January 15, 1825.

15. *Richmond Enquirer*, January 3, 1828.

16. Felton, *Addresses*, pp. 42–3.

17. *Address of the Republican General Committee of Young Men of the City and County of New York Friendly to the Election of Gen. Andrew Jackson* (New York, 1828), p. 38.

18. 'Address of the Herkimer Convention,' *Jackson Republican*, October 4, 1828.

19. *Jackson Republican*, October 15, 1828. Compare Emerson's dictum that books are for the scholar's idle times.

20. *Jackson Wreath*, p. 56. The biographical sketch in *The Jackson Wreath* is an abridged version of an earlier sketch by Robert Walsh which appeared in *The American Monthly Magazine*, I (January 1824), 68–82. The latter was reprinted entirely in *The Casket, or Flowers of Literature, Wit, and Sentiment*, n.s., No. 1 (January 1828), 1–6; in part in *American Magazine of Useful and Entertaining Knowledge*, III (September 1837), 468–70. Walsh's sketch was also issued in book form as *Biographical Sketch of the Life of Andrew Jackson, Major General of the Armies of the United States, The Hero of New Orleans* (Hudson, N.Y., 1828).

21. Bethune, *Discourse*, p. 351.

22. In addition to the above citations, compare the following:
'Natural': Wise, *Seven Decades*, pp. 102–3; Felton, *Addresses*, pp. 42–3; Merrick, 'Eulogy,' p. 169; Stevenson, 'Eulogy,' p. 254.
'Native': *Address of the Republican General Committee of Young*

Men of the City and County of New York, p. 15; *New-Hampshire Patriot and State Gazette*, January 14, 1828; Dallas, 'Eulogy,' p. 53; John Van Buren, 'Eulogy Delivered at Albany, June 30, 1845,' Dusenbery, comp., *Monument*, p. 99.

'Intuitive': Bancroft, 'Eulogy,' pp. 37, 41, 50; A. F. Morrison, 'Eulogy Delivered at Indianapolis, June 28, 1845,' Dusenbery, comp., *Monument*, p. 142; Hugh A. Garland, 'Eulogy Delivered at Petersburg, Va., July 12, 1845,' Dusenbery, comp., *Monument*, p. 206; Stevenson, 'Eulogy,' p. 268; Smith, 'Eulogy,' p. 273.

'Instinctive': George Bancroft, 'General Order [on the occasion of Andrew Jackson's death] Issued by the Acting Secretary of War and Navy,' June 16, 1845, Holograph Original in the Jackson Papers, New York Public Library; *Boston Post*, July 1, 1845; Dallas, 'Eulogy,' p. 53; Garland, 'Eulogy,' p. 199.

23. *The New York Times*, October 18, 1834; cited *The Political Mirror, or Review of Jacksonism* (New York, 1835), p. 46.

24. Jackson's temper may be gauged by the letter he wrote to the Secretary of War just before leaving Nashville: 'I have the pleasure to inform you that I am now at the head of 2,070 volunteers, the choicest of our citizens, who go at the call of their country to execute the will of the government, *who have no constitutional scruples;* and if the government orders, will rejoice at the opportunity of placing the American eagle on the ramparts of MOBILE, PENSACOLA, AND FORT ST. AUGUSTINE, effectually banishing from the southern coasts all British influence.' Parton, *Life*, I, 372 (my emphasis).

25. James Wilkinson to Jackson, January 22, February 22, 1813, Bassett, *Correspondence*, I, 273, 281–2.

26. John Armstrong to Jackson, February 5, 1813, Bassett, *Correspondence*, I, 275–6.

27. Bassett, *Correspondence*, I, xiv–xv.

28. See Jackson's blistering reply to Armstrong, Bassett, *Correspondence*, I, 291–2.

29. Jackson to Willie Blount, March 15, 1813, Bassett, *Correspondence*, I, 295. This letter also expresses the fear that his men 'would have been a fine harvest for petty recruiting officers to have taken advantage of their necessities, which would constrain them to enlist in order [to] get the means of subsistence.' Wilkinson had hinted at such a

course (Bassett, *Correspondence*, I, 291) and Jackson was suspicious of Wilkinson even before leaving on his expedition (Bassett, *Correspondence*, I, 244–5).

30. Bassett, *Correspondence*, I, 303n.

31. Both Parton (*Life*, I, 382) and Marquis James (*Andrew Jackson, The Border Captain* [New York, 1940], p. 159) regard the 'Old' as an affectionate augmentative, but it also has patriarchal overtones with the connotation of the father and, hence, ruler. Jackson was only 45 at this time but he tended to see himself as a father to the men under him on this campaign (see Jackson's letter to Mrs. Jackson, Bassett, *Correspondence*, I, 296).

32. Philo A. Goodwin, *Biography of Andrew Jackson, President of the United States* (New York, 1834), p. 40.

33. Waldo, *Memoirs*, p. 58.

34. Garland, 'Eulogy,' Dusenbery, comp., *Monument*, p. 189.

35. Cartwright, 'Eulogy,' Dusenbery, comp., *Monument*, pp. 293–4.

36. William Irvin, 'Eulogy Delivered at Lancaster, Ohio, July 12, 1845,' Dusenbery, comp., *Monument*, p. 310.

37. Goodwin, *Biography*, p. 40. For other accounts to the same point: *National Intelligencer*, December 29, 1818; *Richmond Enquirer*, January 14, 1819; Reid and Eaton, *Life*, pp. 18–24; Matthew Hall McAllister, 'Eulogy Delivered at Savannah, July 8, 1845,' Dusenbery, comp., *Monument*, pp. 124–5; Lewis, 'Eulogy,' Dusenbery, comp., *Monument*, pp. 158–9.

38. John M. Lea, Biographical Sketch of John Overton, in the Overton Papers (microfilm), Joint University Library, Nashville, Tenn.

39. Jackson to Monroe, November 29, 1818, Jackson Papers, second series, Library of Congress.

40. John Spencer Bassett, *The Life of Andrew Jackson*, 2 vols. (Garden City, N. Y., 1911), I, 233–93.

41. The much discussed question whether Jackson had President Monroe's tacit approval to invade Florida and to take Spanish possessions need not concern us here. The controversy, which pivots on the famous 'Rhea letter,' had no bearing on the discussion by Congress in 1819 of Jackson's course in Florida. See Richard R. Stenberg, 'Jackson's "Rhea Letter" Hoax,' *Journal of Southern History*, II (November 1936), 480–96.

42. *Niles' Weekly Register*, XVI (March 6, 1819), 25. This editorial was reprinted in *Liberty Hall and Cincinnati Gazette*, March 23, 1819, and *Knoxville Register*, April 13, 1819.

43. *The Indiana Gazette*, February 27, 1819, reprinted an editorial from the *Pittsburgh Gazette* to this point on the same day that it recorded the favorable vote of the House for Jackson.

44. The editorial of the *Boston Patriot* was reprinted in *The Indiana Gazette*, March 27, 1819. See also the *Argus of Western America*, April 2, 1819.

45. *The Nashville Whig and Tennessee Advertiser*, May 30, 1818.

46. *The Nashville Whig and Tennessee Advertiser*, July 18, 1818.

47. *Richmond Enquirer*, July 28, 1818.

48. *National Intelligencer*, January 23, 1819.

49. See especially the number of January 7, 1819, which relies heavily upon interpretations of Vattel.

50. January 26, 1819.

51. *Liberty Hall and Cincinnati Gazette*, July 9, 1819.

52. Samuel Swartout to Andrew Jackson, April 26, 1819, in the Jackson Papers, second series, Library of Congress. For the approbation of the people see the accounts in the local papers of the receptions accorded Jackson in Baltimore, Philadelphia, and New York on his tour of the east in February 1819. *Niles' Weekly Register*, XVI (March 6, 1819) devoted seven pages, 28–33 inclusive, to extracts concerning Jackson's eastern tour; it commented, 'Whenever the general went into the streets, it was difficult to find a passage through them, so great was the desire of the people to see him.' (p. 29.) The editor of the *Boston Patriot* wrote that 'this plan of censuring Gen. Jackson is altogether distinct from public sentiment. There was no feeling of disapprobation on the part of the people.' (*The Indiana Gazette*, March 27, 1819.) The *National Intelligencer*, February 2, 1819, carried a letter from 'a highly respectable gentleman in Albany, N. Y.,' which commented that 'the popular feeling is almost wholly on the side of the General. He is clearly the Ajax of the day.'

53. Wise, *Seven Decades*, pp. 151–2.

54. Edwin Mims, Jr., 'The Will of the People: Studies in the Background of the "Constitutional Democracy" of the Jacksonian Period,' Unpublished dissertation (Harvard, 1938), *passim*.

55. Henry Adams, *The Education of Henry Adams, An Autobiography* (London, n.d.), p. 28.

56. *Address of the Great State Convention of Friends of the Administration, assembled at the Capitol in Concord, June 12, 1828, With the Speech of Mr. Bartlett* (Concord, 1828), p. 12.

57. *The Middlesex Journal* had reprinted such a letter from the *Washington Journal* and then apologized for being taken in and denounced such tactics, *New-Hampshire Patriot and State Gazette,* April 21, 1828.

58. Anon., *An Impartial and True History of the Life and Services of Major General Andrew Jackson* (n.p., n.d. [1828?]), p. 40.

59. Eugene H. Roseboom and Francis Phelps Weisenburger, *A History of Ohio* (New York, 1934), p. 206.

60. *Address of the Republican General Committee of Young Men of the City and County of New York,* p. 41. Adams's poetry dogged his whole campaign. John Henry Eaton asked 'Will it be pretended that the President of this Union should be considered wanting in qualifications, because of his inability . . . in sybil strains to turn trifles into things of seeming consequence?' *Letters of Wyoming,* p. 9.

61. *Jackson Republican,* November 1, 1828.

62. *Ohio State Journal,* November 29, 1827.

63. *Address of the Committee Appointed by a Republican Meeting in the County of Hunterdon, Recommending Gen. Andrew Jackson, of Tennessee, to the People of New Jersey, as President of the United States* (Trenton, 1824), p. 13.

64. *The* [Frankfort, Ky.] *Argus, Extra,* February 13, 1828.

65. Levi Woodbury, 'Eulogy Delivered at Portsmouth, New Hampshire, July 2, 1845,' Dusenbery, comp., *Monument,* p. 81 (my emphasis).

66. Stevenson, 'Eulogy,' Dusenbery, comp., *Monument,* p. 253.

67. [Eaton], *Letters of Wyoming,* pp. 47–8.

68. Compare the attitude of the schoolbooks of the time. The McGuffey readers, decidedly anti-Jacksonian in other respects, spoke of the interior in the same accents as John Henry Eaton: 'Our literature [went one reader] cannot fail to be patriotic, and its patriotism will be American; composed of a love of country, mingled with an admiration for our political institutions. . . The literature of the whole union must be richly endowed with this spirit; but a double portion will be the lot of the interior, because the foreign influences,

which dilute and vitiate this virtue, cannot reach the heart of the continent where all that lives and moves is American.' (*McGuffey's Newly Revised Eclectic Fourth Reader* [Cincinnati, 1853], p. 313, cited Richard D. Mosier, *Making the American Mind: Social and Moral Ideas in the McGuffey Readers* [New York, 1947], p. 34.)

69. *The Western Sun and General Advertiser,* September 20, 1828. This, of course, falls into the category of 'hard primitivism,' which I discussed before, p. 25. Compare Bancroft's statement: 'And there he stood, like one of the mightiest forest trees of his own West, vigorous and colossal, sending its summit to the skies, and growing on its native soil in wild and inimitable magnificence.' ('Eulogy,' Dusenbery, comp., *Monument,* p. 41.)

70. *Address of the Republican General Committee of the Young Men of the City and County of New York,* pp. 14–15.

71. Dangerfield, *Era of Good Feelings,* p. 385. Dangerfield gives a good account of the spartan regimen of John Quincy Adams during his stay in the White House.

72. *Washington Gazette,* September 7, 1824.

73. *Western Sun and General Advertiser,* April 17, 1824.

74. Frost, *Pictorial Life,* pp. 148–9; Garland, 'Eulogy,' Dusenbery, comp., *Monument,* pp. 192–3; Dallas, 'Eulogy,' Dusenbery, comp., *Monument,* p. 56; Lewis, 'Eulogy,' Dusenbery, comp., *Monument,* p. 160; Parton, *Life,* I, 446–7, where the story is referred to as an 'oft-told anecdote.' Thomas Low Nichols (*Forty Years,* p. 307) blended this anecdote with the origin of the nickname 'Old Hickory' by having Jackson eat hickory nuts.

75. *National Republican,* May 15, 1827.

76. Also involved was the assumption that the simple task of republican government did not require special training.

77. Richard Mather, 'Preface to the Bay Psalm Book,' in Perry Miller and Thomas H. Johnson, *The Puritans* (New York, 1938), p. 671.

78. Above, p. 70. Compare also a toast given at a banquet in commemoration of the Battle of New Orleans in Concord, N. H.: 'Gen. Andrew Jackson. The hero who fought and bled in the defence of our liberties, needs not the polish of European courts to recommend him to the heart and suffrages of a free and grateful people.' (*New-Hampshire Patriot and State Gazette,* January 14, 1828.) See also the *Argus of Western America,* February 6, 1828.

79. George Bancroft, 'Progress of Civilization,' *Boston Quarterly Review*, I (October 1838), 391.

80. [James Hall], 'On Western Character,' *The Western Monthly Magazine*, I (February 1833), 51, 55.

81. Benjamin Chew Howard, 'Funeral Address,' *The Daily Union*, July 2, 1845. Compare the similar sentiment of Henry D. Gilpin (*A Speech*, p. 8): 'From the forests of the West, so late a wilderness, are returning, even to ourselves the wisest political lessons.'

82. Bancroft, 'Eulogy,' Dusenbery, comp., *Monument*, p. 42. Bancroft made the relation between physical nature and human mind even more explicit in treating Jackson's childhood: 'On [the] remote frontier, far up on the forest-clad banks of the Catawba . . . his eye first saw the light. There his infancy sported in the ancient forests and *his mind was nursed to freedom by their influence.*' (p. 33 [my emphasis].)

83. Bancroft, 'On the Progress of Civilization,' pp. 390–91. In the last paragraph of this quotation Bancroft is consciously invoking for the Transcendental audience of Orestes Brownson's journal the distinction between Reason and Understanding in order to demonstrate the political implications inherent in Transcendentalism.

84. Bancroft, 'On the Progress of Civilization,' p. 400 (my emphasis).

85. *The Daily Union*, July 2, 1845. The editor of the *Union* was moved to comment on Howard's address that 'his picture of western energy, and its comparative freedom from the shackles of the more ancient institutions and prejudices of the other states, is particularly fresh and striking.'

86. Garland, 'Eulogy,' Dusenbery, comp., *Monument*, p. 206.

87. Butler, 'Eulogy,' Dusenbery, comp., *Monument*, p. 63.

V   THE WHIGS TAKE TO THE WOODS

1. *Downing Gazette*, February 28, 1835, quoted in Mary Alice Wyman, *Two American Pioneers: Seba Smith and Elizabeth Oakes Smith* (New York, 1927), p. 49.

2. Wyman characterizes the Crockett letters as stiff and formal and suggests that they are not Davy's. Constance Rourke (*Davy Crockett* [New York, 1934]) does not mention them.

3. Charles T. Congdon, *Reminiscences of a Journalist* (Boston, 1880), p. 60.

4. Wyman (*Two American Pioneers*, pp. 32–4) has a good discussion of the forerunners of Jack Downing. Wyman places primary emphasis on Seba Smith's ingenuity and power of re-creating New England life and manners to account for his success, although she does recognize that Jack Downing reflects the unconscious self-satisfaction of a democratic society in full swing (pp. 34–5).

5. Jennette Tandy, *Crackerbox Philosophers in American Humor and Satire* (New York, 1925), pp. 24–42.

6. Tandy, *Crackerbox Philosophers*, p. ix.

7. Wyman, *Two American Pioneers*, p. 4.

8. Wyman, *Two American Pioneers*, p. 70.

9. Wyman, *Two American Pioneers*, p. 69.

10. Andrew McFarland Davis, 'A Tempest in a Teapot: Jackson's LL.D.,' *Massachusetts Historical Society Proceedings*, 2d series, xx (December 1906), 490–93.

11. Josiah Quincy, *Figures of the Past From the Leaves of Old Journals* (Boston, 1883), p. 361.

12. *Memoirs of John Quincy Adams, Comprising Portions of His Diary from 1798 to 1848*, ed. Charles Francis Adams, 12 vols. (Philadelphia, 1876), VIII, 546.

13. Quincy, *Figures of the Past*, p. 354. Jackson's momentary popularity in New England was decidedly at variance with the normal attitude of that region toward him. Quincy remembers that 'the name of Andrew Jackson was, indeed, one to frighten naughty children with.' (p. 363.)

14. [Seba Smith], *The Life and Writings of Major Jack Downing, of Downingville, Away Down East in the State of Maine. Written By Himself* (Boston, 1834), pp. 175–7. Uncle Joshua was right. See Samuel Eliot Morison, ed., *The Life and Letters of Harrison Gray Otis, Federalist, 1765–1848*, 2 vols. (Boston, 1913), II, 291–3. Van Buren ('Autobiography,' p. 549) relates how narrowly the supporters of Jackson were able to postpone a resolution by the opposition calling for an expression of Jackson's views of the origins of the national government.

15. [Smith], *Life and Writings of Major Jack Downing*, pp. 211–15.

16. The letter which resulted, describing the preparation and the final disappointment over Jackson's expected visit, is perhaps the

finest letter in either collection. [Smith], *Life and Writings of Major Jack Downing*, pp. 206–10.

17. [Charles Augustus Davis], *Letters of J. Downing, Major, Downingville Militia, Second Brigade, to His Old Friend, Mr. Dwight, of the New-York Daily Advertiser* (New York, 1834), p. 26.

18. Wyman (*Two American Pioneers*, p. 69) refers to such a letter by a third hand without citing its source.

19. Quincy, *Figures of the Past*, p. 365.

20. Edmund Quincy, *Life of Josiah Quincy of Massachusetts* (Boston, 1868), p. 454 (my emphasis).

21. Quincy, *Figures of the Past*, p. 364.

22. John P. Dix, 'Andrew Jackson, Representative of American Frontier Democracy,' *Social Studies*, xxxix (April 1948), 163.

23. Quincy, *Figures of the Past*, p. 365.

24. Jackson himself took delight in the Downing letters and when in Boston had Josiah Quincy read them to him from the papers. Jackson seems to have thought that Downing may have been Martin Van Buren in disguise. (Quincy, *Figures of the Past*, p. 359.) Mr. Stanley Horn, Sr., of Nashville, Tennessee, very kindly showed me various newspaper clippings which he purchased from the Jackson estate; presumably they are Jackson's own collection. Two Downing letters are included, both, judging from the tone, the work of C. A. Davis or someone following Davis closely. The clippings which carry these letters have no markings to indicate their source.

25. Elkanah Hogg [pseud.], *The Lay of the First Minstrel, or The Court of King Andrew the First* (New York, 1834), pp. 10–11.

26. *Salem Register*, July 10, 1833, cited Davis, 'Tempest in a Teapot,' p. 503. By this date the Charles Augustus Davis letter concerning Jackson's use of Latin had already appeared in the *Boston Daily Advertiser* (July 4, 1833).

27. [Seba Smith], *Jack Downing's Letters by Major Jack Downing* (Philadelphia, 1834), p. 26.

28. Davis, 'A Tempest in a Teapot,' p. 503.

29. Charles H. Haswell, *Reminiscences of New York By an Octogenarian (1816 to 1860)* (New York, 1896), p. 310.

30. James Parton, *Caricature and Other Comic Art in All Times and Many Lands* (New York, 1877), facing p. 323. The Tennessee State Library has a similar mock paper note.

31. The collection in the Library of Congress has a lithograph cartoon by Anthony Imbert, New York, *c.* 1832, dealing with the bank question in which Jackson is pictured as a braying jackass kicking to death little chicks which represent the branch banks of the United States Bank. Van Buren is pictured as a sly fox creeping up on the mother hen, 'U. S. Bank,' while the 'collar press,' as dogs in the background, bay their praise of the whole procedure. Jack Downing, as a rooster, crows on the fence and the caption is 'Let Every One Take Care of Himself (As the Jack Ass said when he was dancing among the Chickens).' The famous New York lithographer, H. R. Robinson, who did most of the anti-Jackson cartoons in the collection of the Library of Congress, did a drawing now in the Tennessee State Library which shows Jackson dying in the form of a jackass with a Catholic priest in his robes saying the last rites over him in a thick Irish brogue. The caption of this cartoon, which is probably trying to use anti-Catholic sentiment against Jackson, is 'Old Jack in the Last Agony.'

Thurlow Weed's stunt has a complicated background. Weed meant to confuse the voters as well as to ridicule the Democrats. He had been accused of exploiting anti-Masonic sentiment by finding a corpse and claiming it was William Morgan whose abduction had set off the anti-Masonic craze. Others claimed the body to be that of one Timothy Munroe and that Weed had caused Munroe, a bearded man, to be shaved in order to provide a suitable corpse for the forthcoming election. Weed is supposed to have said that the corpse was a 'good enough Morgan' until after the election. The opposition, which was largely Democratic, immediately set out to capitalize on its version by snipping at Weed and his followers with shears, all the while crying 'Good Enough Morgan' at them. Weed, in order to confuse the issue, shrewdly adopted the gesture and turned it on his opponents. The important point here is, of course, that Weed was sure his identification of the Democrats with the jackass would be immediately understood. Thurlow Weed, *Autobiography of Thurlow Weed,* ed. Harriet A. Weed (Boston, 1883), pp. 313–19.

32. Jay Monaghan, 'The Origin of Political Symbols,' *Journal of the Illinois State Historical Society,* xxxvii (September 1944), 205–12.

33. Walter Blair, 'Six Davy Crocketts,' *Southwest Review,* xxv (July 1940), 443–4.

34. Blair, 'Six Davy Crocketts,' p. 447.

35. Blair, 'Six Davy Crocketts,' p. 449.

36. See, for example, Henry Clay to Seba Smith, August 9, 1834, Wyman, *Two American Pioneers*, p. 48.

37. Anon., 'Review of *A Narrative of the Life of David Crockett* (Philadelphia, 1834),' *The Western Monthly Magazine*, XVII (May 1834), 277–8.

38. See [Davis], *The Letters of J. Downing, Major*, pp. 4–5.

39. Freeman Cleaves, *Old Tippecanoe, William Henry Harrison and His Times* (New York, 1939), p. 312.

40. Weed (*Autobiography*, pp. 480–82) gives a good description of the difficulty in by-passing Clay. See also, Cleaves, *Old Tippecanoe*, p. 318. The rules of the convention can be conveniently consulted in A. B. Norton, *The Great Revolution of 1840. Reminiscences of the Log Cabin and Hard Cider Campaign* (Mount Vernon, Ohio, 1888), pp. 20–22. The title of this book is a misnomer since it is not a 'reminiscence' but rather a collection of official documents, campaign material, and speeches, and for that reason even more valuable.

41. *William H. Seward: An Autobiography From 1801 to 1834. With a Memoir of His Life, and Selections from His Letters, 1831–1846*, William H. and Frederick W. Seward, eds., 3 vols. (New York, 1891), I, 447.

42. Harrison to the Whig Members of the legislature of New York, May 23, 1840, Norton, *The Great Revolution of 1840*, p. 40.

43. Weed, *Autobiography*, pp. 466–7.

44. Norton, *The Great Revolution of 1840*, pp. 33, 35, 309–13.

45. Richard Smith Elliott, *Notes Taken in Sixty Years* (St. Louis, 1833), p. 120; Norton, *The Great Revolution of 1840*, p. 10.

46. Seward, *Autobiography*, I, 448.

47. Weed, *Autobiography*, p. 482.

48. *The Rough-Hewer*, I (March 26, 1840), 45.

49. Congdon, *Reminiscences of a Journalist*, p. 69.

50. Congdon, *Reminiscences of a Journalist*, pp. 69–70; Linda Rhea, *Hugh Swinton Legaré: A Charleston Intellectual* (Chapel Hill, 1934), pp. 191–2.

51. Elliott, *Notes Taken in Sixty Years*, p. 127.

52. *The Log Cabin*, October 17, 1840.

53. Robert Gray Gunderson, 'Webster in Linsey-Wooley,' *Quarterly Journal of Speech*, XXXVII (February 1951), 23.

54. *National Intelligencer,* September 4, 1850; *The Log Cabin,* September 5, 1840. Norton (*The Great Revolution of 1840,* p. 11) reports that when Webster came to the reference to his father his voice became 'inarticulate with emotion.'

55. Resolution of the Ohio State Convention, February 21, 1840 (Norton, *The Great Revolution of 1840,* p. 47).

56. [Cincinnati] *Daily Gazette,* January 3, 1843; *Cincinnati Chronicle,* January 3, 1843; Cleaves, *Old Tippecanoe,* p. 319; Norton, *The Great Revolution of 1840, passim.*

57. Norton, *The Great Revolution of 1840,* p. 50.

58. New York Public Library has a copy of *The Harrison Almanac;* the cover is reproduced in Cleaves, *Old Tippecanoe,* facing p. 321.

59. Lithograph by Henry R. Robinson, New York, *c.* 1840, courtesy of the Library of Congress.

60. Reproduced in Rhea M. Knittle, 'Mementos of a Colorful Campaign,' *Antiques,* xxxviii (November 1940), 217.

61. Reproduced in Knittle, 'Mementos of a Colorful Campaign,' p. 218.

62. Cleaves, *Old Tippecanoe,* p. 326.

63. Van Buren, *Autobiography,* pp. 8, 394.

64. *United States Magazine and Democratic Review,* viii (October 1840), 390.

VI   GOD'S RIGHT-HAND MAN

1. Latour, *Historical Memoir,* pp. 199–200.

2. Latour, *Historical Memoir,* Appendix xxxiii; Bassett, *Correspondence,* ii, 150, has a slightly different version.

3. Bassett, *Correspondence,* ii, 150n.

4. Latour, *Historical Memoir,* Appendix xxxv. The Abbé Dubourg's address and General Jackson's reply were copied from the New Orleans papers by the *National Intelligencer,* March 2, 1815; Dubourg's address alone appeared in *The Enquirer,* March 8, 1815; *The Albany Argus,* March 14, 1815. When Jackson revisited the scene of his triumph on the eve of his election, the Abbé's address was repeated in the reception at New Orleans and again widely reprinted: see the *Louisiana Advertiser,* December 3, 1827; *Richmond Enquirer,* January 8, 1828.

5. Latour, *Historical Memoir,* p. lxxiii.

6. Letter of John Pope of Kentucky, July 8, 1828, *Jackson Republican,* September 13, 1828.

7. *National Intelligencer,* February 14, 1815.

8. February 15, 1815.

9. See, for example, the *Louisiana Gazette,* quoted in the *National Intelligencer,* March 6, 1815; *Boston Yankee,* quoted in the *National Intelligencer,* February 16, 1815; *Boston Daily Advertiser,* February 23, 1815; *New-Hampshire Patriot and State Gazette,* February 14, 1815; *Kentucky Palladium,* January 30, 1815; *Liberty Hall,* February 4, 1815; *National Intelligencer,* February 7, 1815; *Boston Patriot,* February 11, 1815; *Niles' Weekly Register,* VIII (March 4, 1815), 417.

10. For historians, see Ingersoll, *Historical Sketch,* pp. 215–16; [Thomas O'Connor], *An Impartial and Correct History of the War Between the United States of America and Great Britain,* 2nd ed., rev. and corr. (New York, 1815), p. 6; Professor Linebaugh, 'Faith and Fate: The Battle of New Orleans,' *De Bow's Review,* n.s., III (April 1867), 374. For poets, see Anon., *An Epick Poem,* p. 21; W. Ray, 'Jackson's Victory,' *The Albany Argus,* February 28, 1815; Anon., 'The Delivery of New Orleans: A Sacred Song,' *The Nashville Whig,* April 11, 1815; Anon., *The Battle of New Orleans; or, Jackson's Victory, a Poem by a Citizen of Baltimore* (Baltimore, 1825) which according to the introduction was first published in a Baltimore newspaper immediately after the battle.

11. October 3, 1815.

12. General John Adair to Governor Shelby, January 13, 1815, *Kentucky Palladium,* January 30, 1815; also in *Liberty Hall,* February 4, 1815; *Spirit of the West,* February 5, 1815. See also Colonel Robert Hays of the Tennessee Militia, to his father, January 9, 1815, Jackson Papers, Library of Congress. For a similar expression by Jackson's aide, Major Reid, to his father, see *The Enquirer,* February 18, 1815, which reprinted Reid's letter from the *Lynchburg Press, Extra,* February 10, 1815.

13. Latour, *Historical Memoir,* p. clxxxiv.

14. Arda Walker, 'The Religious Views of Andrew Jackson,' *East Tennessee Historical Society's Publications,* No. 17 (1945), p. 61.

15. *National Intelligencer,* January 10, 1824. For other expressions of Jackson's belief in the role played by Providence in the Battle of New Orleans see his letters to Governor Holmes and to Colonel Robert

Hays, Bassett, *Correspondence,* II, 145, 153. For many expressions by Jackson concerning Providence's solicitude in other instances see Walker, 'The Religious Views of Andrew Jackson,' p. 62.

16. *The National Advocate,* February 7, 1815; *The Albany Argus,* February 10, 1815. For a brief discussion of the comparison of Americans to the Israelites, see Albert K. Weinberg, *Manifest Destiny: A Study of Nationalist Expansionism in American History* (Baltimore, 1935), pp. 39–40, which has examples in other contexts including Jefferson's suggestion that the national seal be the representation of the children of Israel led by a pillar of light.

17. February 7, 1815; reprinted in *The Enquirer,* February 11, 1815, and in *The Nashville Whig,* February 28, 1815.

18. November 21, 1815.

19. *National Intelligencer,* February 9, 1819. For another use of the 'wine press' image in establishing Jackson as 'destined by Heaven,' see Stevenson, 'Eulogy,' Dusenbery, comp., *Monument,* p. 261.

20. See, for example, *The Globe,* June 16, 1831, quoting the remark of the *Rochester Republican* that at the time of crisis 'Providence had sent a deliverer'; speech of Joseph Allen as reported in the *New-Hampshire Patriot and State Gazette,* January 21, 1828; Isaac Hill, *Address Delivered at Concord, N. H., Being the Thirteenth Anniversary of Jackson's Victory at New Orleans* (Concord, 1828), p. 4; Robert Alcock to the editors, *New-Hampshire Patriot and State Gazette,* December 17, 1827.

21. Butler, 'Oration,' *Report of the Committee of Arrangements,* p. 273. For other attributions of Jackson's success to God's grace by eulogists at his death, see McCandless, 'Eulogy,' McAllister, 'Eulogy,' Irvin, 'Eulogy,' Dusenbery, comp., *Monument,* pp. 108, 128, 311.

22. James Nelson Barker, 'Prologue,' to Richard Penn Smith's *The Eighth of January, A Drama in Three Acts* (Philadelphia, 1829); see also, Grice, *The Battle of New Orleans,* p. 20.

23. *New-Hampshire Patriot and State Gazette,* January 14, 1828.

24. Charles Francis Adams, ed., *Memoirs of John Quincy Adams, Comprising Portions of His Diaries* (Philadelphia, 1876), VIII, 478–9. For further discussion of George Washington as the agent of Providence, see William A. Bryan, *George Washington in American Literature, 1775–1865* (New York, 1952), pp. 52–5.

25. *Western Monitor,* August 18, 1830. For a fuller discussion of the

impact upon the American imagination of the simultaneous deaths of Adams and Jefferson, see Merrill D. Peterson, 'The Jefferson Image, 1829,' *American Quarterly*, III (Fall 1951), 205–6.

26. [Eaton], *Letters of Wyoming*, p. 93.

27. Frost, *Pictorial Life*, p. 67.

28. McCandless, 'Eulogy,' Dusenbery, comp., *Monument*, p. 109.

29. Stephen Douglas, 'Oration on the Installation of Mill's Statue,' *Graham's Magazine*, XLIV (January 1854), 88.

30. Anon., *An Epick Poem*, p. 24.

31. *The Albany Argus*, August 5, 1828.

32. Undated newspaper clipping in the Jackson Papers, New York Public Library.

33. Robert Rantoul, *An Oration Before the Citizens of Gloucester, Massachusetts, on the Fourth of July, 1833* (Gloucester, 1833), p. 51.

34. Butler, 'Eulogy,' Dusenbery, comp., *Monument*, p. 59.

35. Cartwright, 'Eulogy,' Dusenbery, comp., *Monument*, p. 292.

36. Woodbury, 'Eulogy,' Dusenbery, comp., *Monument*, p. 85.

37. Andrew Jackson, as we have seen, was as ready as any of his contemporaries to see the intervention of Providence in the astounding success he had at New Orleans. Although he could refer to himself as the 'humble instrument of a superintending Providence,' the attitude was not nearly so humble as it might at first appear: a strong self-trust underlies the ostensible humility of the claim to be but the chosen agent of God. The pastor of the Presbyterian Church at Nashville, who finally baptized Jackson, told James Parton that Jackson joined the church as the result of a sermon which stressed the impossibility of chance. The minister, a Dr. Edgar, delivered a sermon on the interposition of Providence in the affairs of men, 'a subject congenial with the habitual tone of General Jackson's mind.' (Parton, *Life*, III, 644.) The sermon so impressed Jackson that during that very night he decided to join the church. As a contemporary later remembered Jackson, 'he was a believer in predestination, and trusted and believed in special Providence, *considering the Battle of New Orleans as an evidence of Divine favor vouchsafed him.*' (H. S. Turner, 'Andrew Jackson and Davy Crockett,' *Magazine of American History*, XXVII [May 1892], 386–7 [my emphasis].) George Bancroft accounted for Jackson's calm determination by the fact that he never lost faith in his eventual success. His attitude, says Bancroft, always was that 'Provi-

dence will take care of me.' (Bancroft, 'Eulogy,' Dusenbery, comp., *Monument*, p. 44.) Martin Van Buren remembered that 'the remarkable success which crowned [Jackson's] efforts in [the service of the people] had inspired him with a firm belief that to labour for the good of the masses was a special mission assigned him by his creator.' (Van Buren, 'Autobiography,' p. 255.) In view of this testimony from his closest friends, one is inclined to accept the witness of Josiah Quincy, to whom Jackson is supposed to have blurted, 'Heaven would not suffer [my] opinions to be other than *right*.' (Quincy, *Figures of the Past*, p. 355.) The dangerous quality implicit in such a view of one's self is even more obvious in the editorial comment of *The Globe* after Jackson's successful fight against the bank: 'What would now have been your condition [the editor asked the people], had not Presidential power been interposed *to save you from the effects of your own votes;* had it not been for that man whom Providence seems to have preserved for the perpetuation of the liberties of our common country?' (August 31, 1833 [my emphasis].)

38. *Washington Telegraph*, February 2, 1835; *Niles' Weekly Register*, XLVII (February 14, 1835), 420.

39. Marquis James, *Portrait of a President* (New York, 1940), p. 391.

40. *Baltimore Patriot*, in *Niles' Weekly Register*, XLVII (February 7, 1835), 392.

41. Harriet Martineau, *Society in America*, 2 vols. (New York, 1837), I, 60.

42. *United States' Telegraph*, January 31, 1835.

43. William T. Ritchie to Thomas Ritchie, February 2, 1835, Thomas Ritchie Papers, Library of Congress. See also William T. Ritchie to Thomas Ritchie, January 30, 1835, Ritchie Papers.

44. *The Globe*, January 31. 1835. For expressions to the same point and in almost identical language, see the *Baltimore Patriot*, in *Niles' Weekly Register*, XLVII (February 7, 1835), 392; Frost, *Pictorial Life*, pp. 529–530. Blair not only editorialized that Jackson was under the special care of Providence, he had a fondness for stories with Biblical and Providential overtones. See, for example, the two stories he told Parton (*Life*, III, 493, 553–4).

45. Bassett, *Correspondence*, VI, 391–2.

46. Poore, *Perley's Reminiscences*, p. 331.

47. [Russell Jarvis], *A Biographical Notice of Com. Jesse D. Elliott;*

Containing a Review of the Controversy Between Him and the Late Commodore Perry; and A History of the Figure-Head of the U.S. Frigate Constitution. By a Citizen of New York (Philadelphia, 1835), p. 313.

48. [Jarvis], *A Biographical Notice*, pp. 318–19.

49. [Jarvis], *A Biographical Notice*, p. 322.

50. [Jarvis], *A Biographical Notice*, p. 326.

51. See the report of Elliott to the Secretary of the Navy, July 3, 1834, in [Jarvis], *A Biographical Notice*, pp. 334–5.

52. *Niles' Weekly Register*, XLVI (July 12, 1834), 329.

53. [Jarvis], *A Biographical Notice*, pp. 359–60.

54. *The Diary of Philip Hone, 1828–1851*, ed. Allan Nevins, rev. ed. (New York, 1936), pp. 130–31. For another use of the same pun, see Hogg [pseud.], *The Lay of the First Minstrel*, p. 42.

55. [Jarvis], *A Biographical Notice*, pp. 335–6.

56. Haswell, *Reminiscences of an Octogenarian*, pp. 302–3.

57. Poore, *Perley's Reminiscences*, pp. 186–9.

58. Frederick A. Carfield ('The Figurehead of Jackson,' *Proceedings of the New Jersey Historical Society*, n.s., VII [July 1922], 222–3) quotes the passage from Dickerson's diary.

59. There is a crude reproduction in Poore, *Perley's Reminiscences*, p. 189.

60. The original is in the Prints and Photographs Section of the Library of Congress; it is unfortunately not attributed. My guess that it appeared in New York is based on the fact that Henry R. Robinson, who was doing most of the political cartoons of that time, was in New York and about the same time the *New-York Daily Advertiser* carried an editorial with the sentence that 'the frigate, however, with whatever block she may have for a head, go where she may, will have the best wishes of every American.' (*Niles' Weekly Register*, XLVIII [March 21, 1835], 42.) The repetition of the phrase, blockhead, Robinson's whereabouts, the fact that the frigate went to New York City from Boston, all seem strong circumstantial evidence in this instance. For an appraisal of Henry R. Robinson's work in lithography, see Harry T. Peters, *America on Stone: The Other Printmakers to the American People. A Chronicle of American Lithography Other than that of Currier and Ives, from its Beginning, Shortly before 1820, to the Years When the Commercial Single-Stone Hand-Colored Lithograph*

Disappeared from the American Scene (New York, 1931), pp. 13, 337–42, which contains high praise indeed for Robinson as an early practitioner of lithography in this country.

61. The pictorial statement of this cartoon is somewhat muddled. The epigrammatic reference to Jackson as a 'great Blockhead' leaves little doubt of the hostile intention of the cartoon; the sentinel guarding our independence carries out this intention by suggesting that the decapitation of Jackson is a stroke in behalf of liberty. These two items, taken by themselves, bear out the interpretation that the bolt of lightning is an act of God, since presumably God acts for good. But the visual presentation of the moral is somewhat confused by the presence of what are obviously two imps of satan with saw and axe in hand; if without the implements of cutting, they could be interpreted as Jackson's aides, thus strengthening the moral, but as given they confuse the agency which accomplished the deed. In either case, the cartoon gives covert expression to the belief in supernatural intervention in human affairs. I cannot comprehend the reference to the 'claret-coloured coat' which might solve the meaning of the satanic figures. Dorothy Waples (*The Whig Myth of James Fenimore Cooper* [New Haven, 1938], p. 95) identifies a contemporary pamphleteer, Edward Sherman Gould, as the man in the claret-colored coat but does not explain the significance of the reference. There was also published anonymously a novel, *The Sleep Rider; or, The Old Boy in the Omnibus. By the Man in the Claret-Colored Coat* (New York, [1843]), which, in the copy in the Rare Book Collection of the University of Pennsylvania Library, is attributed to Gould. Here again, however, the significance of the phrase is not revealed.

62. Ira N. Hollis, the accepted historian of the ship, confuses the two figureheads and describes the second figurehead as the mutilated one (*The Frigate Constitution, The Central Figure of the Navy Under Sail* [Boston, 1931], p. 222). The second figurehead still survives and is in a niche in Bancroft Hall at the United States Naval Academy, Annapolis, Maryland. I have been informed by the Office of Naval Records and History, Department of the Navy, Washington, D. C., that the original figurehead was restored but its whereabouts at present is unknown.

63. For further discussion of Napoleonic imagery in connection with Jackson, see below, pp. 182–5.

64. March 7, 1815.

65. Waldo, *Memoirs of Andrew Jackson*, p. 236.

66. Clark, 'The Influence of Science on American Ideas,' pp. 305–49; Walker, 'The Religious Views of Andrew Jackson,' p. 62.

67. Paul G. Brewster, 'The Battle of New Orleans (An Example of Communal Composition),' *Southern Folklore Quarterly*, I (September 1937), 25.

68. February 25, 1815.

69. Andrew White, *A History of the Warfare of Science with Theology in Christendom* (New York, 1910), p. 109.

70. *National Intelligencer*, July 21, 1819.

71. Garland, 'Eulogy,' Dusenbery, comp., *Monument*, pp. 197, 198.

72. Kendall, *Autobiography*, pp. 637, 634.

73. Woodbury, 'Eulogy,' Dusenbery, comp., *Monument*, pp. 78–9.

74. Stevenson, 'Eulogy,' Dusenbery, comp., *Monument*, p. 261.

75. [Williams], *Sketches of the War*, p. 481.

76. Anon., *An Epick Poem*, pp. 13, 21.

77. *The Harbinger*, I (June 28, 1845), 45.

78. *Missouri Intelligencer*, July 25, 1828. The reference to Clay concerns a toast he gave at Baltimore expressing a preference that war, pestilence, and famine should visit the country before Jackson should be elected President.

79. *New-Hampshire Patriot and State Gazette*, December 17, 1827.

80. Parton, *Life*, III, 162.

81. *National Intelligencer*, reprinted in *New-Hampshire Patriot and State Gazette*, February 4, 1828.

82. Emerson, *Journals*, VI, 350–52. Emerson's opinion of Jackson in 1829 is in Rusk, ed., *The Letters*, I, 274. For other expressions of Emerson's distaste for Andrew Jackson, see Ralph L. Rusk, *The Life of Ralph Waldo Emerson* (New York, 1949), p. 153. There is a brief sketch of Major Auguste Davezac's career accompanied by an engraved portrait in *The United States Magazine and Democratic Review*, XVI (February 1845), 109–11. To the writer of this sketch, Davezac said that at New Orleans Jackson 'became my destiny! I instinctively foresaw his greatness and glory. My attachment to him was a religion of the heart.' (p. 110.)

VII EXTENDING THE AREA OF FREEDOM

1. *The Illinois Gazette,* March 19, 1825 (my emphasis). The writer of this editorial was probably Henry Eddy, a prominent early Illinois journalist; see Franklin W. Scott, *Newspapers and Periodicals of Illinois, 1814–1879* (Springfield, Illinois, 1910).

2. Julius W. Pratt, 'The Origin of "Manifest Destiny," ' *American Historical Review,* XXXII (July 1927), 795–8. For a fuller account of O'Sullivan's career, see the same author's 'John L. O'Sullivan and Manifest Destiny,' *New York History,* XIV (July 1933), 213–34. In a letter to me Mr. Pratt says that subsequent to these articles he has not discovered any earlier conjunction of the two words, manifest and destiny.

3. Compare Pratt's conclusion: 'It was into an America seething with such ideas as these, but lacking a convenient phrase to sum them up, that O'Sullivan introduced the *Democratic Review.* . . His "manifest destiny" was a perfect expression of current enthusiastic belief in American democracy and in the mission of the United States to carry it throughout the North American continent.' ('John L. O'Sullivan and Manifest Destiny,' p. 221.) Weinberg (*Manifest Destiny, passim*) has abundantly demonstrated this point.

4. 'Annexation,' *The United States Magazine and Democratic Review,* XVII (July and August 1845), 5.

5. *New-York Morning News,* December 27, 1845, in Pratt, 'The Origin of "Manifest Destiny," ' p. 796.

6. Jackson to Aaron V. Brown, February 12, 1843, in Parton, *Life,* III, 658. Compare this version with Bassett's (*Correspondence,* VI, 201). Bassett observes that the changes may be the work of Francis P. Blair, the editor of *The Globe.* In the Library of Congress' fair copy of the original letter, Jackson's phrase is 'extending the area for freedom.'

7. Weinberg, *Manifest Destiny,* pp. 100–107.

8. Paul M. Spurlin, *Montesquieu in America, 1760–1801* (University, La., 1940), p. 261.

9. Edwin Forrest, *Fourth of July Oration at New York City* (New York, 1838), p. 7.

10. Miller and Johnson, *The Puritans,* p. 199.

11. William Plumer, *An Address Delivered at Portsmouth, N. H.,* *on the Fourth of July, 1828* (Portsmouth, 1828), p. 23.

12. Compare Caleb Cushing in 1839, speaking of America after the Revolution as 'like a monumental column on a hill-top, a spectacle and a beacon to the nations alike of the old World and the New.' (*An Oration on the Material Growth and Territorial Progress of the United States, Delivered at Springfield, Mass. on the Fourth of July, 1839* [Springfield, 1839], p. 6); John Quincy Adams in 1821: 'It [the United States] stands, and must forever stand alone, a beacon on the summit of the mountain, to which all the inhabitants of the earth may turn their eyes for a genial and saving light.' (*An Address, Delivered at the Request of the Committee of Arrangements for Celebrating the Anniversary of Independence, at the City of Washington, on the Fourth of July, 1821, upon the Occasion of Reading the Declaration of Independence* [Cambridge, Mass., 1821], p. 23.) For other instances see: Glenville Mellen, *Address Delivered Before the Citizens of North Yarmouth, on the Anniversary of American Independence, July 4, 1825* (Portland, Maine, 1825), p. 4; Gilpin, *A Speech*, pp. 6–7; Ware, *An Oration*, p. 5; *National Intelligencer*, May 1, 1819; *Nashville Whig*, April 10, 1819; Weinberg, *Manifest Destiny, passim*.

13. [Thomas Hart Benton], *Abridgement of the Debates of Congress*, 16 vols. (New York, 1857–61), XIV, 88–9.

14. William Powell Mason, *An Oration Delivered Wednesday, July 4, 1827, in Commemoration of American Independence Before the Supreme Executive of the Commonwealth and the City Council and the Inhabitants of the City of Boston* (Boston, 1827), pp. 17–18.

15. Jefferson to Joseph Priestley, June 9, 1802, *Writings*, ed. Ford, IX, 380–81; see also Jefferson to Dickenson, March 6, 1801, *Writings*, ed. Ford, IX, 202. James Tallmadge, Sr., to James Tallmadge, Jr., January 7, 1819, Dangerfield, *Era of Good Feelings*, p. 116.

16. *National Intelligencer*, July 4, 1823.

17. Mellen, *Address*, p. 4.

18. Reprinted in *The Globe*, June 14, 1831.

19. Weinberg, *Manifest Destiny*, p. 127.

20. Richard Bland Lee, 'Fourth of July Oration,' *National Intelligencer*, July 14, 1819.

21. Gilpin, *A Speech*, pp. 6–7.

22. 'The Great Nation of Futurity,' *United States Magazine and Democratic Review*, VI (November 1839), 428–9.

23. Adams, *An Address*, pp. 31–2.

24. Dexter Perkins, *The Monroe Doctrine, 1823–1826* (Cambridge, Mass., 1927), pp. 76–7.

25. J. G. Harris, 'Eulogy Delivered at Charlotte, Tenn., July 17, 1845,' Dusenbery, comp., *Monument,* pp. 326–7.

26. See note 6, above.

27. *The Hickory Tree,* June 27, 1844.

28. Richard R. Stenberg, 'Jackson, Anthony Butler, and Texas,' *The Southwestern Social Science Quarterly,* XIII (December 1932), 264–86. I am not willing to accept this article completely. Stenberg, the author of many violently anti-Jackson articles, seizes too readily every shred of evidence, even from obviously partisan sources. However, there can be no doubt that Jackson was cognizant of Butler's shady tactics in Mexico and willingly blinked them until Butler became so outrageous that he had to be jettisoned. The best that can be said for Jackson was that he was willing to pay Mexico the sum of five million dollars for Texas, knowing full well that most of the purchase price would go no further than the pockets of Mexican officials. His ground was that it was none of his concern how the money was disbursed once it was paid to the Mexican government; but he also knew that Butler had made the overtures that had aroused Mexican greed. The contempt Jackson felt for the Mexicans throughout the whole affair is another measure of the danger implicit in the belief in one's self as a member of a divinely favored group.

29. Richard R. Stenberg, 'The Texas Schemes of Jackson and Houston 1829–1836,' *The Southwestern Social Science Quarterly,* XV (December 1934), 229–50. Although Jackson recorded that he thought Houston was 'distempered,' he shortly afterward attempted to secure without competitive bidding a fat contract for supplying Indian rations for Houston and at a price which would have resulted in a profit of over a million dollars. Stenberg plausibly suggests this would have put Houston's random filibustering schemes on a more solid footing.

30. *Young Hickory Banner,* October 15, 1845, quoted in Weinberg, *Manifest Destiny,* p. 119.

VIII   THE MAN OF IRON

1. Garland, 'Eulogy,' Dusenbery, comp., *Monument*, p. 199.

2. *The Enquirer*, February 11, 1815.

3. *National Intelligencer*, March 18, 1815; *Federal Republican* in *The Enquirer*, March 18, 1815.

4. Latour, *Historical Memoir*, p. xvii.

5. Garland, 'Eulogy,' Dusenbery, comp., *Monument*, p. 198.

6. [Salma Hale], *History of the United States, from their First Settlement as Colonies, to the Close of the War with Great Britain in 1815* (Keene, N. H., 1829), p. 281.

7. The entire quotation is taken from Frost, *Pictorial Life*, p. 345; the emphasized portions are also to be found in Cobbett, *Life of Jackson*, p. 107, and in [Smith], *Memoirs of Andrew Jackson*, p. 247.

8. Walker, *Jackson and New Orleans*, p. 214. Compare the similar sentiment of 'an enlightened man of high standing' writing from New Orleans before the battle, in *The Enquirer*, January 14, 1815.

9. February 14, 1815. For the same sentiment, see: H. M. Brackenridge, *History of the Late War Between the United States and Great Britain*, 6th ed. (Philadelphia, 1839), p. 292; Claiborne, *Notes on the War in the South*, p. 57; Walker, *Jackson and New Orleans*, p. 149; Mr. Wells, 'Battle of New Orleans,' *The Illinois Gazette*, March 19, 1825; *The Enquirer*, March 1, 1815.

10. Charles Jared Ingersoll, *Historical Sketch of the Second War Between the United States and Great Britain*, 2 vols. (Philadelphia, 1845–9), II, 269.

11. Anon., *An Epick Poem*, p. 5.

12. Walker (*Jackson and New Orleans*, p. 73) is typical of the writers who poised Jackson's will against the enormous odds he faced.

13. Stevenson, 'Eulogy,' Dusenbery, comp., *Monument*, p. 258.

14. Anon., 'The Battle of New Orleans,' *New England Family Magazine*, I (March 1845), 69.

15. The anonymous author was Nathaniel H. Claiborne who included this sketch of Jackson in his *Notes on the War in the South*.

16. Most of the papers copying Claiborne's piece had it from the *National Intelligencer*; in chronological order the *Enquirer* article appeared in the following papers among others: *Boston Daily Advertiser*, February 8, 1815; *The* [New York] *National Advocate*, February

9, 1815; *The Albany Argus,* February 10, 1815; *Boston Patriot,* February 15, 1815; *New-Hampshire Patriot,* February 21, 1815; *The Liberty Hall,* February 25, 1815; *Intellectual Regale, or Ladies' Tea Tray,* 1 (March 4, 1815), 243–5; *Niles' Weekly Register,* VIII (March 1815), 46–7.

17. In the election of 1824, Claiborne's description was reprinted in the *Address of the Committee . . . in the County of Hunterdon,* pp. 17–18; in 1828, in Hill, *An Address,* p. 17; as part of the funeral ceremonies in the city of New York in 1845, in the 'Resolution of the Democratic Republican Young Men's General Committee,' *Report of the Committee,* p. 170.

18. McAllister, 'Eulogy,' Woodbury, 'Eulogy,' Dusenbery, comp., *Monument,* pp. 130, 70–71.

19. Butler, 'Eulogy,' *Report of the Committee,* p. 277. The occasion of the remark was the settlement of the dispute between France and the United States concerning payment of spoliation claims against France.

20. Wise, *Seven Decades,* p. 119. Compare the account of William Allen Butler who as a boy visited Jackson in the White House and remembered when he came to his memoirs that 'the aspect of command and dominating will . . . were [Jackson's] prominent characteristics.' (*A Retrospect of Forty Years,* p. 53.)

21. Smith, 'Eulogy,' Dusenbery, comp., *Monument,* p. 273.

22. In addition to the previous citations, the following accounts which deal with Jackson's will power all employ the word 'iron': *The Daily Union,* June 17, 1845; *The Richmond Enquirer,* June 17, 1845; *The New-York Morning News,* June 18, 1845; *New-York Herald,* June 18, 1845; *New-York Evening Post,* June 20, 1845; Frost, *Pictorial Life,* p. 16; George Ripley, 'Andrew Jackson,' *The Harbinger,* I (June 28, 1845), 45; 'Fragments of Unpublished Reminiscences of Edward Livingston,' *The United States Magazine and Democratic Review,* VIII (October 1840), 369; Reverend Robert Paine, *A Funeral Discourse on the Life and History of Andrew Jackson, Delivered at Courtland, Ala., on the Fourth of July, 1845* (Huntsville, Ala., 1845), p. 13; Hone, *Diary,* II, 732; Morrison, 'Eulogy,' Dallas, 'Eulogy,' Irvin, 'Eulogy,' Woodbury, 'Eulogy,' Bethune, 'Discourse,' Dusenbery, comp., *Monument,* pp. 42, 57, 313, 76, 350.

23. Walker, *Jackson and New Orleans,* p. 13.

24. Quincy, *Figures of the Past*, pp. 360–61, 370–71.

25. The little-known wood sculpture of Jackson's head by Clark Mills, better known for his equestrian statues of Jackson, is in the private collection of Mr. Stanley Horn, Sr., Nashville, Tennessee. Mr. Horn very kindly allowed me to examine it and the many other items of Jacksoniana which he has amassed over the years. Compare also the comment of the editor of *The Nashville Whig and Tennessee Advertiser*, May 9, 1818, on a portrait of Jackson by Ralph Earl: 'There is a characteristic in the forehead of the original which is rarely to be met with—there is a stubbornness, or perhaps more properly speaking, a firmness almost amounting to obstinacy, which the painter has unequivocally struck.'

26. Waldo, *Memoirs*, p. 131. Compare the reasons given for the destruction of the Creek nation by McAfee (*History of the Late War in the Western Country*, p. 528) who assigns an important place to Jackson's 'unrelenting perseverance and irresistible energy.'

27. Walker, *Jackson and New Orleans*, pp. 149–50.

28. See Francis Tomlinson Gardner, 'The Gentleman from Tennessee,' *Surgery, Gynecology and Obstetrics with International Abstracts of Surgery*, LXXXVIII (March 1949), 404–11, for a clinical description of the ills that afflicted Jackson; based on available evidence this article attempts to diagnose Jackson's complaints and concludes that his death was the result of amyloidosis brought on by chronic suppuration. At the end of Jackson's life, his flesh from the waist down had literally to be wrapped to his body to keep it from falling away. Gardner says that 'no structure ever endured under greater handicaps than the frame that supported the brain of the astonishing, the determined, the invincible gentleman from Tennessee.' (p. 405.) This somewhat lyrical statement from a physician implies, as the tradition has it, that Jackson's will (brain) conquered his flesh. Typical of Jackson's ability to surmount physical pain was his action in taking command of the Creek War. At the time he was suffering from wounds received in his famous affray with Thomas Hart Benton. Enoch Parsons, a member of the Tennessee legislature at the time, wrote out his remembrance of the incident for Nicholas Trist. Parsons was at Jackson's bedside when the order was given by the legislature for the Tennessee Volunteers to muster; Parsons expressed his regret that Jackson was not in condition to take the field. 'To which General Jackson replied: "The

devil in hell, he is not." He gritted his teeth with anguish as he uttered these words, and groaned when he ceased to speak . . . I did not believe he could just then take the field. . . Two hours after, I received fifty or more copies of his orders. . . At the bottom of the order was a note stating that the health of the commanding general was *restored*.' (Parton, *Life*, III, 610.)

Jackson's struggle with ill-health was one of the elements which made him so attractive to Franklin Delano Roosevelt. ('The more I learn about old Andy Jackson the more I love him.' *F.D.R. His Personal Letters, 1928–1945*, ed. Elliott Roosevelt [New York, 1950], I, 433.) In the depths of the depression, in a Christmas greeting to the Nation in 1934, Roosevelt reminded the people of America of the monument in the park before the White House of 'a man who will live forever as the embodiment of courage — Andrew Jackson.' (*Public Papers and Addresses of Franklin D. Roosevelt* [New York, 1938], III, 501; see also, x, 82–7.)

29. *The Rough and Ready*, I (March 13, 1847), 1.

30. Bolles, 'Eulogy,' Dusenbery, comp., *Monument*, p. 232.

31. Bancroft, 'Eulogy,' Dusenbery, comp., *Monument*, p. 48; see also the analysis of Jackson's character by a fellow Tennessean, John Bell: 'Speech by Mr. Bell of Tenn.,' *Addresses on the Presentation of the Sword of General Jackson to the Congress of the United States . . . February 26, 1855* (Washington, 1855), p. 15. Compare Martin Van Buren's account of his reception by Jackson at the height of the bank struggle. Van Buren had just returned from England and found Jackson stretched out in bed 'a spectre in physical appearance but as always a hero in spirit. . . Holding my hand . . . he said . . . "the bank, Mr. Van Buren is trying to kill me, but I will kill it!" ' (Van Buren, 'Autobiography,' p. 625.)

32. Parton, *Life*, III, 397.

33. Marguerite G. Bartlett, *The Chief Phases of Pennsylvania Politics in the Jacksonian Period* (Allentown, Pa., 1919), p. 53.

34. *National Intelligencer*, May 19, 1829.

35. February 26, 1824.

36. *National Journal*, June 24, 1829. For a fuller listing of such characterizations of Duff Green, see Fletcher M. Green, 'Duff Green, Militant Journalist of the Old School,' *American Historical Review*, LII (January 1947), 253; also Culver H. Smith, 'The Washington Press

in the Jacksonian Period,' Unpublished dissertation (Duke University, 1933), *passim.*

37. Frances Anne Butler [Kemble], *Journal,* 2 vols. (Philadelphia, 1835), II, 69n.

38. The best and most complete account of the Jackson-Dickinson is to be found in Parton, *Life,* I, 267–306.

39. Parton, *Life,* I, 295.

40. Parton, *Life,* I, 301.

41. Gardner, 'The Gentleman from Tennessee,' *passim.*

42. Frost, *Pictorial Life,* p. 91; Parton, *Life,* I, 297.

43. Parton, *Life,* III, 683. This anecdote concerning Jackson shows amazing vitality. In a current version, an ancient Negro body servant who was supposed to have been a child at 'The Hermitage' heard this story from Jackson's own lips to emphasize his determination to have his way. (Letter in my possession from F. M. Allen, Paris, Tennessee, March 19, 1952.)

IX   THE SELF-MADE MAN

1. Stevenson, 'Eulogy,' Dusenbery, comp., *Monument,* p. 252.

2. Parton, *Life,* III, 372.

3. Parton, *Life,* III, 697.

4. Irving Gordon Wyllie, 'The Cult of the Self-Made Man in America, 1830–1910,' Unpublished dissertation (Wisconsin, 1949), pp. 10–11; Alfred Whitney Griswold, 'The American Gospel of Success,' Unpublished dissertation (Yale, n.d.), p. 30.

5. Philadelphia Committee of Correspondence, *Jackson Wreath,* p. 72; *Jackson Republican,* October 8, 1828. For contemporary interest in Franklin see, for example, the essay on him in the *National Intelligencer,* July 14, 1819, which begins, 'Every Man is said to be the artificer of his own character.'

6. David Riesman, and others, *The Lonely Crowd: A Study of the Changing American Character* (New Haven, 1950), pp. 14–15, *passim.*

7. S. C. Phillips, *An Oration Delivered at the Request of the Young Men of Salem, July 4, 1831* (Salem, Mass., 1831), p. 16.

8. O. L. Holley, *The Connexion Between the Mechanic Arts and the Welfare of the States: An Address Delivered Before the Mechanics of Troy, at Their Request, on the 4th of July, 1825* (Troy, N. Y., 1825), p. 4.

9. 'Alfred,' 'Decision of Character,' *The Atheneum*, I (September 15, 1817), 887–8.

10. *Argus of Western America*, August 20, 1828.

11. Neal, 'Self Reliance and Self Distrust,' p. 202.

12. Wyllie, 'Cult of the Self-Made Man,' pp. 36–69.

13. Morrison, 'Eulogy,' Dusenbery, comp., *Monument*, p. 134.

14. James, *Andrew Jackson, The Border Captain*, pp. 10–11, 31.

15. Dallas, 'Eulogy,' Dusenbery, comp., *Monument*, p. 53.

16. Riesman, *The Lonely Crowd*, pp. 41–4, *passim*.

17. Andrew H. Fonerden, 'Andrew Jackson,' *Southern Literary Messenger*, XXXII (February 1861), 147.

18. Wright, 'Eulogy,' Dusenbery, comp., *Monument*, pp. 246–7.

19. Compare, for example, the editorial in support of William H. Crawford in the *Rhode Island Patriot* (*National Intelligencer*, September 28, 1824).

20. [Joseph G. Baldwin], ' "Representative Men" Andrew Jackson and Henry Clay,' *Southern Literary Messenger*, XIX (September 1853), 523.

21. Clay is credited with coining the phrase, 'self-made man,' in a debate in Congress, February 2, 1832. Sir William A. Craigie and James R. Hulburt, *A Dictionary of American English on Historical Principles*, 4 vols. (Chicago, [1938–1944]), IV, 2065.

22. Bancroft, 'Eulogy,' Dusenbery, comp., *Monument*, p. 34.

23. 'Fragments of Unpublished Reminiscence of Edward Livingston,' *The United States Magazine and Democratic Review*, VIII (October 1840), 369.

24. Frost, *Pictorial Life*, pp. 556-7.

25. Parton, *Life*, I, 97, 104-5.

26. Garland, 'Eulogy,' Dusenbery, comp., *Monument*, p. 187.

27. Waldo, *Memoirs of Andrew Jackson*, p. 35.

28. Phillips, *An Oration*, p. 19.

29. E. Douglas Branch, *The Sentimental Years, 1836–1860* (New York, 1937), p. 196 (my emphasis).

30. James D. Knowles, *Perils and Safeguards of American Liberty: Address Pronounced July 4, 1828, in the Second Baptist Meeting-House in Boston, at the Religious Celebration of the Anniversary of American Independence, By the Baptist Churches and Societies in Boston* (Boston, [1828]), p. 14.

31. 'The Course of Civilization,' *The United States Magazine and Democratic Review*, VI (September 1839), 215.

32. Woodbury, 'Eulogy,' Dusenbery, comp., *Monument*, p. 71.

33. Lewis, 'Eulogy,' Dusenbery, comp., *Monument*, pp. 165–6.

34. *The Rough-Hewer*, I (February 27, 1840), 13.

35. David Lee Child, *An Oration Pronounced Before the Republicans of Boston, July 4, 1826, The Fiftieth Anniversary of American Independence* (Boston, 1826), p. 8.

36. Bolles, 'Eulogy,' Dusenbery, comp., *Monument*, p. 214. Jackson also subscribed to the belief that poverty was the cause of his later success. See his letter to R. K. Call (Bassett, *Correspondence*, III, 130) in which he rationalizes Call's failure to receive an appointment from the War Department by asserting that his own later eminence was due to the harsh beginnings of his life.

X   THE MAN OF (MALLEABLE) IRON

1. Harold E. Dickson was the first to point out that it is unlikely that Jarvis's portrait was from life since he probably did not see Jackson until 1819 in New York when Jackson toured the eastern cities after the debate over the Seminole controversy. Dickson, therefore, dates the Jarvis portrait about 1819 (*John Wesley Jarvis, American Painter* [New York, 1949], pp. 178, 213–15) but he seems not to have seen David Edwin's engraving of the Wheeler portrait in the Reid and Eaton biography two years earlier. Almost nothing can be discovered about Wheeler. He was probably a local New Orleans artist since in 1816 there was another likeness of Jackson engraved by Gambrede which is marked, 'Wheeler, pinxt. N. O.' (David McNeely Stauffer, *American Engravers Upon Copper and Steel*, 2 vols. [New York, 1907], Check List No. 1055.) Jarvis's copy differs only in matters of minor detail and in the more flowing quality of his line; the Phillips engraving appeared as the frontispiece to *The United States Magazine and Democratic Review*, new series, X (1842). We are fortunate in having pictorial evidence that in 1815 Jackson's hair did not suddenly for a time curl down over his forehead; see the pencil sketch of Jackson's head by Thomas Sully immediately after the Battle of New Orleans, now in the possession of Mrs. Albert Sully, Brooklyn, New York. An art historian has suggested to me that the style of the hair may reflect the traditional representation of Caesar; even so, the point is the same.

2. Parton, *Life*, II, 327–8. Parton's memory has blended Jarvis's portrait with still another 'Napoleonic' likeness of Jackson. Parton says that the Jarvis portrait was a miniature; Jarvis's portrait measures 25-½ x 21 inches. But in New Orleans in 1815 Jean Francois Vallée did a miniature of Jackson which Jackson presented with a testimony of his regards to his aide, Edward Livingston. The miniature and the accompanying note became heirlooms in the Livingston family. For a reproduction, see *McClure's Magazine*, IX (July 1897), 797. The Vallée miniature may even be the source of Wheeler's interpretation of the general; it has the Napoleonic hair-do and the pose is much the same but the features are different. In the case of either portrait, Parton's remark is still justified; Charles Henry Hart, who wrote the note on Vallée's portrait for the reproduction in *McClure's*, also noted 'how thoroughly he has imbued this portrait of Jackson with the Napoleonic feeling.'

3. Mosier, *Making the American Mind*, p. 43.

4. Albert Guerard, *Reflections on the Napoleonic Legend* (New York, 1924), p. 107.

5. Frost, *Pictorial Life*, p. 64.

6. *The Mercantile Advertiser*, in the *National Intelligencer*, February 11, 1815.

7. Philip C. Brooks, 'Diplomacy of the Borderlands: The Adams-Onis Treaty of 1819,' *University of California Publications in History*, XXIV (1939), 125.

8. See, for example, *National Intelligencer*, May 20, 1815; the platform of the Indiana Jackson party in 1824, quoted in Logan Esarey, 'The Organization of the Jacksonian Party in Indiana,' *Proceedings of the Mississippi Valley Historical Association*, VII (1913–14), 231.

9. Ingersoll, *Historical Sketch*, II, 272.

10. Charles M. Wiltse, *John C. Calhoun: Nationalist, 1782–1828* (Indianapolis, 1944), p. 38.

11. Jackson to James Robertson, January 11, 1798, Bassett, *Correspondence*, I, 41.

12. The volumes on Napoleon in Jackson's personal library were: *Napoleon's Own Memoirs Printed from a Manuscript Transmitted from St. Helena through an Unknown Channel. Translated from the French* (Pittsburgh, 1817); *Historical Memoir of Napoleon, 1815. Translated from the Original Manuscript by B. E. O'Meara* (Philadel-

phia, 1820); Barry Edward O'Meara, *Napoleon in Exile; or, A Voice from St. Helena*, 2 vols. (New York, 1823); [Sir Walter Scott], *The Life of Napoleon Bonaparte . . . by the Author of 'Waverly'* (Philadelphia, 1827); John S. C. Abbott, *Biographical Sketch of Joseph Napoleon Bonaparte* (London, 1833).

13. *National Intelligencer*, April 25, 1815.

14. E. Douglas Branch, *The Sentimental Years* (New York, 1934), p. 161.

15. See, for example, *National Intelligencer*, June 11, 1823, January 15, 1824; [Eaton], *Letters of Wyoming*, p. 89; Marguerite G. Bartlett, *The Chief Phases of Pennsylvania Politics in the Jacksonian Period* (Allentown, Pa., 1919), p. 8.

16. *Speech of the Hon. Henry Clay, in the House of Representatives of the U. S. on the Seminole War* (n.p., n.d. [Washington, 1819]), pp. 27–8.

17. *Speech of the Hon. Henry Clay*, pp. 29–30.

18. *New-York Evening Post*, June 20, 1845; *New-York Herald*, June 20, 1845.

19. The chief defense of Jackson was the *Speech of the Hon. Alexander Smyth, in the House of Representatives of U. S. on the Seminole War* (n.p., n.d. [Washington, 1819]).

20. The best source for an examination of the affair usually named after the judge involved is 'Andrew Jackson and Judge D. A. Hall. Report of the Committee of the Senate (of the State of Louisiana, 1843) in Relation to the Fine Imposed on Gen. Jackson, together with Documents Accompanying the Same,' *Louisiana Historical Quarterly*, v (October 1922), 509–70.

21. *New-Hampshire Patriot and State Gazette*, January 14, 1828.

22. [Eaton], *Letters of Wyoming*, p. 3.

23. A thorough examination of the use of Washington by Jacksonians to answer the 'military chieftain' charge would constitute a separate article. Such devices as making amber flasks with bas-relief profiles of Jackson and Washington on opposite sides were employed (Harry Hall White, 'More Light on Coventry and Its Products: Part II,' *Antiques*, xxxviii [November 1940], 225): the campaign between Jackson and Adams was billed as the 'second Washington' *versus* the 'second Adams' (*National Republican*, September 3, 1824). The Jacksonian invocation of the Washington image seems never to have been discomfited by the fact that Jackson, as a member of the House of

Representatives in 1796, was one of twelve extreme Jeffersonians who voted against a declaration of sentiments by the House which voiced high praise of Washington's administration.

Lafayette's triumphal tour of the United States in 1824 provided many opportunities for Jacksonians to toast the three 'military chieftains,' Washington, Lafayette, and Jackson. Later, while President, Jackson was presented by an admirer with a shell comb upon which Jackson's likeness was engraved, flanked by portraits of Washington and Lafayette, the whole surmounted by an eagle with a banner in its beak inscribed, 'New Orleans' (*The Globe*, June 29, 1831).

24. Stevenson, 'Eulogy,' Dusenbery, comp., *Monument*, pp. 268–9.

25. Parton, *Life*, III, 602.

26. Bancroft, 'Eulogy,' Dusenbery, comp., *Monument*, pp. 48, 50.

27. Stevenson, 'Eulogy,' Dusenbery, comp., *Monument*, p. 251.

28. Anon., *An Epick Poem*, p. 26.

29. Reid and Eaton, *Life*, p. 10; Waldo, *Memoirs of Andrew Jackson*, pp. 25–6; [Jerome V. C. Smith], *Memoirs of Andrew Jackson* (Philadelphia, 1831), pp. 13–14.

30. 'Jackson's Oration at the Tomb of Mary Washington,' *American Historical Magazine and Tennessee Historical Society Quarterly*, IX (1904), 277–8.

31. Cartwright, 'Eulogy,' Dusenbery, comp., *Monument*, p. 305.

32. The best review of the complications attending Jackson's marriage is the 'Report of the Committee in Defense of Jackson,' which was written chiefly by John Overton (*United States Telegraph*, June 27, 1827).

33. *Richmond Enquirer*, May 4, 1827, took note of these two epithets, among others, which appeared respectively in the *Commentator* and the *Boston Journal*.

34. Hattie M. Anderson, 'The Evolution of a Frontier Society in Missouri, 1815–1828,' *Missouri Historical Review*, XXXII (April 1938), 28.

35. See the rebuttal of Charles Hammond's charges by the *Richmond Enquirer*, April 27, 1827.

36. Parton, *Life*, III, 462. The story told by Dale is a good example of the mixed character ascribed to Jackson. Right after tears dropped on Jackson's knee, Dale mentioned the nullifiers and expressed the hope that things would go right. ' "They SHALL go right, sir," [Jackson] exclaimed passionately shivering his pipe upon the table.' The more

common pattern is for the description of Jackson as the sentimental hero to *follow* the portrayal of him as the man of will.

37. Parton, *Life*, III, 602.

38. Woodbury, 'Eulogy,' Dusenbery, comp., *Monument*, p. 74.

39. Benton, *Thirty Years' View*, I, 737.

40. Frost, *Pictorial Life*, p. 238.

41. Bolles, 'Eulogy,' Dusenbery, comp., *Monument*, p. 225.

42. Lore, 'Eulogy,' Dusenbery, comp., *Monument*, p. 339.

43. Wise, *Seven Decades*, p. 99.

44. Parton, *Life*, III, 630.

45. Woodbury, 'Eulogy,' Dusenbery, comp., *Monument*, p. 76.

46. Bethune, 'Discourse,' Dusenbery, comp., *Monument*, pp. 350, 352-3.

47. There was, however, a strong current of belief that the surest protection against the wilful man was the self-reliance of other men. James Fenimore Cooper (*Notions of the Americans Picked Up By a Traveling Bachelor* [Philadelphia, 1828], I, 271) has his traveler in America complain of the lack of perturbation in American society over the threat of Caesarism by Jackson, saying that 'it is provoking to find a whole nation dwelling in this species of alarming security, for no other reason than that their vulgar and everyday practices teach them to rely on themselves instead of trusting to the rational inferences of philanthropic theorists.' The argument which Cooper puts so pithily is elaborated at great length in a series of articles which appeared in the *Albany Argus* under the running title, 'Military Chieftains or Political Chieftains.' The series was reprinted in the *Jackson Republican* (August 9, 13, 20, 1828). For other expressions of the same idea, see Woodbury, 'Eulogy,' Stevenson, 'Eulogy,' Dusenbery, comp., *Monument*, pp. 77, 266. But trust in the self-reliance of all members of the society could logically lead to *bellum omnium contra omnes;* most Americans therefore tried to fit self-reliance into a larger and happier scheme of things.

48. Bancroft, 'Eulogy,' Van Buren, 'Eulogy,' Dusenbery, comp., *Monument*, pp. 51, 101-2.

49. 'Resolution of the Democratic Republican Young Men's General Committee,' *Report of the Committee of Arrangements of the Common Council of the City of New York*, p. 170.

50. Frost, *Pictorial Life*, p. 16.

51. *The Daily Union,* June 17, 1845.

52. Rev. Robert Paine, *A Funeral Discourse on the Life and History of Andrew Jackson, Delivered at Courtland, Ala., on the Fourth of July, 1845* (Huntsville, Ala., 1845), p. 13.

53. Irvin, 'Eulogy,' Dusenbery, comp., *Monument,* p. 314.

54. Butler, 'Eulogy,' Dusenbery, comp., *Monument,* p. 68.

55. The Tennessee State Library has four Currier and Ives lithographs of the death-bed scene and one by Kellogg and Thayer. Fig. 5 is by the courtesy of the Library of Congress.

56. *Miner's Free Press,* August 21, 1838. This article is a good example of the borrowing of the press before the telegraph made news simultaneously available throughout the nation. The *Miner's Free Press* copied the article on Jackson's conversion from the Nashville *Banner* which, in turn, had it from the *American Presbyterian.*

57. Lore, 'Eulogy,' Dusenbery, comp., *Monument,* p. 341.

XI   CODA

1. Richard Hofstadter, *The American Political Tradition and the Men Who Made It* (New York, 1949), p. 44.

2. Carlton J. H. Hayes, *Essays on Nationalism* (New York, 1928), p. 110.

3. *Niles' Weekly Register,* IX (December 2, 1815), 238.

4. Anon., 'Self Cultivation,' *The Southern Literary Messenger,* VI (June 1840), 461. Wyllie, 'The Cult of the Self-Made Man,' *passim,* demonstrates the typical nature of this expression.

5. *The Daily Union,* July 2, 1845.

6. John Neal, 'Self Reliance and Self Distrust,' *Brother Jonathan,* III (October 15, 1842), 202.

7. Woodbury, 'Eulogy,' Dusenbery, comp., *Monument,* p. 73.

8. Anon., 'Presidential Inaugurations. Jackson — 1829,' *The Ladies Magazine and Literary Repository,* V (March 1832), 116.

9. *Cincinnati Literary Gazette,* III (June 1825), 193.

10. *McGuffey's Newly Revised Eclectic Fourth Reader* (Cincinnati, 1853), p. 313, cited Mosier, *Making of the American Mind,* p. 34.

11. [Baldwin], ' "Representative Men," ' p. 525. On the same page, Baldwin compares Jackson to Napoleon in describing his will power.

12. Wise, *Seven Decades,* p. 118.

INDEX

Acorn anecdote, 70–71
Activism, 53, 57–8, 76–7, 210, 213
Adair, John, 26, 107
Adams, John, 70, 92, 110
Adams, John Quincy, 62–5, 70–71, 76, 83, 88, 92, 110, 133, 145, 208
Ahab, 201
Alabama, 203
Alger, Horatio, 90
'Algernon Sidney,' 62
Ambrister, 59
America, as example, *see* Manifest Destiny
An Epick Poem, 24
Anglo-Saxonism, 223n
Anti-intellectualism, 52, 64, 71, 73–4, 81, 86, 89, 111, 211
Arabella, 138
Arbuthnot, 59
Aristotelianism, 124, 126
Armstrong, John, 54, 56
Assassination attempt, 114–15

B

Baldwin, Joseph G., 212
Bancroft, George, 30–31, 72–5, 77–8, 161, 175, 192
Barbarism, 35, 37, 43; *see also* Savagery
Barker, James Nelson, 109
Barratarian Pirates, 26

Battle of New Orleans, *see* New Orleans, Battle of
Beale's Rifle Company, 26
'Beauty and Booty,' 34–5, 193–5, 226n
Benton, Thomas Hart, 197
Bethune, Rev. George W., 199
Biddle, Nicholas, 94, 120
Blair, Francis P., 115, 167
Blair, Walter, 89
Blount, Willie, 38
Boston, 83, 94, 118–19, 159
Boston Navy Yard, 115
Boston Patriot, 60
Boylies, Francis, 69
Brownson, Orestes, 97
Butler, Anthony, 148
Butler, Benjamin F., 109, 113, 203
Butler, Robert, 61
Byron, Lord, 32, 33

C

Calhoun, John C., 184
Cassirer, Ernst, 49, 206
Character, 169–70, 177, 211; *see also* Self-made man, Self-reliance, Will
'Character,' 152
Charismatic leader, 113; *see also* Providence
Childe Harold's Pilgrimage, 32

Cincinnati (Ohio), 28, 62
Cincinnatus, 42–4, 229n
Civilization, 32–41, 44–5, 69, 78, 95, 177, 194–6
'Civis,' 60
Claiborne, Nathaniel, 27–8, 36–40, 190–92
Classical imagery, 229–30n
Clausel, Marshal Count Bertrand, 23
Clay, Henry, 6, 60, 67, 91, 128, 174, 186–7, 190
Cobb, Howell, 61
Coffee, John, 26, 47
Cole, Thomas, 230n
Coleridge, Samuel Taylor, 50
Communism, 210
Concord (N.H.), 85
Constitution, 116–17, 121
Cooper, James Fenimore, 264n
Correspondence, Emerson's theory of, 72–3, 75
'Course of Civilization, The,' 177
Crawford, William, 60
Crèvecoeur, St. John de, 29
Crockett, David, 79–80, 88–9, 92, 114
Cromwell, 212
Currier and Ives, 203

D

Dale, General Sam, 196–7
Dallas, George M., 39
Davezac, Major Auguste de, 129–31, 149, 250n
Davis, Charles Augustus, 80, 83–6, 89–90
Davis, Warren R., 114
Davy Crockett, *see* Crockett, David
Decadence, 39–40
Democracy, 49, 137; *see also* Jeffersonian democracy
Democratic party, symbol of, 87–8
Democratic Review, see United States' Magazine and Democratic Review

Desha, General Joseph, 219n
Desnoettes, Count, 23
Dewey, Samuel, 120–21
Dickerson, Mahlon, 120–21
Dickinson, Charles, 163–4
Dickson, Harold E., 260n
Douglas, Stephen, 112
Downing, Jack, 43, 79–90
Downing, Sargent Joel, 92
Downing, Uncle Joshua, 84, 92
Downing Gazette, 79–80
Downingville, Me., 80, 84–5
Dubourg, Abbé Guillaume, 101–5, 123, 131, 153
Duel, 163–5

E

Eastern Argus (Portland, Me.), 62
Eaton, John Henry, 44, 68–9, 181, 189
Eaton, Peggy, 196
Eddy, Henry, 251n
Edinburgh Review, 64
Election, of 1824: 44, 50, 64, 133, 162; of 1828: 41, 51, 63–71, 112, 128, 196; of 1840: 80, 91–7
Elliott, Jesse D., 115–19
Emerson, Ralph Waldo, 12, 72, 129–30, 148, 152, 183
Enlightenment, The Age of, 48
Enquirer, The (Richmond), 6, 61–2, 106, 154, 157–8, 162
Europe, rejection of, 31, 40, 77, 140–41, 146, 149; *see also* Civilization, Past
Everett, Edward, 94
Ewing, Andrew, 198
Expansion, 58, 111, 135, 137, 145, 147, 149, 169

F

Farmer, 7, 9, 24–5, 41–2, 73, 78, 91, 95; *see also* Freeholder, Frontiersman, Yeoman

'Farmer of North Bend, The,' 91, 95–6; *see also* Harrison, William Henry

Felton, Nathan B., 52

Figurehead of Andrew Jackson, 115–23, 183

Florida, 54, 58–60, 63, 186, 188

Folklore, 80, 89, 125; *see also* Downing, Crockett, 'Hunters of Kentucky'

Formalism, rejection of, 9, 47, 52–3, 61, 63, 75, 86, 111, 135–6, 185; *see also* Training

Forrest, Edwin, 138

Fowler, Martin G., 125

France, 32–3

Franklin, Benjamin, 168, 176

Freeholder, 28, 36; *see also* Farmer, Frontiersman, Yeoman

French Creoles, 26

Frontier, 25, 27, 29, 40, 93

Frontier theory of American history, 29, 67, 69, 75, 142

Frontiersman, 16, 22–7, 29, 41, 208; *see also* Farmer, Freeholder, Yeoman

Frost, John, 183

Fundamentalism, 126

G

Gadsby's hotel, 43

Gaines, Edmund P., 59

Garland, Hugh A., 154

Genius, 51, 53, 69, 77, 105; *see also* Reason, Intuition

Gibbs, General, 20

Globe, The, 115

Gloucester (Mass.), 113

Goals in open society, 173

Goodrich, Charles A., 37

Goodrich, Samuel G., 3–4

Gould, Edward Sherman, 249n

Greeley, Horace, 92

Green, Duff, 115, 162

Green Mountain Boys, The, 94

Grundy, Felix, 139

Guerard, Albert, 183

H

Hall, James, 72

Hammond, Charles, 196

Harrisburg Convention, 91, 93

Harrison, William Henry, 91, 93, 96–7

Harrison Almanac 1841, The, 96

Hartford Convention, 4

Hartley, Robert, 177

Harvard, 66, 83–6

Hayes, Carlton J. H., 208

'Hermitage, The,' 43–4, 202

Higher law, 111; *see also* Providence

Historical primitivism, *see* Primitivism

History, projection of ideas into, 16, 24–5, 29, 113, 207–13

Hofstadter, Richard, 208

Holley, O. L., 169

Hone, Philip, 82, 119, 123

Honorary degree, 83–7; *see also* Harvard, Downing

Hopkinson, Francis, 106–7

Horatio Alger, 90

Horseshoe Bend, Battle of, 37

Houston, Sam, 148

Howard, General Benjamin Chew, 75, 77–8

Humor, 81; *see also* Crockett, Downing, Folklore

'Hunters of Kentucky, The,' 13–29; use by Jacksonians, 15; New Orleans victory of frontiersman, 16; distortion of facts, 25–6; and frontier interpretation of American history, 29; and nationalism, 29, 30, 33: 'beauty and booty,' 34–5, 92, 108, 194

I

Illinois Gazette, The, 133–6, 138, 142

Imbert, Anthony, 241n
Indians, attitude toward, 40; re-
  moval, 40, 146; and civilization,
  41; and paternalism, 41; 145,
  198; Creek, 37–8, 58, 70; Semi-
  nole, 57
Individualism, 149, 188, 190, 210,
  212–13
Industrialism, 76
Ingersoll, Charles Jared, 6, 156
'Inner-direction,' 172
Internationalism, 140–41
Intuition, 31, 50, 53, 76–7, 97, 111,
  210; *see also* Genius, Nature,
  Reason
Iron, in symbol of Jackson, 157–8,
  171
Isolationism, 139–40, 142, 145

J

Jack Downing, *see* Downing, Jack
'J. Downing, Major,' *see* Davis,
  Charles A.
Jackson, Andrew, 3, 5; nationalism,
  6; 7; symbol of ideas, 10; 'The
  Hunters of Kentucky,' 14; 16,
  17, 25; nature, 30; Bancroft on,
  30–31; 34; addresses to troops,
  37–8; 39; Indian removal, 40–
  41; 'Farewell Address,' 41; as
  farmer, 42–4; and barbarism,
  43; 46; and untrained troops,
  48; and Transcendentalism, 50;
  as Genius, 50–51; nature, 52; activism, 53, 76; Florida, 54; nickname, 54–7; 56; man of action,
  57–9; Seminole controversy, 57–
  63; impetuous, 59; election of
  1828, 63–71; unqualified, 64; illiteracy, 64; wisdom, 66; repudiation of Europe, 67–9; rejection of training, 68; acorn
  anecdote, 70–71; Emerson's theory of correspondence, 72; Pensacola, 77; and progress, 78;

'Jack Downing,' 80–82; honorary
  degree, 83–7; as Jackass, 87–8,
  241n; lack of training, 88; and
  Davy Crockett, 89–90; and success, 90; election of 1840, 91–7;
  in *Moby-Dick*, 100; and celebration of victory at New Orleans,
  102–3; divine agent, 103–5, 109,
  112–13, 246–7n; religious views,
  107; man of nature and God,
  111; will of the people, 112; will
  of God, 112; his mother, 112,
  195; attempted assassination of,
  114–15; figurehead on *Constitution*, 115–23; tomb of Roman
  emperor, 116; man of destiny,
  123; cosmic imagery about, 126–
  8; election of 1824, 133; symbol
  of manifest destiny, 136; nature
  and providence, 144; 'extending
  the area of freedom,' 146; Texas,
  148; repudiation of Europe,
  149; individualism, 149; nature
  and God at New Orleans, 153;
  self-reliant man, 154; as cause
  of victory, 154; will to win, 155;
  'iron,' 157–8; illness, 159, 256–
  7n; duel with Dickinson, 163–5;
  Promethean defiance, 165; self-
  sufficient, 167; and Benjamin
  Franklin, 168; as orphan, 171–4;
  self-made man, 172–5; as symbol
  of equality, 178; and Napoleon,
  181–5; portraits, 181–2, 260–61n;
  'military chieftain,' 185–90; as
  threat to society, 186–9; and
  George Washington, 188–9,
  262n; as sentimental hero, 192–
  200; Rachel and marriage, 195–
  7; and children, 197–9; religion,
  201–4, 246n; and Ahab, 202; as
  symbol, 207–13
Jackson, Rachel, 195–7
Jackson Wreath, The, 24, 52
Jarvis, John Wesley, 181–3
Jarvis, Russell, 119–20

Jefferson, Thomas, 29, 40, 49, 92, 110, 140
Jeffersonian, The, 92
Jeffersonian democracy, 49

K

Kemble, Frances A. (Fanny), 163
Kendall, Amos, 44, 127
'Kitchen Cabinet,' 163

L

Lafayette, 189
Latour, A. Lacarriere, 47, 155
Lawrence, Richard, 114
Leadership, 55
Lee, Henry, 198
Lee, Richard B., 142, 145
Legaré, Hugh, 94
Letters of J. Downing, Major, 89; see also Davis, C. A.
Letters of Wyoming, 68
Liberty Hall (Cincinnati), 196
Library of Congress, 122
Lincoyer, 198
'Lines of an American Poet,' 106
Lippard, George, 160, 184
Litchfield (Conn.), 184
Livingston, Edward, 102, 129–30, 182
Log Cabin, 94–7; see also Election of 1840
Louisiana, 129
Louisville (Ky.), 127
Love Laughs at Locksmiths, 14
Ludlow, Noah M., 13, 15–16, 23
Lyman, Theodore, 66

M

McGuffey's readers, 182
Madison, James, 3, 54
'Major Jack Downing,' see Smith, Seba

Manifest Destiny, 73, 108, 127, 133–5, 140, 143–4, 148–9, 213; see also Providence
Marigny, Bernard, 223n
Massachusetts, 69, 84, 94
Melville, Herman, 100, 201
Memphis (Tenn.), 198
Metcalf, Governor of Kentucky, 92
'Military chieftain,' 185–90
Mills, Clark, 159
'Miss Baily,' 14
Mississippi Republican, 34
'Mississippi River, The,' 126
Moby-Dick, 100, 201–2
Monroe, James, 57, 60, 127, 145
Monroe Doctrine, 145
Montesquieu, 137
Mullins, Lieutenant-Colonel Thomas, 19–20
Mythology, 208; see also Symbol

N

Napoleon, 23, 122–3, 152, 161, 182–5, 191, 202
Narrative of the Life of David Crockett, A, 90
Nashville (Tenn.), 54–5, 61, 128
Nast, Thomas, 88
Natchez, 54–5
'Natick Cobbler, The,' 94
National Intelligencer, 7, 21, 57, 106, 108, 124, 126, 131, 140, 157, 184
Nationalism, 6, 8, 10, 29, 31, 67–9, 107, 111, 127, 131, 139, 141, 143, 147, 178, 208
Natural man, 49, 86, 89–90, 111
Nature, 8–10, 13–97; and victory at New Orleans, 24; Jackson's training, 31; definition of, 32–45; ambivalence toward, 32–45; rejection of wild, 33; 'cultivated,' 36; and civilization, 39; savage, 40; danger of alienation from, 41; higher reason of, 50;

Nature (*continued*)

  Genius, 51; and Jackson's fitness, 52; Reason, 66; wisdom, 72–4; primitivism, 78; social function of idea of, 90; election of 1840, 91–3; 108; and providence, 111, 132, 140, 144; and civilization, 145; 149, 166, 185; functional relation to providence and will, 207–13; and classical imagery, 229–30n

Neauville, Hyde de, 183

Nelson, Lord, 56

New England, 50, 84, 87, 115–17, 119, 159

New Hampshire, 51, 94

New Orleans, 54

New Orleans, Battle of, 4; effect of victory, 5–10; 8, 15; victory of frontiersman, 16, 22–5; description of, 16–22; disparity of loss, 17; night battle of December 23, 1814, 17; confusion of British, 20; on the scene accounts, 21; Jackson's victory address, 21; 24; actual fighting force, 26; 27, 33, 46, 58, 77; victory celebration, 101–3; providential victory, 105–9, 123–32; folksong of, 125; poem about, 126; omen of victory, 129–30; 149, 153; Jackson as cause of victory, 154; suspension of civil law, 188–9; 194

New York, 52, 82–3, 138, 202–3

New-York American, 141

New York Association for Improving the Condition of the Poor, 177

New York Daily Advertiser, 82–3

New-York Evening Post, 4, 20, 156, 192

New-York Historical Society, 188

New-York Morning News, 135

New York Times, The, 53

Newtonianism, 124, 126

Nichols, Thomas Low, 15

Nickname, *see* 'Old Hickory'

Niles' Weekly Register, 60, 210

Nullification, 84, 86, 113, 115, 117, 197

O

Ohio, 34, 65–6, 203

'Old Hickory'; origin and significance of, 54–7; 63

'Old Oaken Bucket, The,' 13

Optimism, 4, 110–11, 213; *see also* Providence

Orders-in-Council, 4

Oregon, 135, 149

O'Sullivan, John L., 134–5, 138, 140, 143

Otis, William Foster, 39–40

Overton, John, 57, 164

P

Packenham, Sir Edward, 17, 19–20, 23, 194

Paradise Lost, 146

Parton, James, 128, 161–2, 164, 167, 182

Past, rejection of, 48, 73, 75–6, 141, 143, 211; *see also* Europe, Tradition

Pensacola, 38, 61, 77

Pequod, 201

Philadelphia, 43, 120, 199

Phillips, Charles, 181

Pictorial Life, 183

Pittsburgh Committee of Correspondence, 44

Plumer, William, 138

Poindexter, George, 34

Polk, James K., 147

Poore, Ben: Perley, 120–21

Portland (Me.), 79–80

Portland Courier, 83

'Power,' 12

Pragmatism, 49

Presbyterian Church, 202

Primitivism, 25, 27, 32–3, 37, 66–7, 69, 71, 75, 78, 95, 142, 144–6
Progress, 36, 78
Providence, 8–10, 74, 76, 101–49; at New Orleans, 108; and George Washington, 110; optimism, 110; anti-intellectualism, 111; preserves Jackson, 115; and figurehead of Jackson, 121–3; and nature, 126, 132, 140, 144; and manifest destiny, 135; repudiation of Europe, 141; and the past, 143; 166, 200; functional relation to nature and will, 207–13
Puritanism, 210
Puritans, 71, 107

Q

Quaker doctrine of the Inner Light, 74
Quarterly Review, 64
Quincy, Josiah (Pres. of Harvard), 83
Quincy, Josiah, 85, 86, 159

R

Reason, 50–51, 56, 65–6, 71, 74
Reeve, Tapping, 184
Reid, John, 181
Removal of Indians, *see* Indians
Removal of office holders, 162
Rennie, Colonel, 22–3
'Representative Men,' 174
Representative Men, 183
Revolutionary War, 112
Richmond (Va.), 166
Richmond Enquirer, see Enquirer, The
Riesman, David, 172
Ripley, George, 128
Ritchie, Thomas, 115

Robards, Lewis, 195–6
Robertson, Thomas B., 48
Robinson, Henry R., 248–9n
Romanticism, 30, 76; *see also* Nature
Roosevelt, Franklin D., 257n

S

Salem (Mass.), 87
Saratoga (N. Y.), 94
Savagery, 33–4, 39–40, 43–5, 78, 95
Second Bank of the United States, 84, 160
Self-made man, 166–80; origin of phrase, 174; 183, 185; and providence, 201
Self-reliance, 58, 74, 81, 154, 162, 166, 171, 176, 189, 191, 200, 203; *see also* Self-made man, Will
Seminole affair, 57–63, 108, 186
Sentimental hero, 190–200
'Sentimental Years, The,' 192
Sentimentalism, 203
Sentimentality, 192, 198–9
Seward, William H., 91, 93
Shelby, Isaac, 107
Simplicity, 37, 66, 69, 93, 96, 112; *see also* Primitivism, Nature
Smith, Henry Nash, 225n, 225–6n
Smith, Seba, 79–81, 83–7
Smyth, Alexander, 108
Social change, 168–9
Social mobility, 90
Southern Literary Messenger, 174
Spain, 62
Spirit of the West, 34–5
Spoliation claims against France, 32
State Street, 94, 120
Stevenson, Andrew, 166–7, 171–2, 179
Success, *see* Self-made man
Sully, Thomas, 260n
Symbol, 8, 10, 77; function, 173; 206–13; and history, 208; as collective product, 88, 213

T

Talent, 51
Talledega, 70
Tandy, Jennette, 81
Tennessee, 54–5, 59, 80; militia, 54–
  5; Volunteers, 26, 56
Texas, 135, 146–9
Tohopeka, Battle of, 198
Tradition, 48, 67, 73; *see also* Past
Training, rejection of, 9, 46–8, 52,
  64, 67–8, 71–4, 77, 80, 86, 89,
  210–11; *see also* Formalism
Transcendentalism, 50–51, 56, 74;
  see also Genius, Nature, Reason
Treaty of Fort Jackson, 58
Treaty of Ghent, 5
Trist, Nicholas, 192, 197
Troup, George, 7–10, 24, 47, 169

U

'Uncle Sam,' 81
Understanding, 50–51, 56, 65–6, 76
*United States' Magazine and Demo-
  cratic Review*, 97, 134, 136, 177
United States' Telegraph, 115

V

Vallée, Jean François, 261n
Van Buren, Martin, 80, 92–3, 96–7,
  162–3
Volunteers, Tennessee, 26, 56

W

Waldo, Samuel Putnam, 27

Walker, Alexander, 23, 35, 160
Walsh, Robert, 52
War of 1812, 3–5, 36, 58, 106–7
Washington, George, 32, 42, 44, 70,
  110, 184, 189, 262n
Washington, D. C., 43, 85, 129, 145,
  190
Webster, Daniel, 82, 94
Weed, Thurlow, 87, 93
Wheeler, [?], 181
Whigs, 80, 82, 88, 90–91, 94–5, 121
White, Hugh Lawson, 31
Wilkinson, General, 54
Will, 8–10, 152–204; basis for char-
  acter, 169; danger symbolized
  by Napoleon, 185; disguised by
  sentimentalism, 190–200; am-
  bivalent attitude toward, 190–
  200; and providence, 200–201;
  Jackson's will as selfless, 202;
  its functional relation to nature
  and providence, 207–13; *see also*
  Self-reliance
Will of the people, 64, 73, 112
Wilson, Henry, 94
Winthrop, John, 138
Wisdom, 65–6, 69, 72, 76–7, 210; *see
  also* Genius, Reason
Wise, Henry A., 63, 76
Woodbury, Levi, 67, 113, 178
Woodward, Samuel, 13
'Wyoming,' 44

Y

Yeoman, 7, 9, 36, 42, 48, 95; *see also*
  Farmer, Frontiersman
'Young Hickory,' *see* Polk, James K.